THE BIG BOOK OF
ANGELS

THE BIG BOOK OF
ANGELS

CONTENTS

Introduction *by Sharon Linnéa* 1

PART ONE

ANGEL AWAKENINGS: THE BIRTH OF ANGELS IN HISTORY AND RELIGION

ANGELS IN HEBREW AND CHRISTIAN SCRIPTURE...15

Angels in Jewish Tradition *by Rabbi David Wolpe* 23

Angels in the Jewish Mystical Tradition *by Tamar Frankiel, Ph.D.*....................30

Angels in the New Testament *by Dr. William D. Webber* 41

On Religion and Real-Life Angels: An Interview with Joan Wester Anderson
    by Wendy Schuman 50

Do Angels Really Sing? *by Marilynn Carlson Webber and Dr. William D. Webber* 60

All-Star Angels *by Dr. William D. Webber*...66

How Well Do You Know Angels in the Bible?...74

"Take Your Angel with You" *by Therese J. Borchard* 78

ANGELS IN OTHER RELIGIONS 87

Angels in Islam *by Shaikh Kabir Helminski*...89

Angels among the Mormons *by Eric A. Eliason* 96

May Hanuman Be with You *by Shoba Narayan* 105

Devas, Fairies and Nature Spirits *by Dorothy Maclean* 109

PART TWO

ANGELS AMONG US: MOST PEOPLE BELIEVE IN AND MANY HAVE HAD
EXPERIENCES WITH ANGELS

ENCOUNTERS WITH THE EXTRAORDINARY..119

Angels Are for Real *by Dr. Arthur Caliandro*..122

Frequently Asked Angel Questions: Encounters and Sightings
   with Brad and Sherry Steiger 134

How Do I Know It's an Angel? *by Marilynn Carlson Webber and Dr. William D. Webber* ..146

Frequently Asked Angel Questions: Appearance *with Brad and Sherry Steiger* 150

Frequently Asked Angel Questions: Guardian Angels
   with Brad and Sherry Steiger 162

The Human Guardian Angel *by Renie Burghardt* 173

A Firefighter's Angel *by Joan Wester Anderson* 178

Angels by His Side *by Joan Wester Anderson* 183

Angels and Children—A Special Angelic Connection? *by Tobin Hart, Ph.D.* 186

Frequently Asked Angel Questions: Sightings by Children
   with Brad and Sherry Steiger 193

God's Pet Care *by Joan Wester Anderson* 199

Janet and the Angel Musicians *by Joan Wester Anderson* 203

Dream Angels *by Robert L. Van de Castle, Ph.D.* 205

Frequently Asked Angel Questions: Dream Encounters
   with Brad and Sherry Steiger 211

An Otherwise Grey Day *by Joan Wester Anderson* 214

Frequently Asked Angel Questions: Angels and Love
   with Brad and Sherry Steiger 220

Heaven Sent *by Azriela Jaffe* 227

Frequently Asked Angel Questions: Angels of Darkness
   with Brad and Sherry Steiger 230

Four Angels Dressed in Black *by Marilynn Carlson Webber* 241

The Doctor Was an Angel *by Joan Wester Anderson* 248

We Are Not Alone *by Joan Wester Anderson* 252

Frequently Asked Angel Questions: Lending Comfort in Death
   with Brad and Sherry Steiger 254

Caught by an Angel *by Joan Wester Anderson* 262

Angel on the Highway *by Joan Wester Anderson* 266

The Warrior Angels *by Marilynn Carlson Webber and Dr. William D. Webber* 270

An Angel in a Hurry *by Joan Wester Anderson* 279

PART THREE
ANGEL COMMUNICATION: FAMOUS ENCOUNTERS WITH ANGELS AND WAYS TO BRING THEM INTO YOUR LIFE

ANGELS AFFECT HISTORY OR INSPIRE BEAUTIFUL WORK *by Johanna Skilling*......283

George Frideric Handel: Inspired by Heaven *by Johanna Skilling* 285

George Washington: A Vision of His Country's Future *by Johanna Skilling* 289

Joan of Arc: Moving Armies with Angels *by Johanna Skilling* 296

Emanuel Swedenborg: A Sober Scientist's Detailed Vision of God *by Johanna Skilling* ...300

Saint Francis of Assisi: A Friend to Man, Beast and Angels *by Johanna Skilling*..............306

J. R. R. Tolkien: Love Individualized *by Johanna Skilling*..................................312

Marc Chagall: Painter of Angels *by Johanna Skilling*..317

William Blake: A Life among the Angels *by Johanna Skilling*............................320

Charles Lindbergh: A Messenger from the Sky *by Johanna Skilling*................324

Howard Finster: Painter of Sermons *by Johanna Skilling*................................328

Saint John Bosco's Four-Legged Angel *by Joan Wester Anderson* 332

There Are Many Ways to Open a Dialogue with Angels *by Sharon Linnéa* 338

Frequently Asked Angel Questions: Communicating
  with Brad and Sherry Steiger 342

Calling All Angels..350

Frequently Asked Angel Questions: How Not to Seek Angelic Attention
  with Brad and Sherry Steiger 366

How to Hear Your Angels' Messages *by Doreen Virtue, Ph.D.* 369

ACKNOWLEDGMENTS

When I began working at Beliefnet, a relative named Courage sent me a paperweight engraved with an angel and the famous quote from G. K. Chesterton: "Angels fly because they take themselves lightly." Every night for the past two years before leaving the office, I've placed this silver cube on top of an unruly pile of papers and books on my desk as a sort of benediction for the day and expression of gratitude for the kind of work we are able to do at Beliefnet—giving individuals the online tools they need to meet their spiritual and religious needs. It is our hope that *The Big Book of Angels* will further this goal by connecting seekers with the eternally fascinating realm of angels.

As usual, the amazing editors at Beliefnet came through with a host of new content and helpful ideas. Sharon Linnéa did an outstanding job of writing the introduction and the "connective tissue" leading into the chapters. Anne Simpkinson originated Beliefnet's angel page and was a rich source of material and wisdom. In addition, Martha Ainsworth, Deborah Caldwell, Jonathan Lowet, Paul O'Donnell, Rebecca Phillips, Elizabeth Sams, Lisa Schneider, Laura Sheahen and Beliefnet Editor-in-Chief Steven Waldman worked with skill and dedication. Many angel experts and religious historians provided guidance as well as beautifully written stories. Special gratitude is due to Brad and Sherry Steiger, the Reverend Dr. William Webber and Marilynn Carlson Webber, Joan Wester Anderson, Rabbi David Wolpe, Terry Lynn Taylor and Johanna Skilling. To Beliefnet's online community, who openly shared their experiences, inspiration and thoughts on the Angels discussion boards, our heartfelt thanks.

And to our partners and editors at Rodale Inc., our sincere gratitude for making this book possible.

Wendy Schuman,
Beliefnet Books Editor

INTRODUCTION

By Sharon Linnéa

The Lesson of the Well

There once was an orphan named Bette who was adopted as a child by a farm couple. From the beginning, there was no pretense of love. She was there as free labour, nothing more. Worse, the couple lived in their own cycle of violence, and their cruel abuse regularly found a focus in the little girl.

When Bette was twelve, the couple went away and left her to tend the farm. The next morning she rose early. After feeding the animals, she went to the pump to draw water for them, but the pump was broken. When this had happened before, she remembered seeing her "father" open the cover of the well and draw water up in a bucket. She found the bucket and a brand-new length of rope the farmer had just purchased. Fastening it tightly around the bucket handle, she stood by the well and lowered it into the dark hole in the ground.

Unfortunately, the water table was very low, and by the time the bucket hit water, Bette could hardly keep her balance. The bucket filled quickly and began to sink. Although the girl tried desperately to get control, the weight of the bucket and water was too much for her.

Bette immediately knew she had two choices: be pulled down into the well to drown or let go of the bucket, lose the farmer's brand-new rope and suffer the consequences. The answer was simple: She would hang on.

But as the weight jerked her muscles and the pulling rope burned her hands, an unexpected thing happened. A voice spoke audibly and clearly: "Lie down on your stomach!"

Bette heard the words, but she was so surprised by them that she didn't have time to process the command and obey it before she was pulled head-first down into the dark well shaft. Down and down she fell, bracing herself for the icy splash of the water. It never came.

For somehow, something even more unexpected happened: She

1

They are always on deck when there is a miracle to the fore—so as to get up in the picture, perhaps. Angels are as fond of that as a fire company: look at the old masters.

—Mark Twain, *A Connecticut Yankee in King Arthur's Court*

ceased falling down. Then she began falling *up*. She "fell" all the way up the shaft and found herself seated neatly on the ground beside the well. But before she had time to question what had happened, the most incredible thing of all took place. The shaken, terrified twelve-year-old girl felt herself surrounded by a presence. And then she felt something she had never felt in her entire life. She felt totally, completely loved. It was a feeling that bathed her inside and out. She felt peace and happiness—but overriding it all was love. Someone loved her. Someone was watching out for her.

"At the time, I had never heard of angels," Bette told me. "I had heard a friend of mine mention God, and I somehow knew God was behind my rescue. Only later, after I heard about angels, did I recognize that it must have been an angel who saved me from the well."

Like thousands of people—from peasant girls to famous painters—who have experienced angelic encounters through the centuries, Bette Fetters's life was forever marked by that experience. Beyond gratitude for the physical rescue, the sure knowledge of such overwhelming power and love dramatically changed the abused girl and prepared her for a life of hope and wholeness of which she had never dared dream.

Practical Wonder

You hold in your hands a book of wisdom and wonder. It is a book unlike any other. For instead of just one author telling you what his or her tradition believes about angels, you will meet wise men and women of many faith traditions who will tell you what they believe about angels, and why and how their beliefs impact their day-to-day lives.

You'll meet the angels of the

Hebrew and Christian scriptures, angels who dictated to Muhammad and Joseph Smith, angels who led a peasant girl into battle, turned soldiers into monks, inspired classical music and spoke to presidents.

You'll hear some of the most common angel questions answered by experts of many faiths, including Rabbi David Wolpe, Muslim Shaikh Kabir Helminski, and the Reverend Dr. Arthur Caliandro of New York's famed Marble Collegiate Church. You'll hear how various cosmologies of angels have developed, including those in the Hebrew, Catholic and Protestant traditions; the angels of Islam, of the Latter-day Saints, of Emanuel Swedenborg, of the Kabbalah; New Age angels; the Hindu and Buddhist equivalents of angels; and, of course, angels in movies, books and television.

You'll also read angel stories of ordinary people throughout the book. These stories are drawn from the online message boards of the Web site Beliefnet, the Internet's largest interfaith gathering place. Since Beliefnet's beginning in December of 1999, angels have been among the site's most popular topics. Through the magic of electronic communication, each day people from all over the world gather at www.beliefnet.com to share their thoughts and experiences—of angels and a host of other topics. Though their adopted screen-names may seem strange, if you're an "angel person", their personal tales will strike a familiar chord.

Chances are, you already know what you believe about angels. This book doesn't aim to change your beliefs: quite the contrary. It means to give you information about why you believe what you do and an understanding of why your friends and neighbors believe as they do. As Flannery O'Connor says, "The truth doesn't change based on our ability to stomach it." Indeed, the purpose of this book is to fill you with wonder and to help each of us live with a deeper sense of awe and mystery in our everyday lives.

For while facts and cosmology are fascinating and informative, they are not as important as the angels in *your* life. You see, in almost every tradition, almost every language, the word *angel* means "messenger". And as awesome as the messenger's appearance may be, what's really important, according to the scriptures of most traditions, is the content of the message that's received. God almost never uses angels frivolously. They are sent when something significant needs to take place. Someone is being called to do something or be something or stand firm about something, and that person's actions or agonies or spiritual comfort are so urgent that God does the equivalent of sending in the Marines to make certain nothing goes wrong.

But the angels themselves are so fascinating simply because they are supernatural—beyond the natural world as we know it—and the effects of their work are so dramatic. Just feeling their presence can explode a human's concept of the universe. They also give us hints—big hints—about the character, nature and being of God. People who have had encounters with angels tend to fall into two camps: either they're afraid no one will believe them and they keep their encounter a secret, or they're so blown away by the experience that they can't stop talking about it.

So, is an encounter with an angel something to be hoped for?

This is a question that will be explored in this book from several faith traditions. History, however, sounds a word of caution. An angelic visitation is seldom something that happens lightly. True, we'd all appreciate a visit from an angel on a life-saving mission—lifting us out of the well, like Bette Fetters, stopping a traffic accident, repairing a car, healing a child in the hospital, bringing words of peace to those in grief—and this book contains many such stories.

But when angels come to you with a message, it's possible that your life is not about to get easier. An angel in the form of a burning bush sent Moses, content as a shepherd, to confront the Pharaoh of Egypt; Elizabeth and Mary, both mothers of babies announced by angels, saw their sons eventually executed; young Joan of Arc followed angelic instructions only to find herself burned at the stake. It is not an easy path that angels call humans to, and yet so unshakeable is the experience that those who have had such encounters cannot deny the power and reality of their calling, even in the face of death.

"Give to the hungry sweet charity's bread,

For giving is living," the angel said.

"Must I be giving and giving again?"

The weary, wondering question came.

"No," said the angel, piercing me through,

"Just stop when the Lord stops giving to you!"

—Anonymous

The History

It's interesting to note that references to angels have existed as long as recorded human history. (It's also necessary to mention that any "history of angels" discussed here is a history of humans and angels—who knows what they were doing in the millennia before we showed up!)

Hermes, in the Greek pantheon of gods, served the function of messenger and was pictured with wings on his heels. In ancient Egypt, the goddess Nepthys was also winged; reliefs depicting her appear in hieroglyphics in tombs. Griffins, winged animals with human heads, appear in a very ancient Etruscan tomb. (See the biblical Book of Ezekiel for other animal/human-appearing angels.) Many other cultures featured winged lions and bulls with human heads; winged creatures were known to the Vikings as *valkyries*, to the Greeks as *horae*, to Persians as *fereshta*, to the Hindu as *apsaras*.

Yet it's important to note that wings do not an angel make. In fact, in the Abrahamic traditions (Judaism, Christianity and Islam, which trace their heritage to the patriarch Abraham), wings did not appear on angels with any regularity until the time of Emperor Constantine and did not become popular in angel art until the Renaissance. Historically, angels who interacted with humans—such as Abraham and Sarah, Jacob, Lot and his wife—came in human form and were only recognized as angels in retrospect. In Christianity, the angels at the annunciation to Mary and the announcement to the shepherds were instantly perceived as superhuman yet were never described as having wings. The angels that met the women at the tomb with the news of the resurrection of Jesus were simply described as "two men" with extraordinary lighting. It's only when you get into supernatural visions such as those of the prophet Ezekiel or the apostle John or the Persian prophet Zoroaster that wings appear with any emphasis.

While it's interesting to find beings with wings carved into ancient caves in many places in the world, what's even more fascinating is to trace the cosmology—and theology—of angels and to see the similarities that emerge in different cultures.

Many scholars feel that the earliest long-lasting, recorded, monotheistic religion was that started by Zoroaster, who lived somewhere between 1500 B.C.E. and 550 B.C.E. (This is a rather large window of time, but there are compelling arguments for placing him at the beginning, in the middle and at the end of this period.) In a vision that contained many elements familiar to Abrahamic traditions, Zoroaster found himself clearly wrestling with a demon, whom he called Angra Mainyu—the Prince of Lies, or Demon of Doubt and Despair, also called Ahaitin (amazingly close to "Satan," the Accuser). He also became aware of a supreme God of Goodness and Light, Ahura Mazda ("wise lord"), who would eventually overthrow the demon. It was all there, the holy rivers, the "host of heaven", the angels of darkness and light. Some scholars feel that before this vision of Zoroaster's, humans perceived the gods to contain both good and evil within themselves; Zoroaster came away from his vision firmly convinced that the heavens were ruled by a great good God, and people were bedeviled by evil demons and assisted by angels of light. He felt that

humans must make a choice as to whether they would serve the good or the evil side.

In 1931, a fascinating discovery was made in Northern Syria. There, archeologists unearthed the remains of Ugarit, an ancient Arabic city dating from the fourteenth century B.C.E. It was fascinating to find that their language was much like ancient Hebrew, and their religion included the gods El, Baal and others reported in the Hebrew scriptures. Also, the function of angels in their religion very much echoed Zoroaster and the Abrahamic traditions, which we will look at closely in the first part of this book.

It's intriguing to trace how theology and cosmology evolve from one culture to another. Scholars posit that because Ugarit was a seaport, its citizens received much information from other cultures; they theorize that the Jews got a good dose of Zoroastrian theology while doing their stint in Babylon, which shaped their own beliefs. It is possible, as many historians suggest, that the cosmology of angels is like a story that each culture adds to to reflect its experiences. It is also possible that prophets and visionaries have

When I ask the angels for answers to the human

mystery, I find that they guide me to a sense of peace

and comfort in my soul. The angels do this not

by bringing me answers and intricate theories,

but by bringing me creative ways of responding

to life with light in my heart.

—Terry Lynn Taylor, *The Angel Experience*

In this dim world of clouding cares,
We rarely know, till 'wildered eyes
See white wings lessening up the skies,
The angels with us unawares.

—Gerald Massey

made independent reports of their own experiences, many of which contain striking similarities. Which is true? That answer is certainly part of the mystery this book will explore.

The Mystery

But what exactly *are* angels, those "beings of light" that Rabbi David Wolpe calls "God's entourage"? Some traditions, including those of the New Age movement, suggest that angels are beings of energy that exist in between the spaces beyond human perception. We encounter them only when they move into our scope of perception or when we tune into theirs through prayer and ritual. Some traditions hold that each person has a personal angel; some feel we can get to know that angel well and have daily chats, while others feel the contact should only be initiated from the angelic side. Some

believe you shouldn't try to "conjure up" angels because you might end up with a demon who is more than pleased to answer the invitation.

Whatever you feel an angel actually is, or is made of, this just opens the door to the beginning of the mystery. For you certainly cannot believe in angels without acknowledging mystery.

Why are angels—and mystery—so well-accepted and popular now? Only a decade ago, there were a grand total of six books in print on the topic of angels. Today, they number in the hundreds. Why the sudden fascination? Three possible explanations have been suggested: first, that human history goes in cycles, as does the necessary intervention of angels. Some have suggested that angels are, in fact, busier now in human affairs than they have been at other times. Even in an era when membership in some organized religions is declining, angels meet our need to encounter the divine in a direct, personal way.

A second theory is that in the last few decades, we humans have been overcome by science and technology until we feel there is *no mystery left*, and yet we know instinctively that this is untrue. The converse of this has also been suggested: that science is revealing *so many mysteries* that we need to remind ourselves that there is a loving presence in the midst of it all. Have you seen the star show at the Rose Center for Earth and Space's New Hayden Planetarium in New York City? There is no way to digest what we now know about the heavens without being absolutely floored by the enormity and majesty of it all. The same goes for what we're discovering about human biology. The mystery is overwhelming. We need help!

Finally, it is true that we live in a world in which we're bombarded by CNN, watching terrorists rip into buildings, seeing children starving by the tens of thousands, hearing of viruses that cannot be cured. The evil in our world is beyond our control, and we desperately need to know there is a benevolent presence beyond us that is more than a match for the presence of evil and hopelessness we see on our television screens.

But you know what? All these "explanations" put together do not have the power of the experience of one twelve-year-old girl who suddenly, for the first time in her young life, knew she was loved. That is what we all need to know. And that is what the angels tell us.

Sharon Linnéa is a writer in New York and was Beliefnet's founding Inspiration Producer. Currently, she serves as head writer for the New Morning Show *on the Hallmark Network. She is an editor and coauthor of the* Chicken Soup for the Soul *series and has been a contributing editor to* Angels on Earth *magazine.*

PART ONE

ANGEL AWAKENINGS

The Birth of Angels in History and Religion

Angels in Hebrew and Christian Scripture

Those of us in the West probably are most familiar with the angels of the Hebrew and Christian scriptures: Michael, the warrior angel, cherubim and seraphim, the joyful "heavenly host" singing to a field of shepherds at Christmas. Yet, as you read the following pieces, you might be surprised at how much you don't know about the Jewish and Christian traditions—and that's not counting the fascinating angelology of the Jewish mystical tradition, the Kabbalah. For one thing, much of what shapes our thoughts of angels comes from Renaissance painters. Tall, beautiful women with halos, chubby cherubs—none of these appear in scripture. In fact, the halo is an artistic development of the fourth century that is never mentioned in scripture.

Much of the recent interest in angels has focused on the role of guardian angels. Stories abound in magazines and television shows of babies miraculously snatched from traffic or people who fell twelve stories and landed without a scratch. So it's not surprising that one of the most common questions—one that will be asked of experts in several traditions in this book—is, Just where was my angel when tragedy struck? Why is one baby saved from traffic when another is not?

Angels at a Glance

A faith-by-faith comparison of how angels are viewed.   By Rebecca Phillips

	ANGEL BASICS	FORM
JUDAISM	Angels in Judaism, or *malachim*, are messengers of God who help carry out God's work and plans.	Angels are purely spiritual beings who do not have a physical form. Biblical angels do take on physical form, though Maimonides, the great Jewish sage and biblical commentator, later wrote that physical descriptions of angels were metaphorical.
CATHOLICISM	Angels in Catholicism are intermediaries between God and humans. In addition to their roles as servants and messengers, angels are also attendants to God's throne. Catholic angelology, formulated by St. Thomas Aquinas, outlines a complex hierarchy of nine choirs of angels divided into three groups (see "The Nine Choirs of Angels" on page 73): Seraphim, Cherubim and Thrones; Dominions, Virtues and Powers; Principalities, Archangels and Angels. The Catechism of the Catholic Church declares: "The existence of the spiritual, non-corporeal beings that Sacred Scripture usually calls 'ANGELS' is a truth of faith." Angels have a huge role in Christian history— announcing Christ's birth, protecting Christ in the wilderness and battling Satan in the Book of Revelation, and more. Their most important function, however, is as attendants at God's throne.	Angels are pure spirits and remain incorporeal forever. Traditional Catholicism teaches that angels speak "within" a person, not "to" them, thereby maintaining their spiritual nature.
ORTHODOX CHRISTIANITY	Angels and archangels are part of the hierarchy of nine bodiless powers in Orthodox tradition. Angels are workers and messengers of God.	Angels are usually described in a physical way, either as having the form of man or being six-winged. However, angels do not actually have physical bodies.
PROTESTANT CHRISTIANITY	Angels are messengers and carry out God's will but have less elaborate characteristics and less prominence than in Catholicism. Angels are most important in their Gospel role of ministering to Jesus and assisting the disciples.	Angels are created as spiritual beings—not as humans. They can take on a corporeal form if doing so will help them do their work on earth. They are genderless and invisible.

INTERVENTION	IMPORTANT ANGELS
Angels intervene in stories in the Torah (the first five books of the Bible written by Moses) as God's messengers, such as when an angel stops Abraham from sacrificing his son Isaac. There is also the famous story of Jacob wrestling with an angel. But in general, angels initiate the communication from God, not vice versa. There is no angel worship in Judaism, and Jews believe that it is only God who determines what happens on earth—angels merely carry out God's will.	Traditionally, Michael is a guardian of the people of Israel. He carries out God's mission of kindness. Gabriel is the angel of judgment and strength. Uriel is an angel who illumines the right path. Raphael is a healer.
Each individual has his or her own guardian angel. Guardian angels can intervene in human affairs to help people. They can also influence people's senses and imaginations, but not their wills. They remain with their charges even in heaven. The Catechism states: "From infancy to death human life is surrounded by their watchful care and intercession." Catholics pray to angels to ask for their help and intercession in human affairs.	Gabriel, Michael and Raphael are archangels or chief angels. Gabriel announces to Mary that she will give birth to the Son of God. Michael's role includes fighting evil and Satan, and rescuing the souls of the faithful at the hour of death. He will be present at the time of the Antichrist and the end of the world. Raphael appears only in the Apocrypha, as the angel who helped Tobias cure his father's blindness in the Book of Tobit. The unnamed Angel of the Lord in the Old Testament is said by some to be the preincarnate Christ. Lucifer is the fallen archangel who, with one-third of the angelic host, was cast out of heaven for the sin of pride. He presides over hell and seeks to lure mankind to sin.
Of all the nine types of spirit beings, the angels are the closest to man. They are appointed to guard and help believers.	Orthodox Christians follow a hierarchy of angels similar to Catholicism, also divided into three levels. The Seraphim are the closest to the Holy Trinity. The most important of all angels is the archangel Michael. Other archangels include Gabriel, Raphael, Uriel, Selaphiel, Jehudiel, Barachiel and Jeremiel. Satan, the fallen angel, plays a similar role to that of other Christian denominations.
They provide guidance and assurance to believers and pray for them in heaven. John Calvin rejected the concept of guardian angels, saying, "All the angels watch over our salvation." Not all angels are good, however. Satan, or Lucifer, the rebel angel, is a constant threat to unwary souls.	All biblical angels are important. Most Protestant theologians, however, warn against the Catholic practice of praying to angels (which they view as idolatry) and the angel hierarchy of Catholicism because these traditions are not biblical and are seen as having pagan roots. The devil is prominent as the "ruler of this world" whom humanity must struggle to overcome.

(continued)

	ANGEL BASICS	**FORM**
HINDUISM	While not specifically referred to as angels, Hinduism does have many different types of spirit beings who act in a similar capacity. One example is the *devas*, literally "shining ones", who inhabit the higher astral plane. Also present in Hinduism are *asuras*, evil spirits or demons. They are fallen *devas* who inhabit the lower astral plane, the mental plane of existence. If *asuras* do good, they can be reincarnated into *devas* and do not have to remain eternally in the lower plane. Hinduism also includes *apsaras*, who are heavenly nymphs; *angiris*, who preside over sacrifices; and *lipika*, who regulate karma.	*Devas* and *apsaras* are spiritual beings, but they are often depicted in physical form. *Apsaras* are seductively beautiful, and the *devas* often look like royalty, stately and handsome.
ISLAM	Angels in Islam, or *malaikah*, play an essential role as messengers and intermediaries from Allah to the world, beginning with the angel Jabra'il (Gabriel) who revealed the Qur'an, Islam's holy book, to the Prophet Muhammad.	Angels do not have a real physical shape. Though at certain times angels may materialize in different forms in dreams or visions, their true forms are incomprehensible to humans.
MORMONISM	Angels in Mormonism are persons who have lived on this Earth at one time ("resurrected personages") or at some point will be born onto this Earth. They are considered by Mormons to be messengers of God and "ministering spirits".	Angels with a physical body are resurrected persons. Those without a physical body have either not been born yet or have not been resurrected yet. Angels without a physical body still possess a spirit body that is identical in form and appearance to a physical body.

| --- | --- |
Devas and *asuras* can inspire or bring down aspirants, helping or hindering people's spiritual journey. *Apsaras* escort brave Hindu warriors killed in battle to heaven.	No specific individual angels.
Every person has two guardian angels in their lives. Guardian angels watch and record everything people do.	The most important of these messengers was the angel Gabriel, or Jabra'il, who Muslims believe revealed the Qur'an from Allah to Muhammad. The other Islamic archangels are Mika'il (Michael), who patrols the Israelites; Israfil, who will sound the trumpet on the last day; and Izra'il, who is the angel of death. Munkar and Nakir are two other angels who visit graves and test the faith of the recently deceased. Shaitan, the Muslim equivalent of the devil, is also important in Islam. Also called Iblis, Shaitan is the source of evil in the world. He is not considered an angel but instead is a member of the *jinn*, invisible spirit beings who can be good or bad. Shaitan tempts humans and tries to mislead them.
Latter-day Saints believe that angels can appear to people in a very literal sense but not necessarily that each person has a specifically assigned guardian angel. Angels serve to advance the work of the Lord through giving instruction or authority for specific tasks, as was the case with the founding of the Mormon religion. Angels can also impart comfort, warning, protection or knowledge but never in a way that interferes with human free will. Mormons believe that the whispering of the Holy Ghost is a more common and ultimately more effective way in which God communicates with individuals.	Mormons believe that their founding prophet, Joseph Smith, was visited by the angel Moroni who led him to the Book of Mormon. (Moroni, once human, was the son of the prophet Mormon. Moroni became an angel after his death.) A golden statue of Moroni sits atop most Mormon temples.

(continued)

	ANGEL BASICS	FORM
BUDDHISM	The Buddhist equivalent of angels is devas, or celestial beings. Some schools of Buddhism also refer to dharmapalas or dharma protectors. In Tibetan Buddhism, for instance, devas are sometimes considered to be emanations of bodhisattvas, or enlightened beings. Different schools of Buddhism have different important devas, as they are often derived from pre-Buddhist cultures and religions and not from Buddhist philosophy.	Devas are spiritual beings by nature—their form is usually described as bodies or emanations of light or energy. They are, however, often depicted in physical form, and there are many images of devas or dharmapalas, particularly in Tibetan Buddhist iconography.

One hard fact of the Judeo-Christian tradition is that God is much more likely to use angels to get people *through* hard times than to save them *from* hard times. Faithful Jews Shadrach, Meshach and Abednego were not saved from the fiery furnace by an angel—they were joined by one in the flames. Angels appeared to Jesus in the Garden of Gethsemane not to save him from his impending death but to give him the strength to endure it.

Do angels play the same role in today's world as they did in biblical times? Many believe they do. One such instance occurred in a kitchen in the middle of the night, in Montgomery, Alabama. As a protest against segregation, Martin Luther King Jr., then a twenty-seven-year-old minister with a young wife and baby, was called to lead the boycott against the Montgomery city bus system. He believed strongly in the cause, and he also believed strongly in Jesus' teachings of love and nonviolence.

What he hadn't counted on was the personal hatred that would be focused on him and other black people in the Civil Rights movement. He and his wife, Coretta, began to receive many threatening phone calls, including one the night after he had been jailed on a false "speeding" charge. Unable to sleep, he went down to the kitchen. There he had a cup of coffee and began to pray. He was new to this kind of hatred and was frightened for his family's safety. Discouraged and exhausted, he prayed, "I just can't face it alone!"

Devas normally do not interfere in human affairs, but as Buddhist teacher Lama Surya Das notes, they have been known to rejoice, applaud and rain down flowers for good deeds performed in the world. In Thailand, it is believed that devas approve of people meditating and will harass people of whose behavior they do not approve.

The bodhisattva of compassion, known as Kwan Yin in Chinese and Chenrezig in Tibetan, is widely viewed as a sort of Buddhist angel. The bodhisattva's original Sanskrit name, Avolokiteshvara, means "hearer of the ten thousand cries"—that is, he or she (the bodhisattva is male in the original Buddhist texts but is represented as female in many Buddhist schools) perceives the suffering of all sentient beings—and in some sects, reciting her name is believed to summon her aid.

Then, as he would later describe, he suddenly knew he wasn't alone. Not only did he feel a presence, he felt a voice telling him that he wasn't alone, that he was called to fight for justice. It was a religious and moral call. This presence and voice in the kitchen did not save him from what was ahead, but it changed him completely. The next morning, though tired, he felt happy and full of energy. Like many others to whom the word of God came as an angelic message, he knew that no matter what hardships lay ahead, this was what he was supposed to do—and that he had supernatural support.

Days later, his worst fears were realized. A bomb ripped through the Kings' house. Fortunately, no one was hurt. Instead of being terrified, King found himself filled with strength and peace. He exhorted the furious crowd that gathered at his home to meet hatred with love and never to answer violence with violence. His words were so deeply felt and so persuasive that a police officer remarked, "If it wasn't for that black pastor, there'd be many a man dead tonight!"

Many people have found that when they are called to walk a hard path, God sends angels as unseen companions to guide, guard and sustain. It's often in the midst of the "dark night of the soul" that angel whispers can be heard.

Angel Awakenings

Angels in Jewish Tradition

What do the Hebrew scriptures and commentaries say about the heavenly host?

―――○◎○―――

By Rabbi David Wolpe

The Tanakh, or Hebrew scriptures, are made up of the Torah (the first five books of the Bible written by Moses), the Prophets and the Writings. Read how angels fit into ancient and modern Jewish thought.

Why in the world do we need angels? Angels seem not to fit inside a monotheistic faith. God can presumably accomplish anything, so what is the function of an angel? If they are doing God's bidding, they are unnecessary, and if they are opposing God, then how can any heavenly creature thwart the will of an omnipotent God?

Jewish teachings about angels are ancient, going back to the first five books of the Bible, the Torah. Cherubim with flaming swords guard the gates of Eden after Adam and Eve are banished (Genesis 3). An angel arrives to tell Abraham he and Sarah will have a child (Genesis 18), and then an angel stays Abraham's hand when he is about to sacrifice that child (Genesis 22). It is an angel who saves Hagar and Ishmael in the desert (Genesis 21), appears to Moses out of the burning bush (Exodus 3), and announces to Samson's mother-to-be that she is to have an exceptional child (Judges 13). This list is but a sampling of the angelology of the Bible.

God's Intermediaries

Why do angels play such a prominent role in Jewish tradition? Some medieval Jewish commentators propose that angels are necessary because they perform tasks that are beneath the dignity of God's "personal involvement". Others, mostly moderns who understand heavenly agents as a way of giving God "cover", assume that angels

The angels laughed. God looked down from his seventh heaven and smiled. The angels spread their wings and, together with Elijah, flew upward into the sky.

—Isaac Bashevis Singer

permit God to distance Himself, in a way, from certain deeds or obligations. But part of the allure of angels is also the colourful and humanly compelling notion of a representative of God who is more humanlike and therefore, more approachable in imagination. For example, as outlandishly other-worldly as Ezekiel's description of angels may seem to us—with its depiction of four faces, animal countenances, four wings, wheels with eyes, fire and so on—it is still more understandable than a God one cannot see. (For the full fantastic depiction, see Ezekiel 1.)

The Hebrew word for angel, *mal'ach,* means "messenger". One traditional portrait of angels is as functionaries who carry out God's will. The rabbis declare that "wherever the angel appears the shechina [the divine Presence] appears" (Exodus Rabbah 32:9). Angels are used to give God distance from the action. Since it is too anthropomorphic (that is, giving God human

characteristics) to have God wrestle with Jacob, an angel serves the purpose (Genesis 28).

Angels are God's entourage. In the famous scene of Isaiah 6, God is seated on a throne with the angelic host arrayed on the right and the left. But developing hints from the Bible, later Jewish literature ascribes to the angels their own characteristics and personalities.

Angels often appear in the apocryphal literature, books written by ancient Jews that were not made part of the Bible, such as the books of the Maccabees. In that literature and the Pseudepigrapha, literature written in the name of an ancient and important character, angels grow in stature. Enoch 3 explains the functions of various angels in a long list (for example, "Ram'amiel, who is in charge of thunder; Ra'asiel, who is in charge of earthquakes; Shalgiel, who is in charge of snow", and so forth). Apocalyptic writing, which deals with the end of days, is filled with the doings of angels. The

Angel Awakenings

The Angels' Argument: Should Man Be Created?

Ever wonder why in the first chapter of Genesis God speaks in the plural, saying, "Let us make man in our image, after our likeness . . . "? The ancient rabbis interpreted this to mean that God was speaking to the angels, spiritual beings who preexisted man and had some say in his creation. Such commentaries are found in the Midrashim, verse-by-verse interpretations of Hebrew scriptures, consisting of homily and exegesis, by Jewish teachers from 400 B.C.E. through the Middle Ages. The following passage is from the *Midrash Rabbah*, written and compiled by rabbis in the fourth and fifth centuries, among them Rabbi Simon. Here, Rabbi Simon interprets a number of scriptural verses as a debate among warring parties of angels over the creation of mankind.

Rabbi Simon said: "When the Holy One, blessed be He, came to create Adam, the ministering angels formed themselves into groups and parties, some of them saying, 'Let him be created,' while others urged, 'Let him not be created.' Thus it is written, Love and Truth fought together; Righteousness and Peace combated each other. Love said, 'Let him be created, because he will act lovingly'; Truth said, 'Let him not be created, because his nature is to be false'; Righteousness said, 'Let him be created, because he will perform righteous deeds'; Peace said, 'Let him not be created, because he is full of strife.' What did God do? God took Truth and cast it to the ground. Said the ministering angels before the Holy One, blessed be He, 'Sovereign of the Universe! Why dost Thou despise Thy seal [of truth]? Let Truth arise from the earth!' Hence it is written, Let truth spring up from the earth."

—Midrash Rabbah, *Genesis 1:26*

same is true of the Dead Sea Scrolls where, for example, The Manual of Discipline speaks of an angel of light and an angel of darkness.

Although these texts did not become normative in the Jewish tradition, they do reflect what ancient Jews were teaching and learning. And many of the views in texts that did not become part of the Bible endure in rabbinic literature.

Judaism is given shape by the writings of the rabbis. The Talmud, rabbinic commentary encompassing both Jewish law and legend written in the years between 50 B.C.E. and 600 C.E., is full of speculations and stories about angels. In rabbinic literature, angels sometimes show a little independence of mind. They even argue with God, making a persuasive case that human beings should not be created. The angels argue that people will commit offenses against truth and peace. Since the angels' arguments are not refutable—human beings do indeed sin continually against both truth and peace—God dashes truth to the ground and creates human beings in spite of their deficiencies (Genesis Rabbah 8:5).

Angels in Folklore

Jewish folklore sees angels as guardians. A famous passage reproduced in many prayer books asks for the aid of Michael, Gabriel, Uriel and Raphael. Each has a certain guiding function, although their roles vary. Michael, "merciful and forbearing" commander in chief of angelic host, is guardian of Israel. Gabriel is the master of courage. Uriel is the angel of light, whose name means "God is my light". Raphael is the healing angel.

The rabbis teach that two angels, one good and one bad, follow us home on Shabbat. If all is prepared—candles, challah, wine—the good angel exclaims,

Angel Stories
ANGELS OF DARKNESS

To me the "demons" of life are things like fear, hate, greed, envy, jealousy and other negative emotions that lower one's energy, not raise the energy. These are the "real demons" one should look out for and guard against. Love is who you are. Be the love you are and remember God's angels are always with you.

I looked, and lo, a stormy wind came sweeping out of the north—a huge cloud and flashing fire, surrounded by a radiance; and in the centre of it, in the centre of the fire, a gleam as of amber. In the centre of it were also the figures of four creatures. And this was their appearance:

They had the figures of human beings. However, each had four faces, and each of them had four wings; the legs of each were [fused into] a single rigid leg, and the feet of each were like a single calf's hoof; and their sparkle was like the luster of burnished bronze. They had human hands below their wings. The four of them had their faces and their wings on their four sides. Each one's wings touched those of the other. They did not turn when they moved; each could move in the direction of any of its faces.

Each of them had a human face [at the front]; each of the four had the face of a lion on the right; each of the four had the face of an ox on the left; and each of the four had the face of an eagle [at the back]. Such were their faces. As for their wings, they were separated; above, each had two touching those of the others, while the other two covered its body. And each could move in the direction of any of its faces; they went wherever the spirit impelled them to go, without turning when they moved . . .

Such then was the appearance of the creatures. With them was something that looked like burning coals of fire. This fire, suggestive of torches, kept moving about among the creatures; the fire had a radiance, and lightning issued from the fire. Dashing to and fro [among] the creatures was something that looked like flares.

As I gazed on the creatures, I saw one wheel on the ground next to each of the four-faced creatures. As for the appearance and structure of the wheels, they gleamed like beryl . . . Their rims were tall and frightening, for the rims of all four were covered all over with eyes.

—Ezekiel 1:4–28 (The New JPS translation according to the traditional Hebrew text)

One should not stand at the foot of a sick person's bed,
because that place is reserved for the guardian angel.

—Jewish folk saying

"May it be this way next Shabbat as well," and the bad angel responds, "Amen". If the house is not prepared, the bad angel exclaims, "May it be this way next Shabbat," and the good angel, in spite of himself, says, "Amen" (Shabbat 119b). We may think of ritual observances as the force of habit, but the rabbis portray it as the force of angels.

Some angels are less beneficent of course, and Jewish tradition is filled as well with dybbuks and demons, and the omnipresent angel of death. Again the theological aim is to distance God from the devastating consequences of tragedy. The Bible depicts God as slaying the first born in Egypt, but rabbinic tradition has long assured us that it was not God directly, but the *mal'ach hamavet*—the angel of death.

Ultimately, however, angels have an ancillary role. In both the Bible and later literature, Judaism insists God is initiator and arbiter of what happens here on earth. Rabbi Judan teaches in the Talmud that God wishes to be directly addressed: "If trouble comes upon someone, let him cry not to Michael or Gabriel, but let him cry unto Me" (Jerusalem Talmud Berachot 9:12). As Jews recite each year during Passover: "And the Lord brought us out from Egypt—not by an angel, not by a seraph [fiery angel], and not by a messenger, but the Holy One alone ..."

David Wolpe is rabbi of Sinai Temple in Los Angeles. Previously, he taught at the Jewish Theological Seminary, at the University of Judaism in Los Angeles and at Hunter College in New York

Angels in the Jewish Mystical Tradition

*The "hidden knowledge" of Jewish mysticism teaches
that angels are always with us.*

By Tamar Frankiel, Ph.D.

*Have you ever been transported by the beauty of a passage of music? If
so, it's possible that you were being touched by the same angel that influenced
the composer at the time he or she wrote it. Isn't that an inspiring thought?*

*Many established religions eventually develop three branches: the
conservative, the liberal and the mystical. Not surprisingly, angels play an
extraordinary and large role in the Jewish mystic tradition known as the
Kabbalah. Kabbalistic learning has a long and varied tradition. Many
religious movements that include fantastic or mystical experiences refrain
from sharing this "inside knowledge" with outsiders who may not understand
or be ready to accept the extraordinary teachings it contains. So it's especially
intriguing that during the last few decades, study of the Kabbalah has become
very popular, even among many who are not Jewish. Celebrities speak openly
in interviews about what they've learned, and television shows such as* The
X-Files *feature Kabbalistic beliefs (and angels) in their story lines.*

*Just what does the Kabbalah teach about angels? They are
representatives of Divine Energies (Sefirot) that keep the universe in
balance. To know more about the angels and their attributes is to come
closer to knowledge of God (and some say, to access immense power).
The following fascinating essay helps unlock centuries of mystery and
provides a vivid look into the development of this "hidden" tradition.*

The word *Kabbalah*, which comes from the Hebrew root meaning "to receive", is commonly used for the tradition of Jewish mysticism from roughly the first century to the present day (though some scholars restrict the term to medieval and later mysticism). Working hand

Angel Awakenings

in hand with the legal tradition that dominated everyday Jewish life, the mystics developed Kabbalah as a way to understand, to the extent humans can, the hidden workings of God.

Jewish mysticism tells us that angels are guiding us all the time. If we are open to them, they will help us on our path and remind us of our destiny. An ancient teaching tells us that a retinue of angels walks in front of every human being, calling out, "Make way for the image of the Blessed-Holy-One!" If we could all hear those angels, our world would be a far better place.

Classically, there were two focuses of Kabbalistic mysticism: *ma'aseh bereishit*, or "the work of Creation", and *ma'aseh merkabah*, or "the work of the Chariot". One corresponded, roughly speaking, to how God had structured the cosmos and the other to how individuals could approach God. Angels figured in both areas.

Angelic Gatekeepers

While Jewish mystics built on ancient traditions about angels as messengers and guides, new angelic traditions developed as well. First, the picture of angels as the choir, court and/or chariot of God (for example, in Isaiah and Ezekiel) evolved into an extensive cosmology. This is evident in the anonymous mystical literature of the classic period (200–800 C.E.) known as *Hekhalot*, or "palaces". Here, the visionary is presented as ascending to God. On the way, he must confront numerous angels who guard the gates against unworthy practitioners. Mystics learned chants and formulas—a great number incomprehensible, but many including angelic or divine names—to keep consciousness focused and to enable them to move through the many difficult passages.

Our Heavenly Twins

In the *Hekhalot* literature, a few angels stand out, notably the figure of Metatron, advocate for the people of Israel. He becomes a kind of "prince" (*sar*) who embodies the essence of the people. This concept of an embodying presence echoes ancient traditions; for example, classic commentaries suggest that the "man" with whom Jacob wrestled in Genesis was the "angel" or "prince" of Esau, Jacob's twin brother.

I have been on the verge of being an angel all my life, but it's never happened yet.

—Mark Twain, *Autobiography*

It is possible that this concept was influenced by the Platonic concept of every person having a "heavenly twin".

Even without association to a particular person, several angels are distinguished by their names, which indicate their essential nature: Michael (*Mi-cha-el*, meaning "Who is like God") is a high-level messenger angel. Gabriel (Gibor-el, "Strength of God") is a defending warrior, Rafael (*Refua-el*, "Healing of God") a source of healing and Uriel ("Light of God") is a guiding power. According to some Jewish traditions, these angels could be invoked at bedtime as part of a special rite of prayer before sleep; some authorities, however, opposed the invocation of angels. In addition, an angel called either Belial or Samael emerged as an evil angel, roughly the counterpart to Satan or Lucifer in Christianity.

Angels as Energy Beings

At the same time as these views were evolving, mystics were developing the basic structure of Kabbalistic thought, commonly known as the Four Worlds and Ten Sefirot (or Divine Energies). According to this view, all of reality emanated from God according to a structure of four basic levels (Emanation, Creation, Formation and Action), and within each level emerged a dynamic interactive system of ten divine energies or qualities (Crown, Wisdom, Understanding, Loving kindness, Justice, Splendor, Victory, Glory, Foundation, Kingship). Angels were seen as what we would today call energetic beings that seemed to occupy superhuman frequencies. In some cases, an angel might be explicitly associated with one of the Ten Sefirot—for example, Michael with *Tiferet* (Splendor).

By the Middle Ages, mystics had theorized that angels are unique in that they are more spiritual than human beings, but they do not have free will. Each angel has a certain type of mission and a one-pointed consciousness

(continued on page 37)

Angel Awakenings

Archangels of the Ten Sefirot (Divine Energies) in Kabbalah

SEFIRAH	ARCHANGEL	ATTRIBUTES
KETER (Crown)	Metatron	The Angel of the Lord, he is the link between the Divine and mankind. He was Enoch before his physical ascension to heaven.
CHOCHMAH (Wisdom)	Raziel	The personification of Wisdom, Raziel (Ra'asiel) is the Angel of Mysteries.
BINAH (Understanding)	Cassiel	The Angel of Contemplation.
CHESED (Loving kindness)	Zadkiel	Chief of the order of dominions. He is the Angel of Benevolence, the Angel of Mercy and the Angel of Justice.
GEVURAH (Justice)	Samael	The adversary (identified with Satan) who represents the severity of God. A chief of the seraphim and leader of angels of destruction. Also the Angel of Death.
TIFERET (Splendor)	Michael	Prince of the sun, chief of the heavenly hosts, Angel of the Presence, Angel of Repentance, Angel of Righteousness, Angel of Mercy and Angel of Sanctification.
NETZACH (Victory, Perseverance)	Anael	"He who sees God." Said to have transported Enoch to heaven.
HOD (Glory)	Raphael	The Angel of Healing, both of the world and humankind, Angel of Compassion and Love. Chief of the host of angels who unceasingly sing the praises of God.
YESOD (Foundation)	Gabriel	Prince of justice and chief of the Kerubim (wheels or chariots). He is the Angel of Mercy, Angel of Vengeance, Angel of Death and Angel of Revelation.
MALCHUT (Kingship) OR SHEKHINAH (God's Presence in the World)	Sandalphon	Twin brother of Metatron, he is a giant among angels: his feet are on Earth while his head touches heaven. Originally the prophet Elias, Sandalphon weaves the prayers of the faithful into a crown for God. He is the Guardian Angel of Earth who wages battle with Samael.

Angel Stories
ENCOUNTERS AND SIGHTINGS

I saw an angel in a little town called Tempe, Arizona, when I was driving a tractor-trailer coast to coast. I was spending the weekend there. Someone on the CB radio told me about a small place that had good food and was a quiet place to layover.

On Saturday, I awoke and thought I would walk across the street and get something to eat. As I looked around while walking I noticed how quiet it was; there were no people stirring anywhere. As I continued to walk, I kept hearing a small noise getting closer. I turned and looked behind me and was totally amazed. There was an old man right behind me on an old bike, riding like it was nothing. He stopped to say, "My brother, are you hungry and alone? Then let us go over there and have some manna, the best food I have ever tasted."

While still in shock from the bright light that seemed to be around him, he told me everything that had happened to me in days past, and what was going to happen in the days to come. He told me not to be scared and to praise God the Father for sending him to me.

We talked just as anyone would and looking at him was like looking at another person, except for that glow around him. He had no wings.

I got up to go to the men's room when he said, "If you believe in my Lord then I'm with you until the end of your world," and he was gone. He didn't fade away or disappear; he just wasn't there anymore. But it got so quiet that you could hear a pin drop, and I heard that small sound just as I did when he appeared. I was so peaceful with myself. There was no reason to ask anyone if they had seen him for it seemed like I knew him all my life. As the weeks and months went by, everything happened exactly like he said it would. I was and still am amazed at this angel encounter.

I just listened to the crowd and listened to the music and I thought of angels and clouds. I thought, "I can do this," and just enjoyed myself.

—Michelle Kwan, after winning her third U.S. Figure Skating Championships

enabling it to focus completely on that mission. An angel might be sent, for example, to teach a person. One of the most famous examples was the Magid (literally "storyteller", but in this case a teacher) who appeared in the dreams of Rabbi Yosef Karo, sixteenth-century author of the Code of Jewish Law, which still undergirds modern Jewish observance. Karo was a member of the famous mystical circle in Safed in Israel, whose guiding light was Rabbi Isaac Luria, creator of modern Kabbalah. When Karo had a question about some difficult point of Jewish law, he would often receive the answer from his Magid in his sleep.

Further, the mystics extended the idea that every person has an angelic counterpart, usually a "guardian angel", or an angel corresponding to all beings. Baal Shem Tov, founder of Hasidim, is said to have taught that every blade of grass has an angel saying to it, "Grow! Grow!" In addition, according to Avraham Greenbaum of the Breslov tradition, when we say a blessing over food before we eat it, we "awaken" the angel in charge of that kind of food, so that the spiritual essence of the food will be present as we eat. When we say a blessing afterward, we are awakening the angels in charge of making the foods assimilable by our bodily organs, so that we will be spiritually as well as physically nourished.

Touched by an Angel?

Since at least early modern times, Kabbalists have also taught that while some angels are created by God, others develop from the results of human actions. Thus, the angel created by a good deed continues to exist and can return, so to speak, to affect people in a positive way. Angelic energy surrounds many things that have been infused with deep human feeling. For example, when you feel transported by the

Angel Awakenings

*We shall find peace. We shall hear the angels,
we shall see the sky sparkling with diamonds.*

—Anton Chekhov

beauty of a piece of music, it may be that you are touched by the angel that influenced the composer at the time he or she wrote it. Sometimes we experience such an energy even around an object that has been loved. For example, when a Torah scroll is carried around the synagogue, it can be a very moving experience to touch it because it is encircled by an angelic presence. Similarly, a family heirloom that has been used with love is very different from some object that has just been around a long time.

Many people study Kabbalah today as part of regular immersion in Jewish teachings or in combination with other spiritual philosophies. Perhaps, in this context, it should be no surprise that angelic encounters are also reported with some frequency. For example, I recently heard the following story from a woman who has been studying Kabbalah for more than ten years. She had been through some intense personal difficulties during a particular week. That weekend, she went on a spiritual retreat, then she had to dive back into her dizzying schedule of professional school and work.

I was driving home at the end of a long day, when I momentarily lost track of the road. Suddenly I saw a car coming. In a flash, without my conscious awareness, "something" lifted my foot and put it on the brake—just in time to avoid a crash. Stunned, I closed my eyes and, at that moment, became aware that there was definitely someone in the car with me. I took a deep breath, said "thank you"—and started crying.

Dream encounters are perhaps the most common way in which angelic energies appear, in modern times just as in the world of medieval visionaries and prophets. Among North Americans who have been studying Kabbalah and related forms of mysticism, angels seem to appear frequently as light brown-skinned figures who bring them messages and gifts or who help or protect them in other ways. (The colour theory of Kabbalah is quite varied from one school to another, and there seems to be no clear association to the colour brown.) Frequently, such dream angels bring messages of love as well as instruction. Here is an example from my own experience:

In my dream I was at a conference. I listened to one brown-skinned man give a lecture. He was like an elder or chief. I tried to ask him a question but as I closed my eyes, concentrating, he disappeared. I went looking for him and saw him in the crowd, but then found myself in a large open room. A younger brown-skinned young man came up to me and told me that I was too stuck in my old ways of thinking. I started arguing with him. But then the first man appeared. He approached me and handed me a beautiful blue bottle; I knew it was something for me to drink. Then he said, "I don't want you to feel so alone." He hugged me; my daughter appeared, and we all hugged. I felt very loved.

If you wake up in the morning feeling very relaxed and loved, or if your room seems unusually light, you may have been visited by an angel.

Tamar Frankiel, Ph.D., lecturer in Religious Studies at the University of California, Riverside, is author of The Gift of Kabbalah: Discovering the Secrets of Heaven, Renewing Your Life on Earth *and* The Voice of Sarah: Feminine Spirituality and Traditional Judaism. *She has also coauthored, with Judy Greenfeld, two books on Jewish prayer.*

Angels in the New Testament

From the birth of Jesus to the Book of Revelation, angels make their presence felt.

By Dr. William D. Webber

Angels are no fly-by-night fad. These magnificent, mystical, supernatural beings are prominent throughout the New Testament. Angels are mentioned 165 times in fifteen books of the New Testament. You will find them in the teachings of Jesus and in the doctrinal sections of the Epistles. Their appearances at the birth and resurrection of Jesus are so dramatic and compelling that they have become a part of the popular culture. A virtual kaleidoscope of powerful angels heralds the Apocalypse in the Book of Revelation. But the New Testament is filled with many fascinating facts about the heavenly host that are little known even by many who attend church regularly.

Where does the New Testament say these celestial beings come from? Colossians 1:16, referring to angels as "things invisible, thrones, powers, rulers and authorities," teaches that they were created by God as angels; that is, God made them from nothing before the beginning of human history. Angels are not recycled humans. Angels are pure spirit (Hebrews 1:14). If we think of angels as minds without bodies, we will be much closer to their reality than if we picture the popular paintings of the heavenly hosts. The scripture writers mean this to be a source of comfort: Even when we do not see them, angels are with us. Most often the ministering angels are invisible.

But at times they must temporarily take on a form that can be seen by humans if they are to carry out the tasks God has assigned them to do. And how creatively they do this! That first Christmas night, first a single angel, then a multitude of the heavenly host, broke through the consciousness of the wondering

Over my head
I see angels in the air
There must be a God somewhere.

—African-American spiritual

shepherds in the fields near Bethlehem. What did the shepherds see? Who can know, but it must have been awesome, since the first words the angel spoke to them were, "Fear not!" Clearly there was something supernatural about their appearance that struck terror into the hearts of the shepherds.

Fear not!

Throughout the Bible, an angel's presence is so unsettling that it is necessary to begin by saying, "Fear not." But at the defining moment of Christianity, the resurrection of Jesus, the angel did not calm the fears of the guards. There was a great earthquake, and an angel of the Lord came down from heaven. The Gospel writer, at a loss for words to describe the angel who must have looked like a beautiful, blinding light, reported, "His appearance was like lightning, and his clothes were white as snow. The guards were so afraid of him that they shook and became like dead men" (Matthew 28:3–4).

Angels are not always this frightening in appearance. The writer of the Book of Hebrews indicates that sometimes angels mingle with people here on Earth (Hebrews 3:2). "Don't forget to show hospitality to strangers," he warns, "for in doing so, some have entertained angels without knowing it."

There are no "lone rangers" found in the ranks of God's holy angels. The New Testament is clear that, without exception, angels are always on assignment carrying out the will of God. Again and again the scripture writers use phrases like "I am Gabriel, sent by God" to describe the work of the angels. It is amazing but true that in the service of God the angels are commissioned to serve us! "Are not all angels ministering spirits sent to serve those who will inherit salvation?" (Hebrews 1:14)

Angels as Messengers

In the original languages of both the Old and New Testaments, the words that were translated *angel* literally mean *messenger*. Most often in the Bible, when angels poke their celestial heads into the story, they are doing exactly that—bringing messages. Gabriel was sent from heaven to a young Jewish girl in Nazareth named Mary. His task was to bring the most important birth announcement in the history of the world: "Do not be afraid, Mary, you have found favour with God. You will be with child and give birth to a son, and you are to give him the name Jesus. He will be great and will be called the Son of the Most High . . ." (Luke 1:30–32). Angels were dispatched to Joseph three times: once to tell him not to be afraid to marry Mary, later to warn him to take his family to Egypt to escape Herod's

Angel Stories
ENCOUNTERS AND SIGHTINGS

I believe that an angel saved my life in an auto accident. This happened in 1983. I was a passenger in the back seat of a Z28 that hit a telephone pole at 110 mph. I am the only one who believed in God in the car and I flew through the front window and never went unconscious.

I remember asking the Lord if I had any favours coming to please save me as my little boy was only three years old at the time. As I saw the ground coming up, I remember curling up and it was as if a hand caught me before impact and gently put me down. I received a small cut on my right shoulder with three stitches. The doctor in the ER brushed glass off of my face and much to his surprise, I didn't have any broken bones. The doctor looked at me square in the eye and said, "I have never seen anything like this before. You should be dead. Someone upstairs must be watching out for you." The other 2 people in the car are in wheelchairs to this day.

For compassion a human heart suffices, but for full and adequate sympathy, with joy, an angel's only.

—Samuel Taylor Coleridge

wrath, and still later to advise him when it was safe to return—information Joseph had no way of knowing.

What Jesus Taught about Angels

The Gospel writers record that Jesus frequently spoke to his disciples about angels. He taught that angels are not male or female; they have no gender, at least as we know it. They do not marry or procreate because each angel is created directly by God (Matthew 22:30). Angels aren't just "ideas of God" or "God's thoughts", however. They have great intelligence, but they do not know everything—only God is omniscient. For example, the angels do not know the time of the Second Coming (Matthew 24:36). Jesus also taught about guardian angels that they who watch over little children (Matthew 18:10), for example, and watch the activities of individual people with sympathetic eyes, rejoice when they

make the right choices (Luke 15:10). In a parable, Jesus taught that the angels carried the soul of Lazarus to Abraham's bosom or heaven (Luke 16:22), and that at His Second Coming, He would return "and all the angels with him" (Matthew 25:31).

Mission Possible

After the crucifixion of Jesus, angels appear at crucial moments to the apostles, bolstering their faith, clarifying their mission and at times protecting them from the enemies of early Christianity. The first appearance to the disciples occurs right in the middle of Jesus' ascension in Acts 1, when "two men in white robes" suddenly arrive to deliver the important message that Jesus will be returning "the same way as you saw him go into heaven." In Acts 8, an angel dramatically appears and brings Philip an unusual assignment: He is to waylay an Ethiopian official—a eunuch—as he drives in his chariot and explain the

Angel Awakenings

Gospel to him. Philip's successful mission results in the official's conversion and the spread of the Gospel into Ethiopia. Having baptized the eunuch, Philip is snatched from sight by an angel, who drops him in another town. An angel like "a man in dazzling clothes" comes to Cornelius, a Roman soldier, and sends him to meet the apostle Peter. The result of this angelic intervention is a complete change in Peter's theology—he will now preach the Gospel to all people, including Romans.

Angels Bring Encouragement

But it would be a mistake to think of angels simply as some kind of glorified messengers. New Testament angels are especially good at bringing comfort and strength. It is well-known that Jesus was tempted in the wilderness. What is often overlooked is that after the temptation, the angels came, ministering and encouraging him (Matthew 4:11). The role of the angels was not to keep Jesus from the pain and agony of the cross, but rather to help strengthen him for what he had to go through.

During the worst moment of a "perfect storm," an angel appeared to Paul (Acts 27), bringing comfort and encouragement. Paul was not saved from the hardship of shipwreck. But he was encouraged by the angel who also brought the message that everyone on board would survive, and Paul would complete his mission and appear before Caesar. In these instances, angels disappear as suddenly as they appear. Throughout scripture, angels do not linger or develop an ongoing relationship with people. They do their work and then leave so that all the glory will go to God instead of the angel.

Angelic Jailbreaks

As the early church grew dramatically, persecution increased as well. At key moments, the presence and power of God was displayed by angelic interventions, validating their messages and drawing larger audiences for their preaching. In Jerusalem, when the apostles performed many signs and wonders among the people, the jealous high priest had them arrested and put in the public jail. The next day, when it was time for the trial, officials found the jailers standing guard and the doors of the jail locked tightly. But the jail was empty! During the night, an angel had secretly opened the prison doors and miraculously led the apostles past the guards without being seen. Rather than having them hide out, the angel gave the apostles the instruction, "Go stand in the temple courts and tell the people the full message of this new life" (Acts 5:20). And that is exactly where the apostles were found.

Later, when Herod imprisoned Peter (Acts 12), he took no chances. He had Peter chained between two soldiers, with two separate groups of guards stationed between the prisoner and the iron gate of the prison. But an angel appeared, Peter's chains fell off, and the angel led the apostle past the first and second guards who did not see them at all. The heavy iron gate of the prison swung open by itself and Peter walked out a free man.

A Warning against Angel Worship

Angels displayed such awesome power and performed such unbelievable feats

that it would only be natural, especially in a predominately polytheistic culture, that some would be tempted to worship angels. For this reason, throughout the New Testament it is emphasized again and again that angels are created beings and are not to be worshipped. Paul stresses the supremacy of Jesus over the angels (Colossians 2:8). In fact, the entire first chapter of the Book of Hebrews makes the case that Jesus only is to be worshipped, and the angels are subordinate to Him. And when John falls down to worship the angel of Revelation, he is strongly rebuked by the angel itself: "You must not do that! I am a fellow servant with you . . . Worship God!" (Revelation 22:8–9)

Angels in Revelation

The Book of Revelation is a distinct type of literature. Revelation is apocalyptic, a kind of writing that is highly symbolic. The book, written to bring encouragement and hope to persecuted believers, is filled with powerful, almost cinematic, visions of angels. Again and again, we see the angels at worship around the throne of God. So glorious is the vision of the heavenly host "singing with full voice" in Revelation 5 that it inspired the majestic choruses of Handel's *Messiah*. Angels of Revelation are so awesome in their power over nature and humanity that mortals cannot fully comprehend it. The book looks forward to the final conflict between good and evil, when Michael and his holy angels completely defeat the evil angels.

Angelology is one of the most intriguing subjects one could ever study. Leading philosopher Mortimer J. Adler, editor of the *Encyclopædia Britannica* and *Great Books of the Western World*, wrote, "Angels are more fascinating than science fiction and extraterrestrial beings." But the more we learn about the heavenly host, the more we are aware that there is so much more we do not know. Angels usually do their work unnoticed. It is said that only in heaven will we become aware of how often angels were active in our lives and the lives of the people around us. Only then will we learn the extent to which the ministry of angels has changed the course of history.

The Reverend Dr. William D. Webber has been the pastor of American Baptist churches. With his wife, Marilynn Carlson, he is the author of A Rustle of Angels: Stories about Angels in Real Life and Scripture *and* Tea with the Angel Lady. *The Webbers have been frequent guests on radio and television programs about angels.*

On Religion and Real-Life Angels

An interview with Joan Wester Anderson

———

By Wendy Schuman

Few writers today know angels better than Joan Wester Anderson, whose Where Angels Walk *was one of the earliest and most successful angel books of the 1990s, selling nearly two million copies worldwide. Anderson, a practising Catholic, says her Christian faith informs her belief in the immediacy and intercession of angels. She also says her books were inspired by a personal experience of angelic intervention. Alarmed by a feeling of fear for her son Tim and his friend Jim, who were driving home from college for Christmas, Joan prayed earnestly for God to help. The radio reported a record windchill of minus-eighty degrees and warned that stepping outside for just a few minutes could be fatal.*

Hours later, when Tim finally called, he related that he and Jim had indeed been in peril. Their car had stalled on a rural road, and they knew they were in imminent danger of death from exposure. They too prayed for help. Almost immediately there appeared a man rapping on the car window. "Need a tow?" he asked.

Startled, the boys turned to see a tow truck behind them. Its driver towed them back to the home of the friend they had just dropped off— without a word and without asking for directions—and vanished as mysteriously as he had arrived.

Moved and surprised by Tim and Jim's story, Anderson, a magazine writer, put out a request for other angelic experiences through a women's magazine and was astounded to receive hundreds of responses, many of which appear in her books. A decade later, Anderson still revels in "the abundance of God" and the company of the angels.

What in your view are angels? What is their essence? Do you have a working definition?

It's almost more important to state what angels are not—they are not the spirits of people who have died. So often we hear someone say, "My baby died, and now she's our little angel in heaven." It's an understandable sentiment, but it's not accurate. Angels are a separate creation, perhaps the first God ever made. All faiths that accept the existence of angels—and that's all Western religions and many of the Eastern—see them in the same way: spirit beings without bodies but able to take on a human form—or any form—if God requires it to carry out His plan. Human beings will become like angels after death, spirits according to most religions, but they will be saints, not angels.

Are angels really necessary as intercessors? Why can't we communicate directly with God?

We should, can and most of the time do communicate directly with God. To my knowledge, angels are not necessary for anything. But God's creation is abundant, and asking "Why angels?" would be like asking why there are thousands of varieties of trees or stars, when we could get along with so much less. God Himself told us many times that He was sending angels to love and care for us, so He is the one who brought them into our lives. Therefore, even if we don't understand their entire purpose, I vote that we pay attention to them.

Angel Stories
LENDING COMFORT IN DEATH

When our youngest son, age 24, passed away last year, the morning after his death, in a completely frozen pond in our backyard, there appeared a perfect shape of a huge heart melted through the ice and snow. It was as though the hand of God Himself carved it out, or perhaps He sent His Angels to comfort us. And it did.

*May leprechauns strew happiness wherever you walk each day,
and Irish angels smile on you all along the way.*

—Irish blessing

Can anyone who wants to have an angelic experience or encounter?

There are people who profess being able to bring on an angel experience for themselves or others. I am willing to keep an open mind on this, but I believe that angels are God's servants, not ours, and they do not show up or perform miraculous deeds on our timetables. Since God doesn't change, and the angels mentioned in scripture did not spend hours or days interacting with humans, I have to assume that angels haven't changed either and largely do the same things they did way back when.

Is it ever okay to pray to or invoke angels? How do you get in touch?

It's not okay to worship angels—worship belongs only to God. This is a hang-up mainly for Protestants who seem to think that when Catholics and Orthodox Jews state that we pray to angels, we're putting them before God, which is simply not true. I think it is obvious that—if we each have a guardian angel or even if we don't, and angels simply come when necessary—we still should get to know this part of creation. People who do say their lives flow much more easily.

What's the most surprising thing you've discovered about angels?

That so many people believe in them. I thought they were really only accepted or noticed by traditional Catholics. When my first book came out, I thought I was going to have to explain angels to people. I was shocked to be invited on so many talk shows on radio, and people called in without any hint of embarrassment to share their own angel stories.

Has your view of angels evolved in any way over the last ten years since your first book on angels was published?

I have learned to pay a great deal more attention to my own angel. I am in touch

Angel Awakenings

"How many angels can dance on the head of a pin?"

Today we view that question as pretty amusing, an invitation to argue over something so esoteric that it makes no sense. But several centuries ago, in the Middle Ages, scholars spent years debating angelology, or the theory of angels. And when the answer became a matter of doctrine, how you answered could determine whether you were embraced by the Church or cast out as a heretic. How would you answer the following questions, if your immortal soul depended on the correct choice?

Do angels have free will? Do they have spirit bodies or are they pure intellect? Can they grieve for those humans they guard? Can angels eat meat or any human food?

Way back in A.D. 325, the First Ecumenical Council of Nicea was formed when the church fathers were still pulling together what would and would not be accepted as official Christian doctrine. After examining the Gospel texts and letters that would be included in the canon, they concluded that angels were, in fact, an important part of Jesus' life and teaching.

This delighted the ordinary folks, who certainly felt they could use some divine help and intervention, and the first explosion of popular interest in angels was unleashed. So enthusiastic was the acceptance of angels that less than twenty years later, in 343, another council found it necessary to reaffirm the apostle Paul's firm dictates against worshipping angels themselves.

Sometime in the next two centuries, a monk from Palestine came on the scene, having "discovered" several mystical books written by Dionysius, an Athenian convert of the apostle Paul's and the first bishop of Athens. One of the books, *De Hierarchia Celesti*, detailed the hosts of heaven in amazing detail. It gave an exhaustive scheme and hierarchy of the "armies of heaven", which was consequently accepted by the Catholic Church. It wasn't until the fifteenth century that these documents were discovered to be written not by Dionysius but by the monk himself, who was given the unflattering name "Pseudo-Dionysius". Even after his deception was uncovered, the angelic hierarchy he put forth remained intact, and he himself was later sainted as the original Dionysius had been.

It was in 787 that the Catholic Church proclaimed an official "dogma of archangels", which gave detailed lists of angels' names and duties—much of it based on the presumed writings of Dionysius. Things were fairly quiet on the theological front for another five hundred years, until Catholic scholars once again wrestled with angels.

Two rival schools sprang up, with the august John Duns Scotus, a Scottish theologian, positing ideas that were hotly contested by Thomas Aquinas. Scotus believed that angels, though created of spirit only, were made of denser material than God, whose spirit was so pure as to be literally made of nothing. Scotus believed that angels were able to think and reason and were created as many different individuals, much as humans were.

Meanwhile, Thomas Aquinas, who is still revered as one of the greatest philosophers of the Catholic faith, did his own interpretation of angelic theology. In a series of lectures at the University of Paris, Aquinas argued that angels had no corporeal existence at all, that they were "all intellect". They were able, however, to assume human bodies at will, and even to eat human food. (Whether angels could ingest human food or had to make do with manna was another hotly contested theological point.) He further argued that angels had free will only at the moment of their creation, at which time they could choose to follow God.

Very shortly after Aquinas's death, the church again reviewed its teaching and issued the Condemnations of 1277, which made several of Aquinas's widely accepted teachings heretical. Nevertheless, Aquinas was canonized in 1323 and given the title *Doctor Angelicus* of the church in 1567. Catholic children still invoke his aid when they start school.

Although, or perhaps because of, the serious consequences of all this back-and-forth over angel minutiae in the Middle Ages, the common people mostly held their tongues and nodded their heads while the scholars debated. In fact, the question, "How many angels can dance on the head of a pin?" was never a topic of debate—it was a great joke of the Middle Ages, the question ordinary folks used to poke fun at the serious theologians, who seemed to be taking the details just a little bit too seriously.

—*Sharon Linnéa*

with him every day. I've also learned to be open to the ideas that other people, especially in alternative faith situations, have about angels. I am a firm Christian, so I take my knowledge about angels from scripture and tradition. But I have also learned that there are other truths that aren't necessarily written down and many more evolving even now. I want to be discerning, but I've learned to listen to others' views and sort out what I think rings true.

How did you get in touch with your angel? Do you know your angel's name?

He really became real to me when I met a person who told me she could sometimes know what a specific angel's name was. I was kind of iffy about this—was this person weird? But I remained open, and she was relieved about that. It must be hard for her or people like her to approach the rest of us—I'm sure they often get rebuffed. She told me that she felt certain that my angel was a huge warrior angel, whose name was Dominic, and he would protect me, especially as I travelled. It just seemed right somehow, the

name and his mission. Once I began speaking to him using his name, I just wanted to be closer to him, so I spoke more frequently. Dominic is definitely a friend to me now, and I ask him for all kinds of things—mostly help, inspiration and patience.

You mentioned that you believe in bad angels, or negative entities—can you expand on this a little?

In the Bible, it explains that God created angels and about one-third of them rose up against the others to attempt to take over heaven. There was a huge fight, and the good angels tossed the bad ones out of heaven where they "roam the world, seeking the ruin of souls." I do believe in these negative spirits; I believe they wrought much sorrow and fear in this world, but I try not to concentrate on them too much. Why give them publicity when we have so many good things going on?

Where were the angels on September 11?

Right where they always are: with us. There have been stories about

We truly are the tenth Choir of angels—the Angels of Earth.
It is up to us to bring each other God's message of eternal love.

—Jane M. Howard, *Commune with the Angels*

strangers guiding people down the stairs of the World Trade Center buildings, then disappearing. The question really is: Why didn't the angels step in and save those victims? I don't know why. People have free will—it's our greatest gift—and God will not thwart it. But He can also bring good out of any kind of evil, and although we may not see anything good yet, I am sure it will come.

There was a photo of dark smoke around the World Trade Center that looked like a horned being—do you think destructive angels were involved?

People send me photos all the time—they see angels or devils in them. I don't know if they are authentic or not, and I try to keep away from that. It can so often be a fraud or just a natural occurrence.

And, sometimes, horror chills our blood

To be so near such mystic Things,

And we wrap round us, for defense,

Our purple manners, moods of sense—

As angels, from the face of God,

Stand hidden in their wings.

—Elizabeth Barrett Browning,
"A Sabbath Morning at Sea"

Do Angels Really Sing?

By Marilynn Carlson Webber and Dr. William D. Webber

Some people who thrive on trivia love to point out that there is no mention in the Bible of angels singing. They point out that even in the Christmas story the Bible says, "Suddenly a great company of the heavenly host appeared with the angel, praising God and saying, 'Glory to God in the highest, and on Earth peace to men on whom his favour rests'" (Luke 2:13).

While it is true that the verse uses the word "saying" instead of "singing", most people find it more logical to imagine the angels singing a great "Gloria" rather than acting as a speech choir. And doesn't "praising" God imply singing, as well?

We do find the angels singing in Job 38:7. Talking about the time of creation, the Lord says " . . . the morning stars sang together/and all the angels shouted for joy." Most biblical scholars agree that in this passage the terms "morning stars" is another name for angels. This is an example of parallelism in Hebrew poetry, where the second line states the same idea as the first line.

The apostle John heard angels sing. He wrote in Revelation 5:9 about the angels: "And they sang a new song." Perhaps one reason that people do not recognize this as angels singing is that the words "living creatures" ("beasts" in the King James version) and "elders" are used. Chapter four of Revelation clearly describes the elders and living creatures as angels.

In Revelation 5:11 we read, "Then I looked and heard the voice of many angels, numbering thousands upon thousands, and ten thousand times ten thousand. They encircled the throne and the living creatures and the elders. In a loud voice they sang:

Worthy is the Lamb, who was slain,

to receive power and wealth and wisdom and strength

and honour and glory and praise!

Build a chair as if an angel was going to sit on it.

—Thomas Merton

What a song that must have been!

Do angels sing today? Here are a few recent stories of those who have heard them.

Songs My Mother Taught Me

When Lois Ponte was growing up, her mother, Marian Fleming, often told her the story of the day the angels sang. As a child, it was Lois's favourite story. It still is today.

When Marian Fleming was a young wife, she fell down icy cement steps, seriously injuring herself. Worse than the physical pain, which was intense, was the young woman's despair. She knew that there was a possibility that she wouldn't walk again. She had three little children— how would she possibly cope?

Then one day as she lay alone in her bed, music filled her room—the sweetest singing she'd ever heard. She looked around to see if anyone was there, even though she knew that no one was. Still the sweet music continued. The words wound around her, filling her with peace. She'd never heard the song before, but its words were comforting and sung with other-worldly certainty and love.

As the music continued, Marian's despair was turned to trust. She knew that she was hearing angels singing and encouraging her. That song renewed the courage and determination that she needed to fight her way back to health.

Only after she was walking again did she see and recognize in a hymnal the unfamiliar song she'd heard sung. Excitedly, she traced the words: "God will take care of you, through every day, o'er all the way . . ." It became her favourite song because she knew for a fact that the lyrics were credible.

Long after she was walking again, Marian kept these things and pondered them in her heart. Every once in a while, she'd tell her story to her enraptured children.

Many years later, as Marian lay

dying in the hospital, her daughter Lois would sit by her bedside and sing "God Will Take Care of You." She hoped that her mother, though in a coma, could hear it and that it would be a loving bridge between this world and the next as the angels took up the final chorus.

Cherie Hanson and the Complimentary Neighbors

One fall evening, the Hanson family had a strange experience: They heard angels singing around their house. In awe they listened to the incredible music all evening long. They couldn't help wondering if they were sharing some wonderful dream. The next morning, their unbelieving neighbors commented on their beautiful singing the night before. "We had no idea that you folks are so talented," they commented. "We've never heard anyone with such amazing voices!"

Said Cherie, "It was then we knew that what we'd heard had been real and not a dream. God is great!"

Laurel Hammond—Singing Alleluia

Laurel Hammond was singing as she drove to work. Instead of letting the traffic annoy her, she preferred to praise God. This morning, the traffic was low, driving was easy and Laurel was especially happy. Thinking of God's love, Laurel began to sing, "Alleluia, alleluia!"

She became aware that others were singing with her—but she was alone in the car. Laurel checked her radio. It was off.

As she began to sing again, her car was filled with glorious harmony. The unseen voices had a soft, light, ethereal quality. As Laurel sang her alleluias, the unseen voices added harmonies different from any she had heard. The sheer beauty of their voices seemed to urge Laurel to lift her voice in renewed praise. When she stopped, the voices became fainter and slowly faded away.

"But I heard them!" Laurel exclaimed. "It was such a blessing, such a confirmation from God."

The Angels' Song

Jill Richmond and her friend Linda were planning a "Life in the Spirit" seminar for their parish in Orange, California. Their lives had been touched by God, and they were excited about sharing with others. Jill had taken the lead in a similar seminar that had been well-received. Linda had been her "gofer", working largely behind the scenes, making sure that everything needed was ready and when it was needed, to "gofer" what was necessary.

In the next seminar, Linda would be the leader, and Jill would be her "gofer". The two had been planning and praying; now they decided that the time had come to share their plans with the pastor and ask his counsel. They came to

But oh, how fall'n! How changed

From him who, in the happy realms of light,

Clothed with transcendent brightness, didst outshine

Myriads though bright!

—John Milton, *Paradise Lost*

the church and rang the doorbell. Jill and Linda waited. They rang the doorbell again, and waited . . . and waited . . . and waited. The two friends were talking as they waited. Then Linda said, "Jill, do you hear what I hear?"

"Yes!" replied Jill. "It's angels singing!"

It was as though the heavens had opened up and the two women could hear through the opening the angels singing glory to God. The two women had come to glorify God's name. They stood at the steps of the church, bathed in the beauty of the celestial music, their hearts caught up in the sense of worship. The music became softer, then faded away. When the music stopped, Jill and Linda quietly left the church. Their visit had been completely rewarding. There was no disappointment that there had been no one to open the church door, for the heavens had opened. There had been no words of pastoral counsel, but they had shared in the praises of God as sung by the angels. Their prayers had been answered in an unexpected way, their lives had been blessed and they were renewed in their service to God.

The Reverend Dr. William D. Webber has been the pastor of American Baptist churches. He and his wife, Marilynn Carlson, are the authors of A Rustle of Angels: Stories about Angels in Real Life and Scripture *and* Tea with the Angel Lady. *The Webbers have been frequent guests on radio and television programs about angels.*

All-Star Angels

A Guide to the Most Famous Angels in Scripture

———◆———

By Dr. William D. Webber

Countless angels work day in and day out for millennia, and the Bible never mentions their names. In fact, the only angels named in the scriptures are archangels, and even these are mentioned only briefly. Yet what we do learn about these celestial beings in the scattered accounts is fascinating.

How many archangels are there? It all depends on who is counting. Different sources say that there are anywhere from four to seventy angels facing the Divine Presence. The Book of the Angel Raziel (Ra'asiel), a Kabbalist work, cites seven great archangels. But historically, the mainstream Protestant view has been to count only those specifically mentioned in the Bible, and there is only one text that mentions an archangel by name—"Michael the archangel" in Jude 9. Billy Graham writes, "He (Michael) must stand alone, because the Bible never speaks of archangels, only *the* archangel."

The Roman Catholic Church, which uses a larger compilation of the Hebrew scriptures including the books of the Apocrypha, recognizes three: Michael, Gabriel and Raphael. A fourth, Uriel, was sometimes included until A.D. 745, but the Catholic Church does not officially recognize him as an archangel today. His feast day, however, is still celebrated in the Coptic Church on July 28.

Most scholars would also agree that there is biblical ground for believing that Lucifer was an archangel before his fall, equal or even superior to Michael.

There are countless numbers of angels, but these are the only archangels named in Christendom. Who are these angels, and what is so special about them?

Will the Real Michael Please Stand Up?

The name *Michael* literally means "who is like God". (Most angel names end in the suffix "-el", meaning God.) Michael makes every "Who's Who?" list of archangels, whether in or out of the Bible. He ranks as the greatest of all angels in Jewish, Christian and Islamic literature. He is said to be the first angel created by God. There are only four biblical references where Michael is called by name. In Daniel he is portrayed as the defender of Israel and is called "a chief prince" and "the great prince". The word *prince* when used about angels refers to having authority over a host of angels in battle. Thus, Michael, as chief prince, would be in authority over all the other prince angels. In Revelation 12:7–12, Michael leads his angels in the titanic struggle with Satan and his angels at the final conflict of the world. To quote Billy Graham, "Scripture tells us in advance that Michael will finally be victorious in battle. Hell will tremble; heaven will rejoice and celebrate."

According to tradition, Michael was the unnamed angel who carried the stone tablets that contained the Ten Commandments to Moses on Mount Sinai, the angel who stood in the way against Baalam (Numbers 22:22), who appeared with Shadrach, Meshach and Abednego in the fiery furnace, and who held back the arm of Abraham as he was about to sacrifice Isaac. In other Jewish writings, Michael is the "Angel of the Lord" who spoke to Moses from the burning bush.

Gabriel: Mighty One of God

The name *Gabriel* literally means "mighty one of God" or "God is my strength". Apart from Michael, he is the only angel mentioned by name in the Old Testament, unless we include the Book of Tobit, which is usually considered to be apocryphal. Gabriel is mentioned by name four times in the Old and New Testaments, always bringing good news. In Daniel 8 and 9, Gabriel appears to Daniel and explains to him God's purpose and program and the events that will take place in the end times. He interprets Daniel's vision and gives him wisdom and understanding. A clear description of Gabriel is found in Daniel 10:

I looked up and saw a man clothed in white linen, with a gold belt around his waist. His body was like beryl, his face like lightning, his eyes like flaming torches, his arms and legs like the gleam of polished bronze, and the sound of his words like the roar of a crowd. I, Daniel, alone saw the vision; the people who were with me did not see it.

The stories in Daniel give a wonderful sense of how angels work behind the scenes. Gabriel explains to the prophet how he and Michael have been working on Israel's behalf, while the angel who oversees the Kingdom of Persia had been disputing some matter with them. Unlike the usually brief messages other angels bring, Gabriel's explanation goes on for pages, establishing him as the wordiest angel in the scripture.

Gabriel is perhaps best known as the angel who brought the news to Mary that she had been chosen by God to bear the Christ Child. In artists' depictions, he appears with a lily in his hand—a symbol of Mary's purity.

Gabriel is also the angel who had earlier brought the news to the aging priest Zechariah that he and his wife, Elizabeth, who was long past childbearing age, would also have a son, John (the Baptist), who would prepare the way for Christ. His words in

Luke 1:19, "Do not be afraid, Zechariah . . . I am Gabriel. I stand in the presence of God, and I have been sent to speak to you and to bring you this good news," indicate his high placement. Some suggest that he is one of the seven seraphim who stand in the presence of God in the Book of Revelation, indicating they are of the highest rank.

Some Christian traditions hold that it was he who appeared in the Christmas narratives to Joseph and to the shepherds. Some also believe he was the angel who strengthened Jesus in the Garden of Gethsemane and rolled back the stone of his tomb at his resurrection.

For Christians, Gabriel is the angel of the incarnation and consolation while Michael is the angel of judgment. But the Jewish tradition, noting how often words like *great*, *might*, *power* and *strength* are used in connection with Gabriel, regard him to be the angel of judgment while Michael is considered to be the angel of mercy. According to this tradition, Gabriel was the angel who destroyed Sodom and Gomorrah. They also regard him as the angel who buried

Angel Awakenings

Moses and who wrestled all night with Jacob.

In Jewish literature, Gabriel is also prominent in 1 and 2 Enoch and the Lives of Adam and Eve. In Islamic tradition, it was Gabriel who revealed the Qur'an to Muhammad in A.D. 610.

Raphael, the Healer

Raphael is identified as an archangel in apocryphal writings, but he is never mentioned in the Old or New Testaments. His name comes from the Hebrew word *rapha*, which means "healer" (*Raphael*, "God has healed"). The word is often translated to mean "doctor". It should be remembered that our ideas of modern medicine are different from the Hebrew concept of healing, which was one of wholeness. Raphael's concern, then, would be not only for the healing of diseases but for all that is needed to bring about wholeness.

Many commentators identify Raphael as the angel who would come down from time to time and stir up the water in the pool of Bethesda (John 5:4).

Raphael is the central figure in the Book of Tobit (apocryphal in the Protestant scripture, canonical in Catholic). Tobit is a religious story that teaches moral and theological lessons. Probably written by an Egyptian Jew about 180 B.C., it contains a wealth of information about how ancient Judaism viewed angels. It is an exciting story telling how Raphael heals the blindness of Tobias and binds the demon that previously had slain seven husbands of Sarah on her wedding nights. It becomes a love story as Raphael brings Tobias and Sarah together. It is only at the end that Raphael reveals himself by name as "one of the seven holy angels" that attend the throne of God.

Raphael is also prominent in the Book of Enoch. Enoch was never admitted as a part of the canon of Jewish scriptures, but it was very influential in its time and is even quoted in the Christian epistle of Jude. More angels are mentioned by name in Enoch than any other ancient work, but Raphael stands out as one of the most important ones. In Enoch, God commands Raphael to heal the earth and to bind the demon Azazel. He is also a watcher, or observer, of the human race. Enoch takes Raphael on a guided tour of Sheol, a sort of neutral way station for the spirits of those who have died.

In Jewish lore, Raphael is credited with healing Abraham of the pain of circumcision and is one of the three angels who visited him and his wife, Sarah (Genesis 18). In "The Legends of the Jews", God sent Raphael to cure Jacob of the thigh injury that was a result of wrestling with an adversary at Peniel. In "Sefer Noah", after the flood, Raphael gives Noah a book on medicine.

Uriel, the Light of God

In the many lists of archangels in different traditions, Gabriel, Michael and Raphael are the three mentioned most often. But Hebrew, Kabbalistic and some Christian traditions also include Uriel.

The name *Uriel* literally means "fire of God", "flame of God", or "light of God". Uriel is not found in the traditional Bible. He is found in 2 Esdras, which was a part of the canon of the Jews of ancient Alexandria, but was not accepted by the Jews of Jerusalem. Today, Esdras is a part of the Bible for many Orthodox Christian churches. In Esdras, Uriel acts as a heavenly interpreter of Ezra's visions.

Uriel was considered an archangel by many in the Catholic Church, but a church council in A.D. 745 removed him from the list.

Uriel is found in many ancient books that are not a part of the scripture, including The Book of Adam and Eve and Enoch. They place Uriel in several of the biblical stories. It is said he was the angel stationed at the gates of the Garden of Eden with a flaming sword to prevent Adam and Eve from returning. He is also identified as one of the angels who helped bury Adam and Abel. Other roles attributed to him include warning Noah of the coming flood, wrestling with Jacob at Peniel and destroying the hosts of Sennacherib. Of course, different sources credit other angels with some of these feats. In later stories, Uriel is connected with volcanoes and earthquakes.

Satan or Lucifer

In Hebrew, the word from which Satan is derived means the "adversary, resister, or enemy". His other name, Lucifer, meaning "light bearer", refers to his original state.

All three of the Western religions—Judaism, Christianity and Islam—share many of the same beliefs about

The angels are a strange genus: they are precisely what they are and cannot be anything else. They are themselves soulless beings who represent nothing but the thoughts and intuitions of their Lord.

—C. G. Jung, *Memories, Dreams, Reflections*

angels. But the belief in Satan and the fallen angels is most central to Christianity. As the editors of the Blackfriars edition of the *Summa Theologica* of Thomas Aquinas note, Satan "is part and parcel of the Christian religion . . . no Satan, no Christ; that is both a historical and theological truth."

This is their line of reasoning. Satan's sin resulted in his fall from heaven. Satan tempted Adam and Eve, resulting in their original sin. From the fall came the need for Jesus Christ to come to Earth as mankind's redeemer from sin. This is the heart of the Christian faith, but the idea is foreign to both Judaism and Islam.

Nowhere in scripture do we find a detailed description of why an angel would choose to rebel against God. There is some debate as to whether references in Ezekiel 28 and Isaiah 14:12–15 are speaking of the downfall of an angelic or an earthly prince. Isaiah writes, "How you are fallen from heaven, O Lucifer, son of the morning! How you are cut down to the ground, you who laid the nations low! You said in your heart, 'I will ascend to heaven; above the stars of God I will set my throne on high . . .'." Is Isaiah simply speaking figuratively about the king of Babylon, who is referred to in the same chapter? Ezekiel prophesies, seemingly about the king of Tyre, "I will destroy you, O covering cherub." Theologians interpret these passages to mean that Satan was created as the wisest and most beautiful of all the angels. He was the anointed "cherub", the highest of all angelic creation. He was perfect without a single flaw, however, he did have the power of contrary choice— the ability to choose contrary to one's nature. God does not have this ability, which is why God cannot sin. The sin of Lucifer, as seen in his five "I wills" of Ezekiel 28, was the sin of pride.

The New Testament states that Satan was an angel evidently perfect in his original state. 2 Peter 2:4 speaks of God

The Nine Choirs of Angels

How Catholics view the celestial hierarchy

FIRST HIERARCHY	SECOND HIERARCHY	THIRD HIERARCHY
FIRST CHOIR: SERAPHIM The highest order of angels. They guard God's throne and contemplate His goodness directly. They are referred to as the "burning ones" because they are aflame with love for God, which they express by constantly singing, "Holy, holy, holy is the Lord of Hosts; the whole earth is full of his glory." Isaiah envisioned them as having six wings.	**FOURTH CHOIR: DOMINIONS (OR DOMINATIONS)** They regulate the activities of all the other angels (except those in the First Hierarchy) to assure the carrying out of God's will. They are shown holding an orb or scepter as a symbol of authority.	**SEVENTH CHOIR: PRINCIPALITIES** They are protectors of religion, providing strength in times of hardship. They also keep watch over nations and their leaders.
SECOND CHOIR: CHERUBIM Cherubim (literally, "fullness of knowledge") are God's record keepers and observers of the primal creative power of God's glory. God put cherubim at the gates of Eden to guard the way to the tree of life. In ancient depictions, each one had four wings and four different faces.	**FIFTH CHOIR: VIRTUES** They are entrusted with the movement of the heavenly bodies and the operations of nature. They can draw on God's force to work miracles on Earth. They bestow encouragement and blessings on the worthy.	**EIGHTH CHOIR: ARCHANGELS** Archangels are "chief angels". They look after the larger affairs of humankind as they relate to God's will. They are holy messengers of God, carrying important decrees to humans. They also command God's armies and act as guardian angels to leaders of world movements.
THIRD CHOIR: THRONES These are known as the chariots of God, charged with carrying out God's justice according to universal laws ("thrones" are associated with the power of judgment). They are sometimes called chariots. Ezekiel describes them as resembling burning wheels with rims "full of eyes round about".	**SIXTH CHOIR: POWERS** They preserve order in the world and keep it from being overthrown by demons. Powers avenge evil acts and protect human souls.	**NINTH CHOIR: ANGELS** These include guardian angels, who are assigned by God to every human being at the time of his or her birth. Angels of this order are concerned with matters that affect individuals.

not sparing the "angels when they sinned." 1 Timothy 3:6 indicates that pride seems to have caused Satan's downfall. The battle between good and evil, between the fallen angels and the forces of God, is a theme throughout the New Testament. From the teachings of Jesus through the Book of Revelation, it is clear that God will ultimately triumph and Satan will be completely defeated.

Though it would be fascinating to know more details about Satan, Calvin once complained of those who "grumble that Scripture does not in numerous passages set forth systematically and clearly the fall of the devils, its cause, manner, time and character." He concluded that we did not need to know more than the scripture revealed about Lucifer. Ultimately, much of what we would like to know, such as how such a perfect creature would choose to sin, is really inscrutable. Or perhaps Lucifer's thinking was as the poet John Milton proposed in *Paradise Lost*: "Better to reign in Hell, than serve in Heav'n."

The Reverend Dr. William D. Webber has been the pastor of American Baptist churches. With his wife, Marilynn Carlson, he is the author of A Rustle of Angels: Stories about Angels in Real Life and Scripture *and* Tea with the Angel Lady. *The Webbers have been frequent guests on radio and television programs about angels.*

How Well Do You Know Angels in the Bible?

How savvy are you about the angels in the Bible?
Do you know when and where they appeared? To whom?
Test your knowledge by answering the following questions.

1. Adam and Eve were banished from the Garden after eating from the Tree of Knowledge. The angel barring the gate was holding a

a. "No Trespassing" sign

b. Thunderbolt

c. Shotgun

d. Flaming sword

2. In the story about Lot, God sent his angels to
   a. Destroy the lascivious city of Sodom
   b. Find ten good men in Sodom
   c. Warn Lot that the city was about to be destroyed
   d. All of the above

3. A man named Balaam was riding his donkey when the donkey saw something that Balaam couldn't. It saw
   a. A ghost
   b. A choir of angels
   c. An angel with a sword and a message
   d. A woman carrying an enticing bunch of carrots

4. In the Apocrypha, Tobit's son, Toby, is travelling with an angel who tells the young man to
   a. Catch a fish, parts from which would cure his father's blindness
   b. Snag a bird, which would make a very fine meal
   c. Dig in the sand, where he would find a natural spring
   d. Send postcards home so that his parents wouldn't worry about him

5. Daniel was an interpreter of dreams who served many kings, some of whom were not happy with what they heard. One of them threw Daniel into a lion's den where
   a. Daniel was protected by angels
   b. Angels turned the lions into playful kittens
   c. An angel brought an old prophet who had a talisman for Daniel
   d. All of the above

6. Jacob, the brother of Esau, wrestled with an angel one night; the next morning, he asked the angel for:
   a. A coat of many colours
   b. A blessing
   c. Two sheep and a goat
   d. An herbal unguent that was the biblical equivalent of Bengay

7. Isaiah, the prophet, once had a vision in which a particular kind of angel touched his lips with a burning coal. That angel was
   a. One of the cherubim
   b. One of the seraphim
   c. An archangel
   d. One of Charlie's Angels

8. The angel who appeared to Mary, telling her that she was to be the mother of God, was named

    a. Michael

    b. Clarence

    c. Western Unicus

    d. Gabriel

9. When the Christ Child was born, angels

    a. Guided three wise men to Bethlehem

    b. Chastised the innkeepers for not taking in a very pregnant Mary

    c. Sang out the good news to local shepherds

    d. Cleaned out the stable to make it presentable

10. Peter, who was one of the twelve apostles, had an unusual encounter with an angel who

    a. Accompanied him to Christ's empty tomb

    b. Brought him food and water when he was in the desert

    c. Helped him to escape from prison

    d. Taught him how to play the harp

(Answers at bottom of page.)

Answers:

1. (d) Flaming sword
2. (d) All of the above
3. (c) An angel with a sword and a message
4. (a) Catch a fish, parts from which would cure his father's blindness
5. (a) Daniel was protected by angels
6. (b) A blessing
7. (b) One of the seraphim
8. (d) Gabriel
9. (c) Sang out the good news to local shepherds
10. (c) Helped him to escape from prison

"Take Your Angel with You"

A young Catholic mother finds herself passing on the "guardian angel" tradition to her child.

———————

By Therese J. Borchard

It was an all too familiar scene. My two older sisters, my twin sister and I had 8½ minutes before the morning bell rang at Archbishop Altar High School. Our coats were on; we scurried out to the garage and loaded our backpacks and duffle bags into the beat-up Buick station wagon that we were embarrassed to drive. Running 10 minutes late already, we heard the faint call of our mum from her bedroom downstairs: "Wait! Take your angels with you."

"Yeah, yeah, yeah," we thought. This wasn't just a morning ritual. My sisters and I could never leave the house without hearing that brief incantation, as if those five words had the power to keep us out of harm's way every time we stepped five feet clear of

Angel Stories
ENCOUNTERS AND SIGHTINGS

When I was a small child we lived out in the country near a dangerous crossing that had been the site of several accidents. I had just got off my school bus and was crossing the highway when a car came barreling down the road at me. I knew I could not possibly get out of the way in time and accepted the fact that I was going to die. Suddenly I was out of the path of the car and standing safely by the side of the road. My brother saw me spinning away from the car like a top. I did not feel this—I just knew that in an instant, I was safe.

The three Divine are in this hierarchy,

First the Dominions, and the Virtues next;

And the third order is that of the Powers.

Then in the dances twain penultimate

The Principalities and Archangels wheel;

The last is wholly of angelic sports.

These orders upward all of them are gazing,

And downward so prevail, that unto God

They all attracted are and all attract.

—Dante Alighieri, *The Paradiso*, Canto XXVIII

Angel Awakenings

The mystic chords of memory, stretching from every battlefield, and patriot grave, to every living heart and hearthstone, all over this broad land, will yet swell the chorus of the Union, when again touched, as surely they will be, by the better angels of our nature.

—Abraham Lincoln, in his first Inaugural Address, March 4, 1861

the front, back or side door of our home.

But it worked, I swear.

It worked all the times we smashed the big boat of a car into a concrete wall, another car, or a building. Somehow we walked away from the crash alive and with no broken bones. And it worked when one or all of us would have a little too much to drink at a party and wound up somewhere we definitely shouldn't be. At some hour the next day we made it safely back to home base.

It worked when I was stranded late at night in an airport in Calcutta, India, a foreign exchange student alone and panicked. A fellow passenger appeared from nowhere, called my host family and waited with me until they arrived.

I could go on and on with examples of "guardian angel" moments. Do I really believe that some feathery friend

Angel Stories
ENCOUNTERS AND SIGHTINGS

I know nothing about the mechanical aspects of automobiles, so I was in despair when my car broke down. A man suddenly appeared and told me that it was probably my battery. He fixed my car. I was going to give him something but he refused and went away. I kind of felt bad for not thanking him enough, so I returned the next day to the same gasoline station. But I could not find the gasoline station, the sign, or the man.

is leaning over my shoulder, watching my every move, like the sexy, winged John Travolta in the 1996 film *Michael*? Or that some heavenly helper is assigned to me like Nicolas Cage was to Meg Ryan in *City of Angels*? Well, I doubt they look like Hollywood actors, but yes, I do believe God commands His angels to watch over His children on earth, responding to their 911 calls with a team of invisible emergency workers.

Granted, angels aren't the most

Orthodox Angel Icons: Windows into Heaven

Frederica Mathewes-Green, Beliefnet columnist and author of several books on Orthodox Christianity, talks about the glorious angel icons and the role of angels in the Eastern Church.

What is the purpose of icons of angels—the magnificent paintings embellished with gold leaf. Are they mostly decorative or used to keep the mind focused on the veneration of saints or angels?

In Orthodox Christianity, you will find many icons of Gabriel and Michael and other angels, as well as the Andrei Rublev "Old Testament Trinity", painted in 1411—this depicts the three angels who came to Abraham (the faithful believe they were the Father, Son and Holy Spirit in the guise of angels) and is one of the most famous icons.

The classic definition of icons is "windows into heaven". They don't capture divinity and aren't intrinsically holy in themselves, but they are portals leading our attention and our minds into heaven. It's probably analogous to the way Protestants treat a Bible; they would say that it's just a book, just paper and ink, not in itself holy. But they would treat it with respect nevertheless and expect that they can meet God "through" it. The analogy is pretty nearly literal, since icons began as a "picture Bible" for people who were illiterate, in an age when it was rare to have a copy of the scriptures available.

An icon of an angel would be a visible reminder of an invisible reality— that angels are all around us and praying for us constantly. Angels are sophisticated stuff of the Catholic faith. Many theologians dismiss their roles as peripheral and overrated. However, they aren't just Hollywood fluff and cute little pins sold on Hallmark's spin rack. They're real.

Most of us have experienced the feeling of assurance referred to in Psalms: "For he will command his angels concerning you to guard you in all your ways. On their hands they will bear you up, so that you will not dash

examples, primarily, of worship; they worship God continuously with full attention, and we should too.

Do the Orthodox feel that they can directly receive messages from angels?

The Greek word *angelos* means "messenger", and a messenger goes between the real sender and the recipient. Like a messenger, an angel just delivers but does not generate the content. So the message might be delivered *by* an angel, but it would not be a message *from* the angel—it would be a message from God.

A person can receive a message directly through an angel, but we should never *expect* to do that and not seek it. Mary received a message through the angel Gabriel, for example. There are other stories of saints being visited by angels to deliver warnings or encouragement. These aren't everyday experiences, and it would be presumptuous and spiritually dangerous to seek them. Those who seek these experiences are just about guaranteed to begin seeing something, but the likelihood is of encountering demons instead, disguised as angels of light. This is called *prelest*, spiritual self-delusion. Demons seek to puff up the person's pride and lead them astray, and the process goes from confusion to delusion to insanity. It's something that folks who spend intense time in prayer—for example, monastics—have to guard against, and a checks-and-balances situation with other monks and a spiritual mother/father is essential.

Angels are spirits, but it is not because they are spirits that they are angels.
They become angels when they are sent,
for the name angel refers to their office, not their nature.
You ask the name of this nature, it is spirit; you ask its office,
it is that of an angel, which is a messenger.

—Saint Augustine

your foot against a stone." And parents (whose ranks I recently joined) can heartily second Jesus' command to his disciples in the Gospel of Matthew, "Take care that you do not despise one of these little ones; for, I tell you, in heaven their angels continually see the face of my Father in heaven."

According to the Catechism of the Catholic Church, angels are among us here on earth, surrounding us with their "watchful care and intercession". I'm embarrassed to admit that I recite the Guardian Angel prayer more often than I do the Our Father or the Hail Mary combined. Whenever I feel the least bit of turbulence on a plane, or my Styrofoam coffee cup moves more than a sixteenth of an inch across my tray table, those words automatically come tumbling out:

Angel of God, my Guardian dear,
to whom His love commits me here,
ever this day be at my side,
to light and guard, to rule and guide.
Amen.

And yes, I've passed on the tradition to my baby boy. Thankfully, he is a bit too young to cruise around in a beat-up Buick and attend parties with no adult supervision. My little prince might not yet appreciate the concept of a guardian angel, but that doesn't stop me from standing over his cot every night as I put him to bed, gently touching his forehead as I ask his angels to watch over and protect him through the night—something I borrowed from Sir Harold Boulton's "All Through the Night":

Sleep, my child, and peace attend thee
All through the night.
Guardian angels God will send thee
All through the night.

I hope and pray that he won't need his guardian angel as much as I did when I was a teenager. But I know he probably will. I just hope the power of those heavenly helpers doesn't wear out before then.

Therese J. Borchard holds a Master of Arts degree in theology from the University of Notre Dame and is coeditor of the best-selling I Like Being Catholic: Treasured Traditions, Rituals, and Stories.

Angels in Other Religions

Those who say, "Our Lord is God [alone]," and wholeheartedly pursue the right way—upon them do angels descend, saying, "fear not and grieve not, but receive the good news . . . We are your supporters in the present life and in the life to come." —The Qur'an

Belief in angels also plays an important role in Islam, which, like Judaism and Christianity, traces its roots back to the patriarch Abraham. Like Christians and Jews, Muslims also believe in an all-powerful Creator God, the angels of the heavenly host and of humankind, and that each person must ultimately choose between good (Allah and the good angels) and evil (Iblis—Satan—a fallen angel, and his followers).

Consequently, it's not surprising that angels play a large part in the practical theology of the Qur'an—the holy book written by the Prophet Muhammad. The man who was to become the prophet was meditating alone in a cave one day when the angel Jibra'il (Gabriel) came to him with instructions to take dictation—of the book that would become the Qur'an. In his essay on Islamic angels, Shaikh Kabir Helminski, a follower of the Sufi branch of Islam, notes that after prayers, Muslims say a greeting over each shoulder to the two angels who accompany them there. Like the angels who are said to follow observant Jews home from Sabbath services, the angels of Islam rejoice

Since angels are men, and live together in society like men on earth, therefore they have garments, houses, and other things familiar to those which exist on earth, but, of course, infinitely more beautiful and perfect.

—Emanuel Swedenborg

in every human step toward holiness.

The Church of Jesus Christ of Latter-day Saints was also started by an ordinary man who was unexpectedly visited by an angel, given very detailed theological information and then was consequently compelled by the urgency of the message to spend the rest of his life proclaiming it. In the case of Joseph Smith, who lived in rural New York, these revelations were already written down on golden plates and were ready to be deciphered by the angel Moroni, who had written them himself with the help of his father, Mormon, when they were alive in their human existence on this Earth. As you'll see, the Mormon theology of angels differs from that of mainstream Christianity in that traditional Christians believe angels are created as pure spirit and remain so; Latter-day Saints believe angels are people at a different "point of progression". The Latter-day Saints have a religion and theology so

fascinating and complex, they often do not share their cosmology with those who are not LDS Church members. Here you will find a wonderful and vivid description of their views and the history of angels by Brigham Young University professor Eric A. Eliason.

Emanuel Swedenborg, while not so well known today as Muhammad and Joseph Smith, had angelic visions that profoundly influenced thinkers as diverse as Rudolph Steiner, William Blake and John Chapman (Johnny Appleseed). Swedenborg was a Swedish scientist and college professor who lived from 1688 to 1772. His descriptions of angels are fascinating because he describes them in great detail from a mystical yet scientific point of view.

Angels almost exclusively inhabit monotheistic religions that worship one supreme Creator God. Other religions, such as Buddhism and Hinduism, which follow very different paths of enlightenment and incarnation, do not have angels in their cosmology but have a rich tradition of other spirits. Still, you'll find here a very sweet contemplation by Hindu writer (and mother) Shoba Narayan about a sort of "angelic equivalent" that she shares with her young daughter.

No matter what your personal beliefs, you are certain to be fascinated and perhaps surprised by the information that the writers of various faiths share with us here.

Angels in Islam

The Qur'an teaches that angels are the medium between heaven and Earth.

By Shaikh Kabir Helminski

Who, if I cried out, would hear me from among the Angelic Orders,
and if just one of them pressed me suddenly to his heart, I'd melt
into his greater Being. For Beauty is nothing
but a terrifying Beginning we can barely endure,
bewildered by the ease with which it annihilates us.
Any angel is terrifying.

—Rainer Maria Rilke, *Duino Elegies* (translated by Kabir Helminski)

These lines by one of the twentieth century's greatest spiritual poets are a fitting introduction to Islam angels. Although not a Muslim, the German poet Rilke (1875–1926) travelled through North Africa and Egypt and was so impressed by the lingering presence of the character of the Prophet Muhammad that he said it felt as if he had passed away only last week. The opening lines are an apt description of the Prophet Muhammad's first

Angel: Greetings, Prophet;
The Great Work begins:
The Messenger has arrived.

—Tony Kushner, *Angels in America, Part One*

unwitting encounter with an angelic presence at the beginning of the whole process of the revelation of the Qur'an.

It came about when Muhammad had been meditating for weeks in a cave on a mountain. Suddenly, a presence commanded him: "Read!" "But I don't know how," Muhammad, not yet a prophet, replied. Whereupon this "being" pressed upon his heart with its full presence and said, "Read, in the name of your Sustainer who created, created the human being from a subtle, clinging substance. Read, for truly your Sustainer is generous!" This being, according to Islamic tradition, was the Archangel Gabriel (Arabic: Jibra'il), the communicator of Divine Revelation.

Spiritual Beings on a Mission from God

According to Islamic tradition, angels are celestial beings or guardian spirits who exist on another plane closer to God. They are therefore mediating agencies between the will of God and the affairs of this Earth. Unlike human beings, they are free of selfish desire and anger and exist in a state of total service to God.

In Arabic, an angel is called *mal'ak*, from *la'aka*, "to send on a mission". This meaning is identical to the original Greek meaning of *angelos*, and to the Hebrew *mal'ach*, "messenger". Angels are considered to be intelligent and living, as well as the *medium* through which communication takes place between heaven and Earth.

Any subject to be discussed within the Islamic context must refer to the Qur'an as its fundamental reference point. Even more than other revealed traditions, the book is the immediate and final source of doctrine and guidance. Muslims search the Qur'an in order to reveal what God would have us know about the angels:

It is He who bestows His blessings upon you, as do His angels, so as to bring you forth from the depths of darkness into the light; and He, indeed, is Most Gracious unto the faithful. (33:43)

He sends down the angels with the Spirit according to His command upon whomever He wills of His servants, saying: "Give warning that there is no God but I, and be, therefore, conscious of Me." (16:2)

The Islamic angelic hierarchy consists, first of all, of four archangels: Gabriel (Jibrail), the communicator of revelation; Michael (Mika'il), the supporter of those contending with evil; Azrael (Izra'il), the angel of death; and Israfil, the blower of the Cosmic Trumpet at the end of time. These are called the Qariibiyyuun (cognate with Kerubhiim in Hebrew, and Christian Cherubim), meaning those who are *near* to God. As a species of invisible beings, they populate a normally invisible universe, which they share with the jinn (genies, sprites) and the shaytans (devils, negative forces).

The Angel Who Wouldn't Bow Down

Our own story, that is, the human story, begins in association with the angels, when Allah commands them to bow before his new creation, Adam. Only Iblis, the equivalent of Satan, refuses. The Qur'anic account goes like this:

We [the Divine We] said to the angels, "Prostrate yourselves before Adam," and they all prostrated themselves except Iblis (Diablo); he was not of those who bowed down. God said, "What has kept you from bowing down when I commanded you?" He said, "I am better than he; You have created me out of fire, but he was created out of clay." God said, "Get down; it is not for you to show insolence here; so go forth, for surely you are one of the least of beings." He said, "Then grant me some respite until the day of resurrection." And God said, "Then, be one of those given leave."

"So now that You have let me go astray, I shall surely do my best to way-lay human beings from Your straight path. I shall place myself ahead of them, or come up behind them, or from the right or the left, and most of them You will find are not among those grateful (for Your mercies)." God said, "Go thee, disgraced and expelled, and those that follow you, I shall surely fill Hell with them." (7:11–18)

A similar incident described in the Qur'an is the first encounter between Adam and the angels in which God announces that he is going to place a "representative" of His own on Earth,

*Every raindrop that falls is accompanied by an Angel,
for even a raindrop is a manifestation of being.*

—The Prophet Muhammad

to which the angels reply, "Will You place there those who will spread corruption and shed blood?" Well, as we know, the angels had a point, but God nevertheless placed within the heart of Adam a knowledge of the divine names and set up a test. He asked the angels the names of various things, to which they could only reply, "We only know what you impart to us." Adam, however, knew the "name" of everything, and all the angels, again except Iblis, prostrated themselves before him.

The significance of this story for us humans is the acknowledgment of the hidden treasure that is latent within our human nature. Knowing the name of something signifies knowing its true, spiritual reality. Within the Qur'anic context, the "word" has a creative power: "God only has to say to a thing, Be, and it is" (2:117). Our human inheritance then, which is the complete knowledge of the divine names, is at the same time a source of creative power.

The human superiority over the angels is also demonstrated in the story of Muhammad's spiritual ascent in which he was taken by Gabriel up through the seven levels of heaven to God's presence, just short of which Gabriel bows out, and Muhammad goes on alone. The mystics explain this as the superiority of love—Muhammad, the *truly human* being—over mere angelic intelligence.

Angels Record Our Deeds

And yet, despite our potential superiority over the angels, they are the medium by which God's mercy is extended to us. We human beings need their support in our own spiritual development; an angel strengthens our hearts, lightens the burden of our human sorrows and delivers our souls to God's forgiveness, where they gain a nobler form. Each human being is accompanied throughout his or her life by two angels, Munkar and Nakir,

Even though you cannot see this guardian tangibly,

when you feel longing, compulsion, or pain you know

that there is such a thing as a guardian. For

example, you feel the softness of the underwater flowers

and plants; but when you go to the farther side you

are scratched by thorns. So you know—even though

you see neither one—that the farther side is where

thorns grow, a place of unpleasantness and pain,

whereas this side is where flowers grow, a place of

comfort.

—Jalaluddin Rumi, *Signs of the Unseen*

who variously record our sins and our good deeds. During the ritual prayer of Islam, called *salaat*, the worshipper ends with a greeting of peace first over the left shoulder and then over the right, acknowledging their presence.

In Islam, belief in angels is an article of faith. *Faith* (Arabic: *Iman*) means not only the conviction of the truth of a proposition, but essentially the acceptance of the proposition as a basis for action. To believe in angels, therefore, is to accept that there are mediating powers by which people are guided and strengthened in their faiths and their positive actions, even while the negative forces, shaytans, may prompt us to evil or bestial behavior. But while belief in angels is an article of faith, because it will help us toward the good, belief in shaytans is not an article of faith, nor a required belief, since we are not required to "have faith in" and act upon evil suggestions.

In summary, the angels are the medium of Divine Mercy (and sometimes of Divine Wrath for those who "spread corruption upon the earth"). They are the interface between the unseen and seen worlds. The Qur'an promises angelic support to those who keep the eye of their hearts focused on spirit:

Those who say, "Our Lord is God [alone]," and wholeheartedly pursue the right way—upon them do angels descend, saying, "Fear not and grieve not, but receive the good news of the Garden that you have been promised. We are your supporters in the present life and in the life to come; therein you shall have whatever you request in a ready, hospitable gift from Him, the All-Forgiving, the Most Compassionate." (41:30–32)

Kabir Helminski is a shaikh of the Mevlevi Order of Muslims (Sufi), which was founded by Rumi, and cofounder and codirector of the Threshold Society in Watsonville, California. He is the editor of The Rumi Collection *and the translator of many poems.*

Angels among the Mormons

From Joseph Smith's angelic visitor to the legends of the Three Nephites, angels play a major role in the theology of the Latter-day Saints.

By Eric A. Eliason

Perhaps the most well-known story from Mormon history involves angels. The angel Moroni appeared to Joseph Smith to tell the young prophet where to find scripture hidden in a hill near his home in rural New York. The golden plates Joseph found contained a sacred history of ancient Christian peoples in America. Moroni had compiled this volume with his father, Mormon, during their lives as mortal men. As Joseph translated with divine help, he received visitations by an angelic John the Baptist and the apostles Peter, James and John, who gave Joseph the authority he needed to organize the Church of Jesus Christ of Latter-day Saints. In 1830, the translation complete, Joseph published the Book of Mormon, from which Church members get their nickname "Mormons" and to which millions turn for guidance and instruction in conjunction with the Bible.

This story tells much about the way Mormons continue to understand angels to this day. First, to Mormons, angels look like people with bodies— glorious and heavenly people—but men, women and children without wings. They are people who can speak, act and be present in a very literal sense. There is very little that is metaphorical about Mormon angels.

This story also reveals a small part of the panoramic sweep of Mormon cosmology and the nature of humans' relationship to angels. In traditional Christian theology, God, angels and humans are seen as being wholly distinct kinds of beings. Angels and humans each glorify God in their own ways.

Angels Are People Too

Latter-day Saints, on the other hand, understand the Bible's teaching that

Angel Awakenings 97

Oh sovereign angel, wide winged stranger
above a forgetful earth,
care for me,
care for me. Keep me unaware of danger
and not regretful and not forgetful
of my innocent birth.

—Edna St. Vincent Millay

we are children of God to mean that a Heavenly Father and Mother were the parents of our spirits before we came to this Earth. In this premortal life we learned many things, but to be whole and complete, we needed physical bodies and an opportunity to grow through exercising faith and making choices. After death, our spirits dwell in a spirit world awaiting resurrection, where we will be reunited with a perfect, eternal, glorified body.

To Latter-day Saints, angels are not a different class of beings, but are persons at a different point along a path of progression. Angels can be spirits from the pre-Earth life, or people who have died but have not yet been resurrected, or people like Moroni who have received their resurrection. Revelations to Joseph Smith indicate that the archangel Michael became the

man Adam on Earth. John Taylor, the third Mormon prophet, identified Gabriel as the biblical Enoch whom God "took" in Genesis 5:24. (Biblical information on Enoch is scanty, but revelations to Joseph Smith tell that Enoch's whole city was taken up with him.) Some Mormons have wondered if Raphael might be Noah.

Mormons believe angelic experiences are not limited to scriptural times but continue today. Many people of various faiths, or no faith, experience visitation by departed loved ones that soothe and comfort them. Latter-day Saint theology welcomes such events, and Mormons who see the spirits of their dear departed sometimes share such experiences with those who they know will respect the sacredness of such events.

Many women (and sometimes

men) have encountered the spirit of a child to be born to them. In the stories told of such experiences, the gender, hair colour and facial features of the angel will be those of the child when it arrives. While such experiences happen to many, Latter-day Saints see them in the special context of a belief in life before birth. Many Latter-day Saints imagine that as preborn spirits, they might have been among the choir of

Joseph Smith's Advice: How to Tell an Evil Spirit from an Angel

According to Mormon teaching, Satan and his angels were cast out of the Lord's presence in the pre-Earth life for trying to thwart God's plan of happiness for His children. They will not receive bodies, but they roam the Earth trying to tempt and frighten us. In this selection from a collection of revelations, Joseph Smith gives advice on what to do if you are not sure a spiritual being you encounter is good or evil.

When a messenger comes saying he has a message from God, offer him your hand and request him to shake hands with you.

If he be an [resurrected] angel he will do so, and you will feel his hand.

If he be the spirit of a just man made perfect [from the spirit world] he will come in his glory; for that is the only way he can appear—

Ask him to shake hands with you, but he will not move, because it is contrary to the order of heaven for a just man to deceive; but he will still deliver his message.

If it be the devil as an angel of light, when you ask him to shake hands he will offer you his hand, and you will not feel anything; you may therefore detect him.

These are three grand keys whereby you may know whether any administration is from God.

—Doctrine and Covenants 129:4–9

An angel can illumine the thought and mind of man by strengthening the power of vision, and by bringing within his reach some truth which the angel himself contemplates.

—Saint Thomas Aquinas

angels who sang to the shepherds heralding Jesus' birth.

Legends of the Three Nephites

Perhaps the most famous of distinctly Latter-day Saint reports of angels are stories of the Three Nephites. The highlight of the Book of Mormon is Jesus' visit to the New World after his resurrection in Palestine. (The people Jesus visited were called Nephites, after one of their ancestors who left Jerusalem six hundred years before.) In ancient America, Jesus blessed and healed the sick, retold his Sermon on the Mount and chose twelve Nephite apostles. When Jesus prepared to return to heaven, he offered to grant each apostle his heart's desire. Nine asked to be saved in the Kingdom of God upon their deaths. The last three wanted to stay on Earth, serving people until the Second Coming.

Jesus promised them that their desire would be so. (See "Jesus Commissions the Three Nephites" on page 102.)

The Three Nephites, having been given a measure of glory and immortality but without death and resurrection, are "translated beings" in Mormon theological terms. They will eventually be instantly changed from their current states to resurrection without passing through death, but for the time being they work among us with seemingly supernatural powers. A large body of Three Nephites stories has developed over the years, but a few examples will suffice to give a picture of the Nephites' characters.

The Winter Traveller. During the Great Depression, many stories circulated of a winter traveller who asks for food at a house in rural Utah. The family invites the traveller in to share their humble meal. The man blesses the house and departs. The family notices

that he has left behind his handkerchief and runs outside to return it. But the traveller is gone, and his tracks suddenly stop a few paces into the snow. They open the handkerchief to find grandmother's gold locket—lost while pioneering years ago.

The Hitchhiker. In another story type, a doubting Mormon picks up a hitchhiker (in his wagon or his car, depending on how old the story is) while travelling far away from home. The conversation turns to religion, and the doubter decides he can confide in the stranger. The hitchhiker listens patiently. In a calm, knowledgeable manner, the stranger resolves every one of the man's concerns. The doubter is so overcome with joy, he bursts into tears. He wipes his eyes for just a

. . . Behold I know your thoughts . . .

Therefore, more blessed are ye, for ye shall never taste death; but ye shall live to behold all the doings of the Father unto the children of men, even until . . . I shall come in my glory with the powers of heaven.

And ye shall never endure the pains of death . . .

. . . Ye shall not have pain while ye shall dwell in the flesh, neither sorrow save it be for the sins of the world; and all this will I do because of the thing which ye have desired of me, for ye have desired that ye might bring the souls of men unto me, while the world shall stand.

And for this cause ye shall have fullness of joy; and ye shall sit down in the kingdom of my Father.

—*Book of Mormon, 3 Nephi 28:6–10*

And they are the angels of God, and . . . can show themselves unto whatsoever man it seemeth them good.

Therefore, great and marvellous works shall be wrought by them before the great and coming day [of judgment].

—*Book of Mormon, 3 Nephi 28:30–31*

moment and looks toward the stranger to thank him, but he's gone.

The Three Missionaries. Many versions exist of the story of Mormon missionaries who arrive on a never-before-visited South Pacific island, only to be greeted by friendly natives who eagerly clamor to be baptized. The confused missionaries ask how the islanders knew they were coming and why they wanted to be baptized. The islanders explain that for the past few weeks, three visitors had been healing their sick children and explaining the Gospel of Christ to them. Right before the three men suddenly disappeared, they told the islanders to expect two young North Americans with white shirts and ties who would come to baptize them.

Yet I am the necessary angel of earth,
Since, in my sight, you see the earth again…

—Wallace Stevens

Protectors of Women. The most common Three Nephites story told among Mormons today reflects anxiety about the dangers of the modern world and the increasing role of women in missionary work. Folklorists have collected this story from all over the world, but it is usually told as if it happened very close by.

Two "sister missionaries", after a long morning of having doors slammed in their faces, decide to be a little more pushy at the next door. The man who opens it says, "I'm not interested," and begins to shut the door. One of the sisters says, "Hey, look: Our message is really important! Listen to us!" The man screams in horror and slams the door. Feeling bad about their pushiness and perplexed by the man's strange behavior, they decide to go to the post office to mail some letters. On the wall, they notice the screaming man's photo on the FBI's most-wanted list. He is a rapist and serial killer whose criminal method is to lure young women into his home. The sisters call the police, who arrest the man and ask him why he did not take advantage of the perfect opportunity to attack the sister missionaries. "I would have," he said, "except that they had three huge dudes with swords standing behind them."

This story suggests that the Lord looks after those who do His work—a great comfort to young Mormon women who brave grave dangers in His service.

All four of these stories follow certain structures and patterns of transmission familiar to folklorists and are found in many cultures. They also display, however, the patterns of behavior one would expect the Three Nephites to follow if the Book of Mormon's explanation of their origin is taken seriously.

Salt Lake City has no office like the Vatican's that investigates miracles for church approval or rejection. Latter-day

Saints are left on their own to make determinations about whether to believe any report of an angelic visitation. Today's church leaders, however, have advised their flocks not to be gullible in believing every sensational story they hear, but at the same time they affirm that the Lord's angelic servants are real and active among us.

Mormons have developed a certain savvy as to the way stories about angels get embellished as they are passed on and as to how some may try to "spice up" an otherwise dull sermon with a sensational story. Just because Mormons may sometimes chuckle at a familiar angel story, however, does not mean that there are not some stories that they firmly believe to be absolutely real, perhaps because of a personal visitation by an angel.

Eric A. Eliason is an assistant professor of English at Brigham Young University in Provo, Utah, where he teaches folklore and Mormon literature.

May Hanuman Be with You

*A Hindu mother talks about the Gods, gurus
and planets that serve as her family's "guardian angels".*

By Shoba Narayan

The other night, my five-year-old daughter, Ranjini, told me that she had a bad dream. "Mum," she asked, "how can I make bad dreams go away?"

I thought for a moment and told her what my own mother had told me when I was afraid of the dark as a child. "Think of Hanuman," my mother always said. "He will protect you." (Hanuman is Hinduism's Monkey-God, known for his strength and benevolence.) With that, she taught me a *sloka* (chant) that I could repeat whenever I was afraid. I taught Ranjini the same four lines and told her to repeat them before she went to sleep to ward off bad dreams.

It seems to work. It's not that my daughter has never been afraid again, but she now has a method for dealing with her fear. Oftentimes, when I put her to bed, she will say in a small voice, "Mum, let's say *Manojavam* together,"

and we begin the chant. Hanuman had, in a sense, become my daughter's guardian angel. He protected her and soothed her fears when she was afraid.

While angels play a strong role in Judaism, Christianity and Islam, there are no angel-like figures in Hinduism. Rather, Hindus look to an array of gods, minor gods (*devas*), planets like Sani (Saturn), gurus (teachers) and ancestors, all of whom can play a protective role during times of crisis or stress: during illness, in the face of physical danger, or when taking a test, trying for a promotion at work, or improving a relationship.

Many Hindus have favourite gods and goddesses, or *Ishta Devatas*, whom they call upon to help, guide and protect them. When Hindus face unexplainable hurdles in life, they might typically ask their astrologers to examine their horoscopes and appease the various planets. I still recall my

*I believe we are free, within limits,
and yet there is an unseen hand, a guiding angel, that somehow,
like a submerged propeller, drives us on.*

—Rabindranath Tagore

brother wearing a black amulet as a child because my parents wanted the planet Sani to protect him. Sani held a strong position in my brother's horoscope and was therefore called on to guard him.

My mother turned to her gurus, who were her guardian angels, guides and soothsayers all rolled into one. She gave us sacred ash blessed by her guru and asked us to wear it on our foreheads before we ventured out of the house. My father still says that he overcame the hardships in his life because of the benevolence and protection of his ancestors. He performs a yearly *shraadam* (ancestor worship) with diligence to sustain their support.

For children, the playful God Krishna or the Monkey-God Hanuman are easy to relate to. Hanuman, in particular, is a favourite protector. A story that is told often about Hanuman relates to Lord Rama's battle against the evil king Ravana. When

Rama's brother, Lakshmana, fell unconscious in the battlefield, a doctor was summoned. After examining Lakshmana, the physician asked for the Sanjeevini herb, which would instantly cure the wounded warrior.

Because he was the strongest of the beings there on the battlefield, Hanuman was asked to fly to the faraway mountain and procure the herb. When Hanuman landed on the mountain, he faced a bewildering array of herbs, all of which looked alike to him. Realizing that time was of the essence, he uprooted the entire mountain and carried it back to the battlefield. The physician plucked out the herb, Lakshmana was cured and Rama's battle against the evil king Ravana continued.

Similarly, Krishna is called upon very often in times of crisis because of the role he plays in Hindu mythology as a savant and protector. The Bhagavad Gita, arguably Hinduism's most

The angel personifies something new arising from the deep unconscious.

—C. G. Jung

famous religious text, came from Krishna. In the Mahabharata, one of Hinduism's most famous epics, Krishna protects Queen Draupadi from being disrobed by the evil Dushasana in court. As Dushasana pulls her sari, Draupadi calls "Krishna," and lo and behold, the sari grows endless. As Dushasana futilely pulls, the sari grows and Draupadi's modesty is saved.

That is another story I frequently tell my daughter, mostly because she relates easily to Krishna. Unlike stereotypical gods, Krishna is not perfect. As a child, he used to steal butter and play tricks on his mother and father. But he also holds the Sudarshana chakra, a flying discus that, as I tell my daughter, "will protect you from that bully in the playground" or whatever that day's crisis might be.

As a practising Hindu, I believe that such protective figures are especially important after September 11. They provide children with a certain amount of psychological comfort. If nothing else, calling on angels and gods gives children, and indeed adults, a weapon against the obstacles that life throws in our paths. Now, more than ever, we need such amulets, armors and mythological weapons.

Shoba Narayan is a freelance journalist in New York City. She has written on finance, technology, food and culture for such diverse publications as The Wall Street Journal, Newsweek, Gourmet *and* Parents.

Devas, Fairies and Nature Spirits

The cofounder of the Findhorn spiritual community attunes to the angels of cities and her native country.

By Dorothy Maclean

Most of us have grown up enjoying tales of fairies with gossamer wings who sip nectar from bluebells, elves that live under toadstools, and sprites both mischievous and helpful. These are storybook versions of the nature spirits known as elementals, which are very real to those who live close to the land. Many native people have long been aware of guardian spirits who look after the well-being of plants, animals and even countries. In the hierarchy of nature spirits, devas (Sanskrit for "shining ones") constitute the highest order. New Age thinkers see them as angels of the natural realm whose job it is to hold nature in balance and teach people to protect rather than pollute the environment. The foremost example of a human partnership with devas is the Findhorn spiritual community in northern Scotland.

In 1962, Dorothy Maclean, a Canadian, and her friends Eileen and Peter Caddy moved to a desolate area of snow, icy winds and sandy soil six hundred miles south of the Arctic Circle. Their hope was to live a life of surrender to God, under divine guidance. As they made efforts to plant a garden in this unpromising location, Maclean found herself being contacted by the angels, or devas, of individual plants. Based on her attunement to the plant angels, the garden flourished remarkably. She and the Caddys grew forty-two-pound cabbages, eight-foot delphiniums and other amazing plants without fertilizers or pesticides. The media picked up the story, and people flocked to Findhorn as a New Age mecca. Others (including national park rangers) told Maclean that they too had experienced contact with

That there is an invisible spirit to all living things is

a common understanding in mystic and tribal religions.

Trees, mountains, animals, rocks, household objects,

buildings, plants, rivers, dances, rituals, healings,

communication, gifts—the list is endless—all have an

invisible spirit. This deva dimension is part of the

creative matrix of everything that exists.

—William Bloom, Ph.D.,
Working with Angels, Fairies, and Nature Spirits

nature spirits but kept quiet for fear of ridicule. Maclean left Findhorn in the 1970s but has continued to help others work cooperatively with nature's intelligence. "Such cooperation is vital for the world," she says.

In the following essay, Maclean discusses her discovery of the angels that animate, govern, or "overlight" everything—from the smallest pebble to the largest manmade creation, including cities and governments.

Years ago while at Findhorn, I was very surprised and sceptical when I was told from my inner divinity that such things as planets, clouds and vegetables had an overlighting intelligence and that I was to attune to and harmonize with these intelligences. When I finally got around to such attunements, I began with the garden pea, my favourite among the vegetables that we were trying to grow. From its intelligence, I received a clear inner message, which I put into words as I had been doing for ten years with my inner attunements. That began my collaboration with the energies of various plants. These I encountered on the soul level: each group or species having a soul, which I called a *deva*, or angel, although to me they were formless energy fields. With answers to our questions and

with our conscious cooperation, we grew remarkably healthy vegetables. The Findhorn garden became well-known for our particular method of gardening.

Almost immediately after my first plant contact, I became aware of a presence that seemed to be in charge of the area in which we were living. I called it the Landscape Angel, and it became my mentor regarding various approaches to gardening and how to cooperate with the devic realm, among other lessons. It, as well as the God within, often urged me to contact other members of these other dimensions, and I gradually attuned to angels of qualities, such as an Angel of Serenity and an Angel of Sound, as these came up in my life. Also, I learned that when a group of people were separate enough to have their

own unique identity, there was also an inner-level identity representing that particular group. My first experience of this aspect was with the angel of our own group, the Angel of Findhorn.

I had long thoroughly disliked cities and wanted to live in the country in harmony with all life, which was the way that I considered that primal peoples lived. While in the United States in 1976, however, I had the opportunity to visit Native American sites and found that my notions were merely romantic dreams, for I learned that the Native Americans had consisted of warring tribes and also lived in conditions that would be very uncomfortable compared to my twentieth-century standards.

The Soul of a City

That discovery broke down my rigid antipathy to cities, and when I next came to a large city, I was open to any spiritual aspect of the city. I experienced a wonderful overlighting angel, from whom I received a message in which I was asked to send love to it. That amazed me, for I thought we receive love from the angels, not send it. On pondering this, I realized that the angels of our large cities must have about the most difficult job on the planet, for they were trying to bring joy and peace to our darkest spots: the crowded, rebellious, poor, drug-filled, criminal districts in our cities. How different from looking after a beautiful nature area!

Are There Pagan Angels?

The Pagan traditions don't include "angels" per se, but we do recognize many helpful and benevolent forces and entities: our ancestors, our spiritual ancestors, those beings we call goddesses and gods. The image of the angel may be an evolution of the ancient, winged bird Goddess, who linked Earth and sky. When we need help, if we ask for it, and open ourselves to the creative and protective powers of the universe, help will come.

—Starhawk, author of *Circle Round* and *The Spiral Dance*

Angels, when the sun is hottest
May be seen the sands among,
Stooping—plucking—sighing—flying—
Parched the flowers they bear along.

—Emily Dickinson

I also realized that I had made the job of the city angels even more difficult, for I had used cities for shopping, movies, museums and so forth, without a word of thanks, quickly getting out of what I considered concrete jungles. This encounter completely changed my view of cities, and I settled in a large city—Toronto—in a downtown area, on an eighth floor, and had no more problems with living in a city. Of course, nothing was different except my attitude. We can all find something to love in a city, such as a tree in a park, which will get love flowing and enable us to make contact with the angel of the city.

Another area of the angelic world opened up to me at that same time. I had considered myself a planetary citizen and even created a planetary passport (though this passport was not recognized by any country). I thought I had outgrown nationalism in my concept of myself as a citizen of the world. In my Toronto neighborhood, I found a deep love and nostalgia for such things as the wonderful wildflowers growing in the Canadian woods before the leaves unfolded—flowers that seemed so much more exquisite than any garden blooms—and for the climate with its rich seasons. I had been bored with the continual rain of Britain or the continual sun of California. And the peaches of the Niagara Peninsula were the most luscious in the world!

Communicating with the Angel of Canada

As a seventh-generation Canadian, I knew the past of the area. Even the present was familiar, for there was a big new library in Toronto named the John Robarts Library, and I had attended the same university at the time he did. As all these familiarities appeared, I began to wonder if there was more relevance in our national and ethnic backgrounds than I had thought. So I wondered if there was an Angel of Canada whose advice I could seek.

With love, I focused on such a presence and got in touch with a wonderful energy, one with quite a feel of nature. It communicated that it could not do its job properly, as it worked through people, and we Canadians didn't know our identity. That motivated me and others on a long search for our identity on the personality level. It also began my inner contact with the angels of other countries that I visited. I learned that it can be helpful to contact such angels, see if they have anything to communicate, and ask questions or offer our love and assistance in whatever way we can.

Dorothy Maclean's books include The Living Silence, Wisdoms, The Findhorn Garden, To Hear the Angels Sing, The Soul of Canada, To Honour the Earth *and* Choices of Love.

PART TWO

ANGELS AMONG US

Most People Believe in and Many Have Had Experiences with Angels

Encounters with the Extraordinary

A disabled girl, lost for hours, reports that a "shining lady" has brought her home. A suicidal woman's silent cries for help are answered by a presence bringing calm and peace. A small child crossing the highway is mysteriously plucked from the path of an oncoming car and deposited on the opposite side of the street. An angel comes to a woman in a dream, shaking her and rousing her from a near-fatal diabetic coma. An American minister lost in Italy is guided to his ancestral home.

Angels, it seems, are all around us. When the Gallup organization did a poll in 1994, they found that an astronomical 74 percent of Americans believed in angels. Canadian researcher and doctoral student Emma Heathcote recently gathered eight hundred eyewitness accounts of angelic encounters. According to the *Ottawa Citizen*, her most amazing report came from a small Anglican church in Hertfordshire, Canada, where five years ago more than two dozen people had gathered for an adult baptism: "Suddenly an angel was standing before them—in the font, actually—and they all saw it. It appeared like a man, beardless in a sort of robe, so shimmering white it was almost transparent. Most people present, including the rector, warden and organist, said they felt a sensation as of warm oil being poured over their skin, and smelled a delicious scent of rose petals . . . The angel spoke not a word, stayed for a few long minutes and then vanished, leaving everyone blinking, bedazzled and in an attitude of quiet, profound love."

When William and Marilynn Webber published a story about a guardian angel, they received *eighty-five hundred letters* in response. Many of their correspondents—such as Maureen Broadbent from Corona, California—detailed angelic encounters. Her dogs and cat were locked behind a chain-link fence when a devastating fire consumed her home. Downed electrical wires prevented anyone from touching the fence, until a mysterious man appeared from nowhere and, using superhuman strength, uprooted the fence and saved the animals—then disappeared as she turned to thank him.

Children and pets are saved from harm, desperate and ill adults are comforted or healed. With such a preponderance of angelic activity encroaching in the everyday lives of ordinary people, it's not surprising that many folks have specific questions about angels. What do angels look like? Can I know the name of my guardian angel? Do loved ones become our guardian angels when they die? Why do angels rescue certain people but not others?

Brad and Sherry Steiger, who have spent years studying angels and have

Angel Stories
ENCOUNTERS AND SIGHTINGS

My encounter came in 1998. I awoke suddenly and toward the ceiling was a being of white light. It had a face, but it was not really defined. It appeared in outline to have on a cowl. This angel was very tall.

I lay awake and just watched. I sensed it did not want to scare me. I eventually fell back to sleep. The next day I said to my son, who had fallen asleep in my bed, "I have something to tell you about what I saw last night," and he said, "What? The white light on the ceiling?"

Everyone who has had an angelic encounter
has seen something different
from everyone else who has seen or experienced an angel.

—Eileen Elias Freeman

published many successful books on the subject, give specific and thoughtful answers to these questions in Part Two. Some of the questions are light hearted: "Do angels have smells?" "Everybody's seeing angels—why can't I?" Others touch on more serious topics, such as how to tell whether a heavenly being is good or evil, and whether an angel's appearance foretells a coming death.

But let's start with two of the basics: one explored by the Reverend Dr. Arthur Caliandro, the pastor of New York's large Marble Collegiate Church (formerly the pulpit of Dr. Norman Vincent Peale), who answers the question, "Are angels for real?", and a fascinating discussion by the Steigers on the difference between angels and spirit guides.

Come along with us to the luminous crossroads where the paths of people and angels intersect, and read the stories of many ordinary folks who have encountered the extraordinary.

Angels Are for Real

*A sermon from a renowned minister recalls his brush with angels
both in his congregation and his personal life.*

By Dr. Arthur Caliandro

Years ago, my family and I enjoyed a wonderful vacation in Italy. We spent two weeks crisscrossing the country. At the end of our trip, we did something very special. We visited the house where my father was born in a little town called Ciegli, near Bari.

As I stood before that house, I visualized my father as a child, playing in the street. Then I imagined his mother leaning out one of the windows, calling him for dinner, just as my mother had done for me.

After visiting that house, we went to find the summer home of my father's family. We drove out into the countryside and got lost. After searching for an hour-and-a-half, I was still making many wrong turns down many wrong roads. It was getting late, my family was impatient and I felt a growing desperation. I didn't know what to do. Then I recalled something I had learned from Dr. Norman Vincent Peale. I said to my family, "I need a few moments to be quiet while I figure this out."

I stopped the car and worked to relax my mind and my body. I spent two or three minutes getting centred in that place of stillness within, and then I addressed my father with my inner voice.

"Daddy," I said, "please show us the way to the house."

In a second, my inner voice answered, "Go down the road about a half-mile. There's a driveway. Turn left." I followed those directions, and there was the house.

For me, those events seemed so simple and natural at the time. But when I thought about them later, I realized that, in that instant, I had experienced the intersection of this earthly experience and a higher realm. It was a supernatural moment for me.

When I ask the angels for answers

to the human mystery, I find that they guide me

to a sense of peace and comfort in my soul.

The angels do this not by bringing me answers

and intricate theories, but by bringing me creative ways

of responding to life with light in my heart.

—Terry Lynn Taylor, *The Angel Experience*

For years, I believed that the voice I heard was my father's. But I have since come to believe that the presence that interceded on our behalf that night was probably a guardian angel. Because—hear me—angels are for real.

Visitors from Another Dimension

Even most sceptical people believe our earthly life is not all there is. We know there's another level of reality, another dimension, a spiritual dimension. If

Angel Stories
ENCOUNTERS AND SIGHTINGS

I know that angels can assume apparently human form, because my family was saved by two "men", who suddenly appeared on a deserted country road, as our car was about to roll over a dangerous cliff.

My husband had been changing the tire, and was outside the car, when it started rolling over the curb toward the edge of the cliff! I was seated in the backseat, holding our newborn son. My daughter was in the front seat, but she could not pull the emergency brake. A car appeared, two "men" got out and, without a word, held the car while my husband opened the car door and stepped on the brake. They told my husband to calm down, because he was in a panic. They left suddenly as we were calling out our thanks.

We lived in a very small community where everybody knew everyone else, and we had never seen those two men before, nor did we ever see them again. They looked like salt and pepper shakers, just alike, except one was white and one black. They each had a beard. Since my husband is black and I am white we felt that those "men" had to be our guardian angels.

O passing angel, speed me with a song,
a melody of heaven to reach my heart, and round me
to the race and make me strong.

—Christina Rossetti

you have trouble accepting that idea, think about radio waves. We know there are radio waves, even though we can't see them, touch them or feel them. Like radio waves, a spiritual wavelength also exists. When we tune in to it, extraordinary things happen.

Angels are the messengers from this other dimension. Think for a moment about the wonder of the nativity. One day, a young woman named Mary was astounded when an angel appeared and told her she was to bear a child and that child was going to make an enormous difference in the world.

Months later, angels appeared to shepherds in a field. They were scared, and the angel reassured them by saying, "Don't be afraid. I've got good news for you. Not far from here, in the city of David, a savior has been born, who is Christ the Lord."

When Jesus' work was nearly done, he was praying in the Garden of Gethsemane. He knew that the next day would bring an agonizing death on the cross. Jesus felt abandoned by friends—even by his God—and in desperation he cried out, "Father, if you are willing, let this cup pass from me. Not my will, but let yours be done." Then, the Bible tells us, "An angel came from heaven and gave him strength."

At Easter, the two Marys went to the tomb to pray. The Bible says that an angel rolled away the stone. When the women saw that Jesus was not there, the angel told them, "Don't be afraid. He's not here. He is risen." Again an angel came bearing momentous news.

Angels in Our Church

Are angels still around? Are they here with us in this church?

I know they are. Over many decades, countless prayers have been

Angel Stories
Encounters and Sightings

I had the first angelic encounter that I recognized about three years ago.

There is a place close to where I live that is very peaceful, very close to the water and sky. I often visit there just to make a fire, listen to the waves and look at the sky. This particular day, I headed up to "my thinking spot" after dark. I had been there so many times and even though it was rough hills and bluffs, I felt safe.

After making a beautiful fire high atop the bluffs of Lake Michigan, I headed back. On the way home, I slipped on some wet clay and tumbled down the bluff. I grabbed onto brush and small trees and still kept falling. At the bottom of the hill I hit my head on a rock. I called and yelled out my name and phone number. I was in a remote location and did not expect to have anyone hear me.

When I had despaired, I heard a voice and [felt] a soft comforting touch. I looked up and saw a young man with long light hair and rough, almost burlap-type material for his clothes. He knew my name and my husband's name. He told me that he knew my husband from "school" and that he would take me home. Next thing I remember I was laying at my back porch. My husband had come out to look for me and found me sleeping outside the back door.

Our house is at least ¾ mile from the lake bluff. Dan asked how I had gotten back, and I told him that "Gabe had brought me. You know, that friend of yours from school." My husband had not gone to school with any "Gabe" but did attend Abbott Pennings Academy and did indeed pray to the angel Gabriel for guidance on the soccer field. I ended up with 25 stitches in my head. I know that somehow I was brought home by that angel. Gabe and I have had many conversations since and I am so grateful for his presence in my life.

Angel Stories

ENCOUNTERS AND SIGHTINGS

Have I had an encounter with an angel? Yes. And to this day it fills me with the most unmeasurable joy, love and humility!

I was a nurse's aide in a hospital in South Dakota in the mid-'90s. One morning I arrived at work to find that a three-year-old boy had come in on life support. He had been sexually assaulted, attacked by his mother's boyfriend, then thrown against a bathroom sink, shattering his skull.

The pediatric intensive care unit (picu) was a madhouse; doctors, specialists, administrators, police and family were all there. It was bad. All morning I wanted to be able to go in and just silently say a prayer over the child. But it was too busy, and I had no need to be in there. Early in the afternoon I decided to walk by the doors and say a prayer.

What happened next left me stunned. The whole ceiling suddenly and literally vanished.

There were angels everywhere! There were several angels for every person in the room; doctors, nurses, police, family members. The love and joy that the angels were pouring into everyone was overwhelming. To the right, I saw what I call the ramp, the "stairway to heaven". Halfway up the ramp was the little boy, with an angel on each side, holding his hands, several in front of him showing and pointing up towards the top of the ramp where there was the most beautiful multi-colour light streaming down upon all. It was incredible! I stopped in mid-stride, totally stunned by all this.

Then an angel came up to me, smiling and sending the same love and light directly into my heart and mind. I can still remember the unfathomable joy radiating from its face—so beautiful.

"It's okay," it told me. "We have him now. He is going home. Thank you for your prayers. They are always welcomed."

Then it was over. I had to immediately duck into the staff lounge bathroom where it took me awhile to stop crying. Then I returned back on the floor. Within moments the child passed away.

To this day, I have only told a few people of this.

Who has not found the Heaven—below—
Will fail of it above—
For Angels rent the House next ours,
Wherever we remove—

—Emily Dickinson

said here, and I believe our walls still hold the power and faith contained in all of them. Only last year, two women were sitting in our balcony. One was a church member; the other was here for the very first time. As the visitor was listening to the choir, she thought she saw something out of the corner of her eye. She looked again and thought she saw the wings of an angel. She turned away, then turned back again and the wings were still there. She turned to her friend and said, "Do you see what I see?"

The other woman said, "Yes. I see an angel."

About a dozen years ago, I was about to marry a certain middle-aged couple. Some people said, "Don't do it, Arthur. This marriage is not going to work; it's the wrong thing."

Yet the wedding was very uplifting. After the service, a man who had been sitting in the back of the church came forward and said, "Arthur, did you notice anything different about that service? Did you feel any special presence?"

"No, why?" I asked.

"During the entire ceremony, a group of angels was hovering over you and the wedding party."

Years later, that man and woman remain wonderfully happy in their marriage. I believe their happiness is due to the angelic presence in their lives.

I also know there is a connection between prayer and angels. I once read, "When you pray for someone else, an angel goes and sits on that person's shoulder."

Prayer Brings Angels to Protect a Missionary

Not long ago, I heard a wonderful true story from a friend. A missionary, on furlough from his assignment in Africa, was visiting his family in Michigan. While there, he preached a sermon in his home church, which was supporting his missionary work.

He talked about the small field hospital where he worked. Every other week, he had to make a two-day bicycle trip to a nearby city to obtain supplies, medicine and cash. On one of his trips, he witnessed a fight between two young men. One of them was injured, and the missionary went to him. While treating his injuries, he told him about Jesus' and God's love.

Two weeks later, when the missionary was again in the city, the same young man stopped him and said, "I want to tell you something. After you were here two weeks ago, five of my friends and I followed you to where you were camping by the road. We knew you had money and drugs, and we intended to kill and rob you. But when we approached where you were sleeping, we saw twenty-six armed guards, who scared us away."

As the missionary was telling this story, a man in the congregation stood up and said, "Excuse me, but I

Angel Stories
ENCOUNTERS AND SIGHTINGS

When I was 18 years old, I was quietly meditating on my bed one summer evening. The window in front of me was open and the curtains were drawn back to let the moonlight in. I was quite upset about myself and the way things were going in my life. I asked God to show me the right way so that I could begin living a more useful, purposeful, joyful life. Suddenly, in front of my very big bedroom window, there appeared what I can only describe as a HUGE "sparkle". It was brilliant and seemed to shine its light directly into my heart and soul. I felt a tremendous love-energy flow through me. The light swirled around in front of the open window for a while and then disappeared. I was not afraid for one second. I immediately realized that it was an angel or some kind of holy energy.

I remember reading the story of Mary Martin,

who as a little girl in Weatherford, Texas,

made a wish that she could fly—

not in an airplane—but like an angel through the air.

Years later, Mary's wish came true

when she was offered the role of Peter Pan

on Broadway.

—Jane M. Howard, *Commune with the Angels*

need to interrupt you and ask a question. When was the date of that incident?" The missionary thought a moment and then told him.

The man responded, "On that day, I was going to play golf. But I had a very strong urge to pray for you. It was so compelling that I called a group of people and said, 'Meet me in the sanctuary. We have to pray for our missionary friend.' So we met here, and we prayed. Would all of you who were with me that morning stand up?"

They all stood up. And then he

Angel Stories
ENCOUNTERS AND SIGHTINGS

When my daughter's boyfriend was in college he was hurrying to class one night. By mistake, he placed his backpack on the top of the car and forgot it there. He and his friend rushed to class, only remembering the backpack when they arrived way across town. They immediately retraced their route to school, but the backpack was gone. Not only were his expensive college books in the pack, but also his tools and wallet. Replacing everything would be out of the question because he was from a poor family that had trouble making ends meet.

Instead of going to class that night, he came to our home to tell me and my daughter what had happened. I immediately started praying and asked God to send a guardian angel to somehow protect the backpack and get it safely back to him.

The next day my daughter was walking home from a friend's house when an elderly man walked up to her. "You look like a college student," he said. "Do you know anyone who lost a backpack?"

My daughter told him that her boyfriend had. The elderly gentleman then opened a large paper bag and pulled out the pack. My daughter bent down to look inside. Everything was there, even the wallet with the money in it. When she looked up to thank the man for his kindness, there was no one in sight.

counted the men who were standing—ten, fifteen and finally twenty-six.

So I say again: Angels are for real. Give them the time. Give them the space. Heed the messages they bring from that other higher realm and they will surely serve you.

The Reverend Dr. Arthur Caliandro has led the Marble Collegiate Church congregation in New York since 1984. He shared the pulpit at Marble Church with Dr. Norman Vincent Peale for several years before assuming his position as Senior Minister. This article is reprinted by permission of MarbleVision, the media ministry of Marble Collegiate Church.

Frequently Asked Angel Questions
Encounters and Sightings

With Brad and Sherry Steiger

WAS IT AN ANGEL?

I have neither seen nor felt an angel. What's wrong with me?

Our immediate response is, "How can you be so certain that you have never seen nor felt an angel?" As scripture says, we may often entertain angels unaware. Perhaps what may be "wrong" with you is that you need to become more aware and more cognizant of the marvellous and mysterious ways that angels move among us, for not all heavenly beings appear in a traditional manner.

A friend told us of the time that he was standing on a New York subway platform waiting for his train. As the train approached, he began to feel sick and dizzy and found himself falling forward toward the tracks. Suddenly, he felt strong hands on his coat, pulling him back to safety. The shock of his near-death and sudden rescue cleared his head, and he turned around to thank his benefactor. Everyone near him appeared oblivious to the terrible accident that had been averted. Only as he peered farther back toward the turnstiles did our friend see someone with a St. Louis Cardinals baseball cap walking away. In another blink of his eyes, the man was gone.

Our friend had grown up in St. Louis and as a boy had been an avid Cardinals fan. Was it a coincidence that some unknown hero with a Cardinals baseball cap just happened to be there to rescue him? Or was the cap a sign to remind him that he was not alone, that a guardian angel was watching over him?

Not long ago we received an intriguing account from a woman who was involved in an automobile accident. Both she and the other person involved in the mishap were grateful to a young man who came on the scene in a new model white car and who directed traffic until the police arrived. When they turned to thank him, they were astonished to discover that he had disappeared in what had to have been a matter of seconds.

Our correspondent was convinced that the young man was an angel. Others will say, well, yes, he was an angel in the sense that a human "Good Samaritan" is a messenger of God. But if he were simply a helpful human, how could he and

Angel Stories
ENCOUNTERS AND SIGHTINGS

In 1991, I was suicidal and desperate to leave an abusive marriage. I'd already attempted suicide twice. I'm not a believer of a particular dogma, but I prayed for two solid hours. My bottle of pills was in my hand. I prayed to an unseen and not-certain-I-believed-in angel to save me. Whatever the reality, I felt a calming presence, a love. I shared this at my 12-step meeting. It is important that I add the fact that I was clean and sober for nearly one year at this time. My fellow 12-step members simply accepted this as another of the many grace moments we are blessed with. In spite of the fact that this occurred over 10 years ago, I hope I will never forget my angelic salvation.

Angels Among Us

*The Prince of Peace was anxious to come to earth
and an angel was used
to bring the good news that the Creator
would become a little child.*

—Mother Teresa

his automobile have disappeared from everyone's sight in the time it took to turn around?

Just because you believe that you have neither seen nor been touched by an angel doesn't mean that they are not involved in your earthly existence. Think back on the many times when a kind stranger just happened to appear to be of service during a crucial moment in your life. Yes, of course, many of these "angels" may have been considerate and thoughtful fellow humans. On the other hand, you may well have interacted with a heavenly being unaware.

Angel Stories
ENCOUNTERS AND SIGHTINGS

It was around Christmastime and we had no presents, food or winter coats. One day my mother went to an Alcoholics Anonymous meeting and told everyone how she felt. She said that she was at the end of the road. When the meeting was over, a man came up to her and gave her a hug. He told her everything would be okay and to keep praying and not to lose faith. That man shook her hand and in his hand was money. She thanked him, thinking it was only going to be $10. When he left, she opened her hand to find $300—enough to get food, presents and coats for Christmas. She looked everywhere for that man and asked everyone in that building. They told her they never saw him hug her or even saw him at the meeting. She has never seen him again.

In heaven an angel is nobody in particular.

—George Bernard Shaw

WHY ARE PEOPLE AFRAID OF SEEING ANGELS?

Why do so many people make fun of others when it comes to talking about angels and other spiritual beings? I have seen angelic beings since I was little but whenever I talk to others about my experiences, they either laugh or appear frightened. Even my pastor seems frightened when I share my stories of angels with him. Why is this?

For the past couple of centuries, the Western world has done little to encourage individual's mystical experiences. Until quite recently, even clergy were reluctant to discuss angelic manifestations or any other kind of spiritual phenomena with their parishioners for fear of being branded primitive or superstitious. Lay people who described their mystical experiences were approached with great caution, and their stories were considered suspect unless some kind of so-called "scientific" proof could be offered. Unfortu-

nately, even learned men and women often express their lack of awareness or their ignorance of the unknown by laughing nervously or by recoiling in fear.

The great philosopher William James once observed that the fountainhead of all religions lies in the mystical experience of the individual. All theologies, all ecclesiastical establishments, he contended, were but secondary growths.

If you are experiencing angelic or other spiritual manifestations, be assured that you are not alone. On January 23, 1994, *USA Today* published the results of a national survey conducted for the National Opinion Research Center at the University of Chicago. The data collected on private spiritual experience revealed that two-thirds of all Americans claim to have had at least one mystical experience.

Of the millions of Americans who acknowledge a mystical encounter, 67 percent claim to have experienced some form of extrasensory perception, such as telepathy, with someone far away from them; 28 percent say that they have seen events occur as they happened at a great distance; 40 percent are convinced that they have communicated with spirits; and nearly 32 percent have experienced the elevation of consciousness by a connection to a powerful spiritual force.

Until only recently, observed Dr. Jeffrey S. Levin, an associate professor at Eastern Virginia Medical School in Norfolk who was one of the experts to analyze the survey data, some kind of social stigma may have prevented more men and women from acknowledging such paranormal encounters, which, he says, have been around "since time immemorial".

Angel Stories
ENCOUNTERS AND SIGHTINGS

I had just lost my mother in a car accident. I was going through a very hard time. She was my best friend. I would lie in bed every night and cry myself to sleep. I was also going through a rough divorce and had battled drug addiction. My mother always told me, put your life in the Lord's hands. He will guide you and give you strength to handle anything.

Well, that is what I did. I turned to the Lord to help me. I went to bed and cried myself to sleep. About 3:00 A.M. I awoke to this white cloud hovering over me. As I focused my eyes on this white cloud, it began to back up to the end of my bed and take the shape of an angel. I sat up and just stared in amazement. The angel never spoke to me and I never spoke to the angel. But I had the most calm feeling.

As I looked at this angel, I remember every detail. This angel was a bright white. Behind the angel were two very large wings. The angel had the most beautiful face. The angel's gown hung in folds. But what brought me the most comfort was when the angel lifted up her wings—they were very large—and placed them around me. I had the most empowering sense of peace and love that I have ever experienced. The next thing I knew I was waking up. I will never forget her.

He who loves goodness harbors angels, reveres reverence, and lives with God.

—Ralph Waldo Emerson

ANGEL OR SPIRIT GUIDE?

What is the difference between a spirit guide and an angel?

Traditionally, an angel is sent by the Supreme Being for the purpose of delivering a message, offering spiritual counsel or, in some cases, healing a physical malady or rescuing a person from threatening circumstances.

For many people, the term *spirit guide* refers to the entity utilized by spirit mediums or channels to establish contact with the deceased.

Angel Stories
ENCOUNTERS AND SIGHTINGS

The angel that is always with me is named Michael. He came to me a little over three years ago, about six months after my husband died unexpectedly. I was contemplating suicide because I could see no way out from the pain and chaos inside. I was standing at my kitchen window, saying the prayer that had become a constant whispering for me: "Please God, I don't ask for happiness and I know this will hurt for a long time. Just let me find some peace."

I felt a movement behind my left shoulder and saw in the reflection of the window a HUGE pair of wings enfold me. I have never before or since felt such total peace. There was no pain, no chaos, not even an awareness of any feeling, just total calm. In my head I heard, "I am Michael. You will have peace. You will also have miracles which I will show you until you can see them for yourself."

He has not left my side since that afternoon and I have seen miracles now with and without his help. I have seen more angels and have even asked that an angel be sent to friends who were in need. Those angels were shown to me before they went and in later talking to the friends, they described exactly the one that was sent.

Angel Stories
ENCOUNTERS AND SIGHTINGS

Two days before Thanksgiving I was driving 65 mph on a highway with traffic when a drunk driver rammed me and sent me through fencing and trees until I smashed into a building. I stepped out of my completely wrecked car without any injuries or pains—without a scratch.

I never hit the brakes so my car went [along] a path that completely missed a highway streetlight and concrete wall. My friends and relatives said, "Thank God you made it out alive." Three days later while waiting for a train, I encountered a street-worn older man. We talked for a half-hour about many things and then he told me he was my guardian angel and that it simply wasn't my time to go. He said he wanted to get a good look at me and stared into my eyes for a few minutes. He said I was very fortunate to find a good life's path already by the age of 30. He said I found it exactly two years ago and I did agree that just around that time I really was getting my act together.

He seemed to know a little too much about me, yet it wasn't uncomfortable. The whole encounter wasn't strange, mystifying or awkward, but no one else was around to witness him. He told me to promise to think of him the next time I ever felt really sad. A few months later I had a moment where I really was in the dumps. I remembered to think about him and an overwhelming "high" came over me. I felt as if my life was very safe.

While angels are said to be spiritual beings created by God, spirit guides usually have lived as ordinary humans before their deaths and graduations to higher realms. Another essential difference is that angels are thought to be sent by a Higher Power and therefore lie beyond a human's desire to initiate contact. Spirit guides are spirit helpers who may be summoned and who facilitate communication with those on the other side.

Many Native Americans have told us that they would not think of summoning their guides during even the most dire circumstances. They do, however, trust that their guides are concerned about them and will provide guidance or counsel if it appears that their human charges have truly exhausted all their energies and possibilities.

DO ANGELS DRAW CLOSER AT THE HOLIDAYS?

Each year, beginning at Thanksgiving and continuing on through Christmas, I feel as though I am in touch with angelic beings and the spirits of certain family members who have died. Is this simply the power of suggestion since this is a season of spiritual significance for so many people? Or, is it possible that angelic beings and the spirits of our beloved departed truly do draw nearer to the earth during this wonderful, yet sometimes melancholy, time of year?

For many years now we have attempted to derive meaningful and definitive answers to questions like yours. We receive so many reports of spirit and angelic visitations at this time of year that we have considered writing a book called, *Home for the Holidays*, which would be devoted solely to accounts of men and women who have welcomed the spirits of their departed loved ones and/or angelic beings during the period from Thanksgiving through Christmas.

Angel Stories
ENCOUNTERS AND SIGHTINGS

About three years ago, I was going through a bad breakup. I was sitting on the sofa thinking, "Lord help me. I have never felt as alone as I do right now." Suddenly I saw a bright white light fly by my face. At first I thought it was a fly and tried to fan it away, but it continued flying. It stopped right in front of me and took the form of an angel. It stayed that way for at least two to five minutes and then it started flying again.

Angel Stories
ENCOUNTERS AND SIGHTINGS

I converted to Islam a few years back, and as you probably know, devout Muslims pray five times a day. This is a set ritual of prayer [salaat]—asking God for help and giving thanks to Him [known as du'a] can be done whenever you want. After each prayer you are supposed to say "Peace be upon you" over each shoulder. It is said that you are greeting your angels, who stay with you as you pray, and that when you say amen, they say amen, too. I thought this was just a superstition that crept into Islamic folklore, and though I did it, I did not feel I was actually greeting anyone.

Now, when I get into prayer, I am standing there and within seconds of beginning the recital of a part of the Qur'an, I often feel a very warm sensation on my lower back. Sometimes it is very warm and I thought it must be my prayer shawl trapping warm air or something, but when I went to the UK to visit my mum, I prayed at her house and the feeling was much stronger. It could not have been my prayer clothing because I was wearing regular clothes. I also had the feeling that someone was standing right behind me. This unnerved me a little, so I prayed with my back to a wall to stop feeling like I ought to look at who is behind me.

Mum has a very spiritual friend, who was explaining that you can feel the presence of supernatural beings through a touch or a feeling and that got me thinking. Perhaps the angels behind you when you pray are not some superstition. So ever since then, after my prayers, I'll smile as I say "Peace be upon you" to my angels.

Sceptics might dismiss such stories as nostalgia, melancholy or the power of suggestion, and we surely cannot deny that the holiday season for many people is a time of loneliness, depression and a great longing for "the good old days". Music has a magical ability to rekindle memories associated with significant moments in our lives, and Christmas carols and hymns bring back the enchantment and the wonder of Christmases past.

Unfortunately for many, the sounds of the holiday can also revive sad memories that are subdued during the rest of the year. Many people have lost loved ones during the holiday season. In our own case, Sherry lost her nine-year-old son in an automobile accident at Christmas, and Brad's first wife died at Christmastime, as did his father. Thus, while the cheery melodies about happy snowmen, little drummer boys and red-nosed reindeers add to the holiday merriment for some, for others the same tunes bring back feelings of loss.

Is it such commingled emotions of Christmas joy and personal sorrow that make us susceptible to a desire to once again glimpse our departed loved ones and receive assurance that they are all right?

Judging by the testimonies of hundreds of sincere men and women who have written to us over the years, the holiday season and all its attendant emotions truly do open doorways between dimensions that may allow deceased relatives to manifest before their families and, in a way, permit them to come home for the holidays—at least in spirit. Perhaps these "furloughs" are gifts to those men and women who believe in such miracles.

Brad Steiger is the author of 140 books, both fiction and nonfiction, with more than 17 million copies in print. Sherry Hansen Steiger is the cocreator of the Celebrate Life program, the founder of the Butterfly Center of Holistic Education and a founding member of the Holistic Healing Board in Washington, D.C. She is the author or coauthor of more than 20 books, including Seasons of the Soul, The Power of Prayer to Heal and Transform Your Life *and* Angels around the World.

How Do I Know It's an Angel?

By Marilynn Carlson Webber and Dr. William D. Webber

It would seem to be a safe rule that when a person appears in a way that defies our usual explanation and performs some act or service usually associated with angels, it is an angel. That is also the simplest explanation.

At other times, individuals have been helped by someone who appeared to belong in that setting. Yet when they tried to locate the person who had been their helper, they discovered that there had been no one present who fit that description.

These mysterious people are probably angels. One cannot be certain, but it does seem to be the best explanation. The authors would not be dogmatic about any one occurrence, but since we have received so many reports of this kind, we are convinced that angels do appear in this way. We believe they may purposely appear as a person but choose a form (including colour of hair, size, with or without glasses and so on) so that no one else in that setting has a clue that this was an angel encounter.

But what about strangers who come in a normal way, give words of encouragement or perform a mission of mercy and then leave in a perfectly ordinary manner? One cannot state with certainty that an angel was present. It could be coincidental—that someone was passing by just when needed. Some people believe there are no coincidences—that everything is ordered by God. Others believe that some things do happen by chance. Regardless of one's theology on this point, it could also be that God in His mercy used a human to meet the need. If God was behind it, He is to be thanked whether the ministry was done by humans or by angels.

There is good reason to believe that many times these strangers are actually angels. There are examples in the Bible of angels having appeared in human form. The writer to the Hebrews thought this happened often enough to admonish, "Do not forget to entertain strangers, for by so doing some people have entertained angels without knowing it" (Hebrews 13:2).

How can you be certain that such a stranger is an angel? You can't! And it really doesn't matter if God meets your need through a person or an angel. If it were important for you to know, the good Lord would certainly give you a clue. But to be safe, follow the teaching of the scriptures and treat each stranger as though that individual is an angel. The implication of the Bible is that more often than we suspect, angels do walk among us in the form of humans. You can add excitement to your life if you are always anticipating that the next person you meet may be an angel in disguise. It's also fun to look back and wonder if you have met any angels on assignment today. That can be a practical part of faith: expecting God to be at work.

We asked a friend, "Have you had any experiences with angels?"

She answered, somewhat reprovingly, "No, but I have had many experiences with the Holy Spirit."

We understood her gentle rebuke. She was certain that God was active in her life and did not want anyone giving credit to an angel for what God was doing, attributing every act of providence directly to God. Others we know see their guardian angel at work in everything. Which perception is correct?

It must be said from the outset that God is free to do what He knows is best. If He wants to work directly in someone's life, that's His prerogative. It's also His choice if He wants to work through an angel. Perhaps some of our confusion is owing to the fact that God may choose to work directly with one person and sometimes through angels with another.

For example, if we are given a message, how do we know whether it is from God or from an angel? It's easy if the message includes some identification of the speaker, such as, "I am Gabriel, the angel of the Lord." Most often this is not the case. Rather, the message is given usually without words that are heard, without identifying the speaker as God or an angel. From the Bible we know that God does speak in both ways. We also know that angels never seek credit for what they do. In fact, angels characteristically do not wait around to be thanked. Perhaps one reason for there

being so many stories of angels disappearing right after their work is done is to direct the thanks and the glory to God.

Again, when there is no way of knowing whether it is an angel or God, one may speculate about how God works but realize that whichever one it is, it is still God. If it is important for us to know how God chooses to work in our lives, He will let us know.

Sometimes in the Bible, angels are clearly angels. At other times, the angel is identified with God. This is the case with the Old Testament use of "the angel of the Lord". Many believe that the angel of the Lord was Jesus Christ, coming to Earth in a visible form before the incarnation. Here is some evidence to support that view.

In the Bible, there are times when the angel of the Lord turns out to be none other than God himself. When Hagar ran away from Sarah, the angel of the Lord found her. The angel of the Lord promised to do himself what only God can do (Genesis 16:10–12). The account continues in verse 13: "She gave this name to the Lord who spoke to her: 'You are the God who sees me.'" The "angel of the Lord" and the "Lord" (Yaweh or Jehovah) are clearly one and the same.

When this angel appeared to Moses in the well-known account of the burning bush, "the angel of the Lord appeared to him in flames of fire from within a bush" (Exodus 3:2). Two verses later it says, "God called to him from within the bush." Here and other places in the Old Testament the words for "God" and "the angel of the LORD" are used interchangeably.

Yet the angel of the Lord is separate from God. In Zechariah (and elsewhere), the angel of the Lord talks to the Lord Almighty. How can the angel of the Lord be God and be separate from God at the same time? This mystery can be understood if we recognize it as being similar to Christ in his earthly life: being truly God, yet being separate from God. So we find Jesus praying to the Father, as in John 17.

It is possible that the angel of the Lord was simply an angel with a special commission. There seem to be fewer difficulties in understanding the ministry of the angel of the Lord if we see the angel as a momentary revelation of God on this Earth.

When we read in the Bible the many references to the angel of the Lord, we ask, "Was it an angel? Or was it God?" There are times today when we are aware of divine intervention in our lives that we ask the same question.

The Reverend Dr. William D. Webber has been the pastor of American Baptist churches. He and his wife, Marilynn Carlson, are the authors of A Rustle of Angels: Stories about Angels in Real Life and Scripture *and* Tea with the Angel Lady. *The Webbers have been frequent guests on radio and television programs about angels.*

Frequently Asked Angel Questions

Appearance

With Brad and Sherry Steiger

WHAT DO ANGELS LOOK LIKE?

I heard or read somewhere that angels are not the beautiful beings depicted in art. Even though they have beautiful souls and heavenly missions, physically they are ugly, repulsive creatures that you really would not want to see. Do you believe there is any truth to this?

The Bible records many awesome appearances of angelic beings that might incline one to believe that at least some of the heavenly messengers are not the beautiful entities depicted in art or in the accounts of the men and women who have reported angelic encounters. The "living creatures" described by Ezekiel and identified as cherubim, guardians of the throne of God, certainly border on the grotesque as judged by contemporary human standards.

As the Old Testament prophet beheld them, each had four faces, that of a man, a lion, an ox and an eagle. Regardless of whether Ezekiel actually saw four separate visages on a single head or was simply using metaphorical language to describe a single face that reflected the attributes of human, lion, ox and eagle, the cherubim in the prophet's vision would have had us trembling in fear and, yes, revulsion.

The figures seen by Ezekiel are suggestive of the *lamassu*, the ancient Mesopotamian spiritual guardians, which are described as rather grotesque creatures that often appear as lions or bulls with human faces and large wings. Such images were often placed at the entrances of temples to ward off evil. Although from our perspective and acculturation, we may consider the *lamassu* to be ugly monstrous beings, the people of Mesopotamia cherished them as accessible guardian spirits and didn't

Let the angelic energy come through to you. It may be as a soft whisper, a picture in your mind, or a feeling of knowing. Your angels have the same loving voice you have heard many times before.

—Barbara Mark and Trudy Griswold, *The Angelspeake Storybook*

seem to mind their appearance in the slightest.

The prophet Daniel probably felt he was in no position to complain about the looks of the angel who may have spared him from death in the lions' den. While we have no physical description of the angel who kept the great beasts at bay, Daniel did perceive a heavenly messenger shortly afterward at the Tigris River. This being wore linen and a solid gold belt and

Angel Stories
APPEARANCE

If angels exist, then they walk the earth in the form of dogs. They:

- help the blind to see, the deaf to hear and the physically handicapped to lead fuller lives
- predict the onset of epileptic seizures
- detect certain forms of cancer
- rescue people trapped under earthquake rubble and become depressed if the person they smell in the rubble is not alive
- help law enforcement detect drugs, explosives and track down criminals, often giving their lives in the process
- guard our homes and protect our families
- give total love
- are totally without prejudice, loving their owners for who they are and not what they are

All they ask in return is an occasional pat on the head or a belly rub. If this isn't angelic behavior, then I don't know what is.

Their faces had they all of living flame,

And wings of gold, and all the rest so white

No snow unto that limit doth attain.

From bench to bench, into the flower descending,

They carried something of the peace and ardour

Which by the fanning of their flanks they won...

And at that centre, with their wings expanded,

More than a thousand jubilant Angels saw I,

Each differing in effulgence and in kind.

I saw there at their sports and at their songs

A beauty smiling...

—Dante Alighieri, *The Paradiso*, Canto XXXI

Angel Stories

APPEARANCE

My experience has been that angels can be male, female or neither. God seems to delight in creating male and female, or we—all of His creation—would be both. There are very few examples in nature of this occurring. As it is below, so it is above, and my belief is that what we know now is God's creation and that when we reach higher levels, God has only added, not taken away. I have had encounters with three angels. Two were male and one was female. When I asked this question to them they said that some were male and some female and some neither or both.

had a face like lightning, eyes like flaming fires and a voice like the roar of a crowd. That angel, too, might well cause us to scatter in fear and hide, just as Daniel's companions did.

We readily concede we'd much prefer to encounter the lovely angels portrayed in religious art—or in the popular television series *Touched by an Angel*. We doubt that any human being has ever seen the angelic beings as they themselves appear to each other. For one thing, angels are spiritual, rather than physical, entities, created to serve God. Throughout our many years of research and our interviews with hundreds of people who have claimed angelic contact, it has seemed to us that

angels always take a form that is most acceptable to whomever they are appearing.

We long ago came to believe that the physical appearance of the manifesting angels depends almost completely upon the witnesses' personal cosmology—their religious backgrounds, cultural biases, levels of spiritual evolution. Therefore, even in this technological, scientific age, a person of a conservative or fundamentalist religious persuasion may behold angels in their traditional winged and robed personas, while a member of a more liberal religious expression may be more likely to perceive an angel minus the wings and other sacerdotal trappings. On the other hand, even those who consider themselves avant-garde may still cherish the traditional and comforting angelic images.

Throughout the years of our research, we have continued to be impressed by the remarkable adaptability of the guardian angels. In one instance, an angel could be the fireman who carried smoke inhalation victims to safety and who later cannot be found by grateful survivors. In another situation, one may be the traffic cop who prevented a fender-bender during rush hour from becoming a twelve-car pileup with inevitable casualties and fatalities—and who then disappears before the real officers arrive on the scene.

Sometimes they are ordinary men and women who just happen to be there at the right time to listen with an attentive ear and offer the right words of advice to prevent a troubled soul from taking his or her life.

Of one thing we are certain: If an angel should appear to you, you will perceive the heavenly messenger in a way most acceptable and understandable to you.

So forget those stories of angels being ugly creatures with beautiful

Angel Stories
APPEARANCE

Angels appear to me as a soft white oval or circular light, more intense at the centre and waning toward the edge. There also seems to be a field outside of where the light fades. It looks as if there is some type of energy there because it appears to distort objects. This is similar to what you see when you look at an object through waves of heat.

I do not consider the ability to see angels anything other than a gift, but it's a gift I believe we all have. Since my encounters began, it feels to me like I've been awakening a part of myself that has long been asleep, like I'm remembering how to do something about which I'd forgotten.

I'm a firm believer in the power of God and that "through God all things are possible". Seeing angels is no exception.

Give ye praise all angels, to him above who is worthy of praise.

—African prayer

souls and hearts of gold, and focus on the gentler, more attractive image of angels as depicted in our religious and cultural traditions. You'll be happier meeting a smiling angel than a scowling *lamassu*.

ARE THERE ANGELS OF COLOUR?

My great-grandfather was born a slave in the American South, and I spent lots of my childhood listening to his stories. Some were funny, but many were filled with pain. My question is, if there are angels or any kind of heavenly being, why didn't they give some comfort to those people? Are there any angels of colour in heaven? Does racism exist even in the hereafter?

None of us is wise enough to provide satisfactory answers to such historical injustices as slavery, the extermination of aboriginal tribes and the merciless deaths of millions during the Holocaust, for example. In times of horrible

Angel Stories
APPEARANCE

I saw an angel last year when I lived in Middle Village, New York. My partner, Vinnie, was out on the deck and he called me to come outside. When I did, he asked me to look up to the sky. She just stood to my left. She was in a white dress very full at the bottom. Her hair was up with flowers. Her hands reached out.

I told Vinnie to get the camera quickly. When he left, she moved to the front of me and stood there while clouds moved beneath her. I thought she had come for one of us, but that was not the reason. We took two pictures each. I have made many copies of her since then.

Whoever these immortal and blessed inhabitants

of heaven be, if they do not love us and wish us

to be blessed, then we ought not to worship them;

and if they do love us and desire our happiness,

they cannot wish us to be made happy

by any other means than they themselves

have enjoyed—for how could they wish our blessedness

to flow from one source, theirs from another?

—Saint Augustine, *The City of God*

persecutions, however, there emerge inspirational accounts of the appearance, counsel and succor of angelic or spiritual beings. Stories of prayers answered, lives spared under miraculous circumstances, men and women inspired to accomplish heroic acts fill the folklore, legends, and scriptures of all cultures and religions.

For instance, from slavery there emerged spirituals and gospel music that still satisfy the soul today. Individuals in the most inhumane of circumstances were inspired to elevate their hearts and spirits by a force far greater than the taskmasters who enslaved them. None of us can possibly excuse the institution of slavery, but we can admire the indomitable spirit of the enslaved that soared high above the evil imposed upon them and achieved the ultimate freedom of their souls.

We doubt if any human has ever seen what a heavenly being truly looks like in that being's dimension of reality. Further, we very much doubt that angels have a complexion of any shade or hue, as we comprehend "colour" in earthly terms. Racism would be non-existent in the heavenly realms because its citizens are spiritual, rather than physical, beings. In other words, they

Angel Stories
APPEARANCE

About seven years ago, I was sleeping on my couch and woke up in the middle of the night. In the corner was a large, greyish figure. It was almost like a statue and was probably about 9 feet tall. It had a gown/robe on and I believe it was floating off the floor, as I could not see the feet because of the end of the couch. I am 100 percent sure that what I saw was real because it was unlike anything I had imagined an angel to look like! The best thing was I remember how I felt when I saw it. Not scared, surprised, anything. It was as if it had always been there and would continue to be there—just like a shadow! I eventually did some research on angels and can identify it as a warrior angel. I am pretty sure that it was Michael or Raphael.

Angel Stories

APPEARANCE

When I was three years old, I almost drowned. My mother and I were staying at a hotel and relaxing by the pool. I guess I decided to investigate and ended up stuck in the bottom of the hot tub. My mother said I was only gone for a few moments when she had this overwhelming feeling of where I was. She caught me just in time, but I guess I had passed out. My mother told me when I awoke she came into the room and the whole room smelled of roses. She couldn't explain where the scent came from. She said that I was sitting up on the bed with a huge smile.

have no material bodies to admire or to fault, to praise or to criticize, to glorify or condemn. And so it will be when we enter the world beyond death. Regardless of our ethnic heritage in our previous physical forms, we shall be beings of spirit, far removed from any prejudices, bigotry or racism that may have afflicted us on the material plane—either as perpetrator or victim.

Here on Earth, in our opinion, angelic or spirit beings express themselves to us humans in a form and manner that would be recognizable and acceptable to our level of comprehension; therefore, they may appear in any complexion, height, gender or ethnic character they choose. For Christians, Muslims and Jews, these spiritual benefactors manifest as angels; for Mahayana Buddhists, bodhisattvas; for Shintoists, the *kami*; for Hindus, the *devas* and *devis*. Chinese religion has countless personal spirits, such as the Spirit of the Hearth; and traditional Native American religions and African religions personify the spirits of nature, together with heavenly beings and their more prominent ancestors, as powerful benevolent entities.

Although we believe that angels and spirit beings are totally nondenominational, nonracial, noncultural entities, we were pleased when the publishers of our *Angels Around the*

Around our pillows golden ladders rise,

And up and down the skies,

With winged sandals shod,

The angels come, and go,

the Messengers of God!

—Richard Henry Stoddard, "Hymn to the Beautiful"

Angel Stories

I was meditating once and suddenly had this overwhelming impression of this enormous figure who stood over me, guarding me. He appeared like a medieval Templar knight—in chain mail and with an enormous sword. It was almost as though his shape was outlined in neon light against the blackness of my closed eyelids. He reminded me a lot of St. Michael. I'll never forget the experience!

World portrayed three lovely angels with Asian, African and Caucasian features to emphasize our opinion that these beneficent beings may appear in any manner revelatory and acceptable to the individual. We heard from many African-American and Asian-American readers who expressed pleasure at seeing angels appear in a manner other than the blond, blue-eyed stereotype so often depicted in religious art.

Is There an Angel Scent?

I was sitting alone at home with my infant daughter asleep in my arms, when I suddenly smelled the aroma of freshly baked doughnuts. I had not made or bought any doughnuts and did not have any in the house. Nor did I have any candle or air freshener that smelled like that. I had a feeling that there was a presence in my home, trying to give me a message. Can angels manifest their presence as a comforting scent, perhaps if they were trying to communicate a calming influence?

The detection of a pleasant aroma in the air has been reported by many individuals prior to their receiving what many have declared a significant, even life-altering, communication from angelic intelligence. The aromas most often reported are those of roses, violets, lilies, and various other flowers. Others have mentioned the smell of a deceased loved one's cologne, aftershave, or body powder prior to spirit contact. If the aroma of doughnuts represents a time of comfort, security, or love to you, then angelic presence might very well surround you with such a smell to bring about a calming of the mind and senses and prepare you for meaningful contact.

Brad Steiger is the author of 140 books, both fiction and nonfiction, with more than 17 million copies in print. Sherry Hansen Steiger is the cocreator of the Celebrate Life program, the founder of the Butterfly Center of Holistic Education and a founding member of the Holistic Healing Board in Washington, D.C. She is the author or coauthor of more than 20 books, including Seasons of the Soul, The Power of Prayer to Heal and Transform Your Life *and* Angels around the World.

Frequently Asked Angel Questions
Guardian Angels

With Brad and Sherry Steiger

HOW TO CONNECT WITH YOUR GUARDIAN ANGEL

Ever since I was very young, I have always felt that "someone" was watching over me. How do I know if this is an angel?

The scriptures of all the major world religions promise that there truly are spiritual beings who are concerned about us. According to the statistics that we have accumulated, thousands of men and women have experienced the feeling that "someone" was watching over them.

Of the approximately thirty thousand individuals who have responded to the questionnaire that we began distributing in 1967, 85 percent indicate that around the age of five, they experienced an interaction with some type of being—an angel, a holy figure, a spirit guide or an entity they believed to be the spirit of a deceased loved one. Nearly all of the respondents who felt the touch of an angel or spirit guide as a child report that they have maintained some kind of communication with this being—or at least from time to time "feel" its presence near them.

The most important aspect of sensing a benevolent presence should

be the wonderful assurance that you are not alone and that a benign entity cares for you in a personal way. If, however, it seems important to you to discover the identity of your guardian, dreams may serve as one reliable means of determining the unseen spirit presence. Keep a note pad at your bedside, and upon awakening in the middle of the night or first thing in the morning, jot down whatever you remember from your dreams. After a few days of keeping a dream diary, you may begin to see a pattern whereby you are receiving useful messages or teachings from a symbolic figure in your night visions. Once you have established a regimen of personal dream analysis, you may also begin to determine specific clues to the identity of the dream teacher, your guardian.

ANGEL NAMES

How can we learn the name of our guardian angel?

We don't think it is particularly important to know the name of your guardian angel. It may even be improper to inquire.

In Judges 13:9–20, when Manoah and his barren wife are informed by an angel that they shall be the parents of a child (Samson) who shall be devoted to God, they ask the heavenly messenger his name "so that when these sayings come to pass we may do thee honour". The angel makes it clear that all honour must go only to God, but as to the matter of his name he answers, in the King James version, that it is secret. In the Contemporary English version, the angel replies, "You don't need to know my

Angel Stories
GUARDIAN ANGELS

His name is Red Cloud. But I'm told he is my spirit guide. He's been around for a long time and just now I'm starting to learn when he's telling me something and what it means. He's VERY important to me. I'm very fortunate to have him with me.

The angels keep their ancient places;

Turn but a stone, and start a wing!

'Tis ye, 'tis your estrangèd faces,

That miss the many-splendoured thing.

—Francis Thompson, "The Kingdom of God"

Angel Stories
GUARDIAN ANGELS

Sixteen years ago I lived in a rat-infested apartment, trying to raise three children while holding down a secretarial job. I had no transportation and was confused and alone. One night when I walked into my bedroom, a light appeared through a dark window and a very large shadow crossed over mine. It was as if I could see the wingspan. The window was not located near any outside light or street, just a very dark brick wall. I felt no fear and knew instantly what it was.

While telling friends at work the next day what had happened, one of them immediately began to cry. She too knew immediately what I had seen. It was my guardian angel. Life is much better now. I have my own business, a wonderful relationship, and great kids and one super great grandchild. But I have never forgotten that I was allowed to see my guardian angel just so I knew he was there. He still is and I carry that very certain knowledge with me always!

name. And if you did, you couldn't understand it."

Some readers may be familiar with our calling our guardian angel or spirit teacher by the name Elijah. In 1972, although we were not yet married— and in fact had not yet even met—we each experienced a physical manifestation of an angelic intelligence. After the manifestation had departed, we were each left with the impression of the name Elijah. Neither of us would claim that we know for certain that this is the name that our angel calls himself. Nei-

ther do we pray to him or call upon him to aid us or serve us in any way whatsoever. We think there is great wisdom in heeding the advice given by the angel who appeared to Samson's parents.

By the same token, we know that for centuries, prophets, teachers and clergy have spoken of angels and archangels, giving them a host of names, and have ascribed to these beings what they deem their specific duties to be. We must also recognize that certain holy men and women may have received a divine revelation that Michael, Gabriel,

O, come, angel band,
Come and around me stand,
O, bear me away on your snow-white wings
To my immortal home.

—Traditional

Raphael and so forth were the actual names of mighty angelic beings, both in heaven and on Earth.

We claim no such divine revelation, so we might best consider "Elijah" as our nickname for our angel guide. We're human beings, after all. We like to have names for everything—from our pets to our automobiles. There is magic in names, an identification, an association. We are compelled by our very nature to want to call our guardian angels and spirit teachers by their names—whether they really are their actual names—so if it pleases you, do likewise.

What impression of a name do you receive while sensing the nearness of your angel guide? What impression of a name do you pick up while meditating on a lovely painting of angels or listening to inspirational music? You, too, can receive a nickname for your angelic guardian. Just remember: To God alone goes all honour, glory, praise, and prayers.

DO OUR LOVED ONES BECOME OUR GUARDIAN ANGELS?

My grandfather passed away two years ago. Ever since his funeral, I have sensed his presence near me. In

Angel Stories
GUARDIAN ANGELS

My little boy has a guardian angel named "service", but he is afraid of him/her. He tells me where the angel is and even describes its appearance.

fact, I believe that Grandpa is my guardian angel. Do our loved ones become our guardian angels when they pass to the other side?

While we are always cautious to avoid any kind of rigid dogma when it comes to discussing angelic beings and the divine order of the universe, we must point out that the holy books of the great world religions agree that angels are an earlier and a separate order of creation from human beings. A human, therefore, does not die and become an angel. We were created a "little lower than the angels", and we join them in the heavenly realm as distinctly human personalities and energy forms.

The teachings of Islam state that there are three distinct species of intelligent beings in the universe. The first are the angels (*malak*), a high order of beings created of light; second, the *al-jinn*, ethereal, perhaps even multidimensional entities; and then humans, fashioned of the stuff of Earth and born into physical bodies.

For hundreds of years, some books and plays have depicted the spirit of a deceased individual sprouting wings and rising to heaven—literally becoming an angel at the moment of death. Often in various productions, such as *Uncle Tom's Cabin*, the actor was outfitted in a pair of wings and hoisted by means of rope and pulley to soar above the scenery to accentuate the portrayal of an ascension to a higher dimension.

Although we humans do not become angels, we have every reason to believe that we are special entities with important earthly responsibilities and missions. So special are we that, according to some traditions, certain of the angels are

Angel Stories
GUARDIAN ANGELS

A three-year-old would pronounce his name keekoo. He was probably less than 5 feet tall, dark hair in a Caesar style with front and middle baldness, dressed like a Roman all in white. He was very kind, helpful and protective. I could feel his love and all-powerful strength.

I felt like angels were lifting and spinning me.

—Brian Boitano, Olympic gold medal figure skater, 1988 Winter Games

jealous of our human attributes— especially our free will—and resent the attention that the Supreme Being shows toward our spiritual evolution.

So while in the strictest definition of the title we do not become angels when we die, there are at least two possible responses to those who feel that a deceased loved one has become their guardian angel. First, souls may temporarily be held earthbound by the grief of their families and appear to assume the role of a guiding presence.

Second, angelic beings, in order to effect more immediate communication, may assume the appearance of a deceased loved one. But these are simply our thoughts. We are not dogmatic nor do we seek to impose our human understanding on others with regard to the limits of God's creative powers.

Do Angels Guard Buildings?

Are there spirits that act as protectors for buildings or businesses? Every time I am at work, I get a very **strong sense of a presence that I only experience in that particular office.**

One possible interpretation of the phenomenon that you describe is that the person who senses such a presence may only be personalizing and projecting their own positive feelings toward that particular work environment. Another explanation, however, is that all edifices contain the dynamics of the people who have lived and worked in them. Nearly every sensitive individual has, at one time or another, sensed the energy in office buildings, hospitals, schools and hotels of people who have conducted their work, spent many hours, experienced a range of emotions, and invested hopes and dreams there. So you may be responding to patterns that have been somehow impressed into the fabric of the environment by former occupants.

Many spiritual theorists also maintain that there are angelic beings who serve as patrons over particular nations, regions, buildings, bridges,

Who does the best his circumstance allows does well,
acts nobly: angels could do no more.

—Edward Young

and so forth (see Devas, Fairies, and Nature Spirits on page 109). Perhaps in response to the prayers of the inhabitants, these angels have been given the assignment of watching over these specific areas.

Regardless of whether these sensations are memory patterns of former occupants, the continuing existence of protective spirit beings watching over their old workplace, or cosmic guardians assigned to watch over an area, one should be respectful toward them and accept the experience as an undeclared "perk" of the job.

CAN ANGELS BE PEOPLE?

Is it true that guardian angels can be living persons, not just unseen entities?

The broadest definition of an angel is simply one who serves as a messenger of God. In this sense, a living person could certainly serve in such a capacity and serve God's purpose by delivering a particular thought, knowledge or

counsel that one might require at a certain crisis point.

Many of us have been privileged to have had a good friend or family member become an "angel" when we really needed the unconditional love and assistance of another, and some of us may even have had such a person assume a protective "guardian angel" role for a time. When we speak of our true "guardian angels", however, we are referring to those unseen, benevolent entities who, according to many traditions, have been assigned to us at birth to guide, direct and on occasion protect us.

ANGELS AND JESUS

Why all this talk of angels? When you speak of guardian angels, you are diverting people from trusting in their savior, Jesus Christ. Why not tell people all they need is their faith in Jesus?

We are delighted that your faith so fulfills you, answers all your questions and helps with your problems. Certainly, we would never suggest that you cease praying to your image or concept of Jesus.

We feel, however, that it is not our place to propagate any one religious view but to celebrate the truth in the belief systems of all sincere spiritual seekers. There is no need, however, for anyone to be forced to choose between Jesus or the angels, for it is clear from the Gospels that the angels consider themselves subordinate to Him.

The Gospels also record a continuing interaction between the angels and Jesus: In Matthew 1:20–21 and Luke 1:26–37, they predicted His birth; in Luke 2:9–14, they announced His birth; they ministered to Him during His time in the wilderness (Matthew 4:11); they sought to soothe His anxiety in the garden before His crucifixion (Luke 22:43); they rolled away the great stone that covered His tomb (Matthew 28:2–4); and they announced His resurrection (Matthew 28:5–7).

We have stressed repeatedly that one does not pray to angels or seek their energy in an attempt to manipulate reality in ways that would be magical, rather than spiritual. We have also reminded our readers that angels are not omnipresent, omnipotent or omniscient. Nor do we humans die, ascend to heaven and become angels.

The angelic beings are a separate creation formed by God to glorify Him and to serve as His messengers. And we have also made a point of recognizing that while the majority of angels remained true to God, the rebellious fallen angels who were turned out of paradise seek always to deceive humans with the temptations and allure of the dark side. To believe that we have guardian angels who guide, direct and protect us is not to deny Jesus but to have the faith of such great heroes of the Bible as Jacob, Daniel, Moses, Elijah, Joshua, Joseph, Peter and John, who also received the benefits of angelic intervention.

Brad Steiger is the author of 140 books, both fiction and nonfiction, with more than 17 million copies in print. Sherry Hansen Steiger is the cocreator of the Celebrate Life program, the founder of the Butterfly Center of Holistic Education and a founding member of the Holistic Healing Board in Washington, D.C. She is the author or coauthor of more than 20 books, including Seasons of the Soul, The Power of Prayer to Heal and Transform Your Life *and* Angels around the World.

The Human Guardian Angel

How come the Russian soldier with the kind eyes was always there at the right moment?

By Renie Burghardt

The first time I saw my guardian angel, he was pointing a machine gun at us. It was the beginning of 1945, and my grandparents and I had just emerged from a bunker, where we had spent a terror-filled night.

I was nine years old then, living in Hungary, and World War II was playing havoc with our lives. My grandparents, who were raising me, and I had been on the road in our horse-drawn wagon for many months, searching for a safe place. We had left behind the village of our birth in the Bacska region because Tito and his Communist Partisans (guerrillas) were closing in on the region. By day we'd move swiftly, ready to jump out and take cover in a ditch if warplanes were approaching. By night, we camped with other refuge-seekers along the roadside. I usually lay bundled up in my feather bed in the back of the wagon, cradling my cat, Paprika. War was almost all I had known during my nine years; there seemed to be no safe place to be found.

After the Christmas of 1944, when we were almost killed in a bombing in the city we were in at the time, Grandfather decided that a rural area would be safer. So we moved to one in northern Hungary and settled in a small house that had an old cemetery as its neighbor. Here, Grandfather, with the help of some distant neighbors, built a bunker in a flat area behind the house. And on that early spring day in 1945, we spent the entire night in the bunker.

Warplanes buzzed, tanks thundered, bombs exploded over our heads all night, but finally at dawn everything grew deathly still. Grandfather decided that it would be safe to go back to our house. Cautiously, we crept out into the light of early dawn and headed toward the house. The brush crackled under our feet as we walked past the cemetery. The markers looked lonely, separated by tall, dry weeds. I shivered, holding tightly onto my cat. He had spent the night in the bunker with us.

Suddenly, there was a rustle in the bushes just ahead. Two men jumped out and pointed machine guns directly at us.

"*Stoi!*" one of the men shouted. Since we were from an area where both Serbian and Hungarian had been spoken, we knew the word meant, "Stop!"

"Russians!" Grandfather whispered. "Stand very still, and keep quiet."

But I was already running after my cat. He had leapt out of my arms when the soldier shouted, so I darted between the soldiers and scooped her up. The younger of the two soldiers, tall and dark haired, approached me. I cringed, holding Paprika against my chest. The soldier reached out and petted him.

"I have a little girl about your age back in Russia, and she has a cat just like this one," he said, gently tugging one of my blond braids. "And she has long braids, too, just like you." I looked up into a pair of kind brown eyes and my fear vanished. Grandfather and Grandmother sighed with relief!

Well, both soldiers came back to the house with us and shared in our meager breakfast, and we found out from them that the Soviet occupation of Hungary was in progress.

Many atrocities occurred in our area, as well as throughout our country in the following months, but because the young Russian soldier took a liking to me, we were spared. He came to visit often, bringing little treats along for Paprika and me, and always talked longingly of his own little girl. I loved his visits, yet I was terrified of the Russians in general. Then one day, almost a year later, he had some news.

"I've been transferred to another area, *malka* (little one), so I won't be able to come and visit anymore. But I have a gift for you," he said, taking something out of his pocket. It was a necklace with a beautiful, turquoise Russian Orthodox cross on it. He placed it around my neck. "You wear this at all times, *malka*. God will protect you from harm." I hugged him tight and then watched him drive

Angel Stories

GUARDIAN ANGELS

He told me his name is Jonas and that he is here to protect and guide me. I talk to him often and get positive responses that he is listening. I visualize him as an older man with long white hair and a long white flowing robe. I hope he remains with me forever.

away, tears welling in my eyes.

World War II was over, but for the people of Hungary a life of bondage was at hand. Many men who had been involved in politics or deemed undesirable were being rounded up by the secret police, never to be seen again. Not long after came the knock on the door we dreaded. They said they wanted to take Grandfather in for questioning. Fortunately, Grandfather managed to sneak out through a window and go into hiding. Then it was just Grandma and I, trying to survive as best we could. Then Paprika died, and life truly seemed unbearable. Sometimes, I would finger the cross my Russian guardian angel had given me and wonder where he was. Was he back home with his own daughter? Did he remember me?

The time passed in a haze of anxiety and depression. Then, in the fall of 1947, a man came to get us in the middle of the night. He said he would take us to the Austrian border, and we'd be reunited with my grandfather. So we travelled all night to a place where the ethnic Germans of Hungary were being loaded into transport trucks and expelled from Hungary. The man would give us counterfeit papers so we could cross the border to freedom together. And when we arrived, a weary-looking man with a thick, scraggly beard and a knit cap pulled low over his forehead was waiting for us.

"Grandpa!" I cried out, rushing into his arms. It was so wonderful to see him again. Then we walked toward the transport truck loaded with dozens of people and got on, fake papers in hand. I knew if we were found out, it would mean Grandpa would get hauled off to prison, and worse yet, he might even be executed. I glanced towards the Russian soldiers who were coming closer to inspect the papers, and I prayed silently to God, to keep us safe.

Then I looked up as a guard boarded the truck. I caught my breath. "Grandpa," I whispered. "Look, it's my soldier, Ivan! He is checking this truck." I wanted to leap up and run to him, but Grandpa shushed me cautiously. "Maybe he won't recognize us," he whispered, pulling the knit hat further down his forehead.

Then he stood before us. My grandfather handed over our papers without looking up. I leaned closer and put my hand protectively on his shoulder while I peered cautiously at Ivan, hoping to see the old kind sparkle in his eyes. But he was intent upon the papers, his expression grave. I didn't dare to breathe. At last he handed the papers back to Grandpa.

"Everything is in order in this vehicle," he announced. Then, winking at me, he jumped down, and the truck began to move on. I looked over my shoulder and caught my guardian angel's eye. "Thank you," I mouthed the words, holding up the cross hanging around my neck. He nodded discreetly, then quickly turned and walked away. As we crossed the border into Austria and safety, we finally sighed a sigh of relief.

Although we had suffered much sadness during the war, one blessing will always stay with me: the memory of a kind soldier who turned my fear to faith and showed me that compassion can be found anywhere, even in the eyes of an enemy.

Renie Burghardt was born in Hungary and came to the United States in the early 1950s from a refugee camp. She is a freelance writer whose work has appeared in many magazines and books, including Chicken Soup for the Christian Family Soul *and* God Allows U-Turns.

A Firefighter's Angel

A firefighter was almost caught in a "flashover," a firefighter's worst nightmare, but then he heard a voice he instinctively knew to obey.

By Joan Wester Anderson

It's not necessary to see an angel in order to feel one's presence. Just ask Mark Kuck.

Mark is a volunteer firefighter in Ohio and also the only paramedic in his district. Usually Mark does not put on an air pack and actually go into a fire because he needs to be readily available to provide medical care. But when an unoccupied mobile home caught on fire—and not enough firefighters had yet arrived—Mark decided to go in.

"My partner and I entered through the back door of the trailer," Mark said (firefighters always travel in pairs). "We kept low to the floor to avoid any superheated gasses that might be higher up." Mark had control of the hose nozzle, and his partner was helping to drag the hose. Mark saw an orange glow, directed the nozzle toward it and easily put out that part of the fire. The men crawled through a doorway into a second room filled with furniture and items lying all around.

"Being in a fire is nothing like what they show on TV," Mark said. "If you are lucky, you might be able to see the hose you are carrying. But the smoke is so thick that everything else is done by feel, and of course you are wearing heavy leather gloves." Eventually, however, Mark located the source of the flames and directed water at it. But it just kept coming back. "This told us that the fire was being fueled by something other than solid material—like propane or heating oil."

It is still possible, Mark said, to contain the spread of such a fire by shutting off the fuel supply or wetting down the materials around the fire. Mark assumed that those outside the trailer had already turned off the fuel supply, so he and his partner opted to stay in the trailer and keep watering the flames. "It was about this time," Mark recalled, "that I began to feel uneasy . . ."

For it is not the shape, but their use, that makes them angels.

—Thomas Hobbes

At first it was just a sense that something wasn't right. Maybe it was just his imagination, Mark thought. But the feeling persisted. Then he heard a clear male voice: "Mark," it said, "you need to go." Mark was astonished. The voice was audible, yet it couldn't be his partner—he was too far away to be heard. And an air pack distorts a voice—"It's kind of a Darth Vader effect," Mark noted. Not like this voice, so distinct and close it was almost at his ear. Nor were there any openings in the trailer where someone outside could yell through. What was happening?

A few moments later, Mark heard the message again. "Okay," Mark said in his mind to the Voice. "I'll go pretty soon. Let me hit this a little more, and see if I can get somewhere."

The Voice was not convinced. "Mark!" it answered, in a no-nonsense tone. "You need to go *now*!" The Voice did not sound angry that he had been ignoring it, Mark said. "It sounded as if it was just giving me an urgent warning." Mark could disregard it no

longer. He turned, motioned to his partner, and the two crouched down to make their way back to the first room. It was difficult, due to all the debris strewn around.

As they entered, Mark suddenly saw a tongue of flame enter the room and heard the terrible *whomph!* sound that all firefighters dread. It was a flashover, something that happens when the contents of a room are so hot that they can instantly explode and just one flame can engulf a room in seconds. "Gear might keep you alive for a few seconds if you are caught in a flashover," Mark explained, "but you will still be seriously burned." (In fact, the survival rate for firefighters caught in a flashover is 3 to 5 percent.)

"Get down! Get down!" Mark yelled as his partner hit the floor. Immediately Mark aimed water at the flash flame and drove it back, just enough for the two to scramble to safety. Had they still been in the second room—or in the first room for just a few more seconds—they never would have lived.

What a piece of work is man,

how noble in reason,

how infinite in faculties,

in form and moving,

how express and admirable in action,

how like an angel in apprehension,

how like a god!

The beauty of the world; the paragon of animals;

and yet to me what is this quintessence of dust?

Man delights not me.

—William Shakespeare, *Hamlet*

As the fire waned, Mark thought more seriously about the Voice. It had been a young voice, something like his own, firm but not intimidating, a voice that he instinctively knew he could trust and obey. And . . . yes, he had heard it once before, when he was seventeen and involved in a serious automobile accident. Wasn't it this same voice that had calmed him as he crashed, reassured him that all would be well? But how could this be?

After the fire, Mark told a friend—another firefighter—about his experience. This man had served more than two tours of duty in Vietnam as a Ranger, extensively involved in com-

bat, as well as a stint in Desert Storm. He immediately knew what Mark was describing. "I heard that voice on a number of occasions, in fires and in combat," the veteran told Mark, "and I learned to listen to it. The times I got hurt were when I didn't."

"I personally believe that I owe my life to whoever's voice that was," Mark says today. "Maybe God, maybe an angel . . . I don't know. But I'm sure glad they were on my entry team."

Joan Wester Anderson is the author of seven books on angels and miracles. Her first book, Where Angels Walk, *has sold more than two million copies and has been translated into fifteen languages. For more angel stories, visit her WhereAngelsWalk Web site at http://joanwanderson.com.*

Angel Stories
GUARDIAN ANGELS

As a child I had little friends, but there were also always unseen friends whom I could address when no one had time for me. In 1981 I started meditating and met my guardian angel. Since then I speak to him almost every day. When I am in trouble he guides me to a good book or makes someone call me. When I was ill my angel stood beside me and comforted me. It is my belief that everyone has at least one guardian angel and that anyone can contact him by speaking to him as to a friend—openhearted and free, allowing space for him to act in his own way. An answer will come most unexpectedly, but it will come.

Angels by His Side

This holy man, who was declared a saint in 2002, often sent his guardian angel to help others.

By Joan Wester Anderson

Padre Pio, born in 1887 of simple farm people in Pietrelcina, Italy, was a monk who had the stigmata—the marks of Christ's crucifixion—etched in his hands, feet and side, as did the founder of his order, St. Francis. Despite his own fragile health, he devoted his life to building homes for the sick, the handicapped and the elderly.

Padre Pio had a particularly interesting relationship with angels. It is said that he "met" his own guardian angel as a youngster and occasionally received counsel from him; later, the two communicated in both prayerful and humorous dialogues.

At times, according to witnesses, Padre Pio was able to read and speak languages he didn't know. When asked how he could do it, he said that his guardian angel translated for him. On occasion, a number of his fellow monks heard voices singing in heavenly harmony but couldn't discover the source of the music. Padre Pio explained that the voices were angels, escorting souls into heaven.

Padre Pio frequently sent his angel to someone who needed help. For example, Father Alessio Parente was assigned to assist the fragile monk from the chapel to his monastic cell every day. But Father Parente had a habit of oversleeping. Often he wouldn't hear his alarm clock or, half-awake, he would switch it off. "Every time I overslept," he says, "I heard a voice in my sleep saying, 'Alessio, Alessio, come down!' and a knocking at my door. Realizing I was late, I would jump out of bed and run out into the corridor to see who called me, but there was nobody there. I would race down to the church and there I invariably found Padre Pio at the end of Mass giving the last blessing.

"One day I was sitting by Padre Pio's side, feeling ashamed at my lack of punctuality. I was trying to explain to him that I never seemed to hear the alarm, but he interrupted me. 'Yes, I understand you,' he said. 'But do you think I will continue to send my guardian angel every day to wake you? You'd better go and buy yourself a new clock.'

"It was only then that I realized who was knocking at my door and calling me in my sleep."

Padre Pio believed that people could send their angels to others to help or intercede. He encouraged his vast network of friends to send their angels to him if they could not come themselves. "Your angel can take a message from you to me," he would say, "and I will assist you as much as I can." On one occasion, Cecil, an English friend of the Padre, was hurt in a car crash. A friend went to the post office to send a telegram to Padre Pio, requesting prayers for the accident vic-

tim. When the friend presented the telegram at the desk, the man gave him back a telegram from Padre Pio assuring him of his prayers for Cecil.

Later, after Cecil had recovered, he and his friend went to see Padre Pio. "How did you know of the accident?" both asked. "We got your telegram before we had sent ours."

"Do you think angels go as slowly as planes?" the monk responded, smiling.

On another occasion, an Italian girl, hearing of this saintly friar, sent her angel to ask for good health for her Uncle Fred. The girl then decided to visit Padre Pio. When she approached him, he joked with her: "Your angel kept me up all night, asking for a cure for your Uncle Fred!"

The mother of a desperately ill infant also sent the baby's angel to ask Padre Pio for prayers. As soon as she

Angel Stories
GUARDIAN ANGELS

Mine are named Galen and Paige. I saw one of them once in a dream, and she was very tall (around 8 feet) and was wearing a royal blue suit, and she was quite overloaded with her caseload.

It is said by some

who ought to understand such things,

that the good people, or the fairies,

are some of the angels

who were turned out of heaven,

and who landed on their feet in this world,

while the rest of their companions,

who had more sin to sink them,

went down farther to a worse place.

—William Butler Yeats, *Fairy Tales of Ireland*

did so, she saw her tiny child shiver as if something had touched her. Although the doctors were mystified, the baby quickly improved and was sent home from the intensive care unit.

"When speaking to people about these stories, the comments are often the same: 'Oh, well, Padre Pio was a very holy man, wasn't he?' or 'I'm just a poor sinner. Why should an angel do anything to help me?'" Father Parente says, "Yes, Padre Pio was a very holy man, but I believe our angels work well for each one of us too—if we only have faith."

When Padre Pio died on September 22, 1968, several American tourists in Italy saw angels in the night sky, angels who quietly disappeared as the sun rose.

Joan Wester Anderson is the author of seven books on angels and miracles. Her first book, Where Angels Walk, *has sold more than two million copies and has been translated into fifteen languages. For more angel stories, visit her WhereAngelsWalk Web site at http://joanwanderson.com.*

Angels and Children— A Special Angelic Connection?

A seven-year-old teaches her dad about divine guidance.

By Tobin Hart , Ph.D.

It was a typical school night; my daughter Haley, seven years old, was settling in after a bedtime story. As I was saying good night, she noticed the cover of a book in my hand that had a picture of a child on it. She asked why I was reading a children's book, and I said that it was not a children's book but a book about children and all the ways that they see and think about the world.

"Oh, you mean like seeing angels?" she said.

As a psychologist and university professor, I was certain that this was not what this developmental psychology

book was about, but I said, "Well, yes, I guess it could be about things like that."

"I see my angel," she announced matter-of-factly.

In that moment, I supposed that for a child who always wanted to stay up later, this had the desired effect. I slowed my exit and said, "Do you see her now?"

"Just a minute," she replied.

As she lay on her bed surrounded by her stuffed animals, I watched her move her spine from side to side, apparently trying to get in the "right

Each corse lay flat, lifeless and flat,

And, by the holy rood!

A man all light, a seraph-man,

On every corse there stood.

—Samuel Taylor Coleridge,
"The Rime of the Ancient Mariner"

*A baby is an angel
whose wings decrease as his legs increase.*

—French proverb

spot." Her eyes were now closed, and she started to take in deeper breaths in a rhythmic beat. My wife and I had never spoken of angels, meditation or the like in front of her, nor had she ever seen anyone do yoga or meditate that we knew of. While I was not sure what she was doing, it was clear that she knew.

After four or five minutes, she calmly said, "Okay, I can see her now."

I asked her several questions, including how she and her angel communicated. She said, "It's kind of like thoughts and pictures all together." I asked if I could speak with her angel, and she paused and then said, "My angel wants to know why you want to

Angel Stories
SIGHTINGS BY CHILDREN

I was four years old and lived with my parents in my grandfather's home. He was a minister. Each night I would walk up two flights of stairs to lie down with my grandmother in her bed and listen to stories and recite poems. After we finished, I would walk down those stairs to the small apartment under the main house, knock on the door so that my mum could open it for me and put me to bed. One night on the way down, I sat down on the top of the last flight of stairs. All of a sudden, arms lifted me and I floated down to the last stair. I looked behind me and no one was there. Unafraid, I got up and knocked on the apartment door as usual. The next day, I told all in the house about my encounter. They told me it was my guardian angel. I am 53 years old and will never forget the feeling of those arms under mine! May we all be blessed with a special angel!

talk with her." I said I was curious and wanted to learn about her angel. She again paused and said, "Okay." She told me that her angel knew my angel and that they seemed to be old friends.

We covered quite a lot of ground in the next fifteen minutes. At first, I asked some fairly trivial questions, and these were politely but clearly dismissed or reframed and turned into questions of more substance. So I sharpened my approach. I began to ask questions about life, about what the angel was there for, about advice she had for Haley and, mostly as a test, about any insight and advice she had for me.

I asked questions to her angel, and Haley seemed to serve as the go-between. She would pause for a moment after I asked something and then offer a reply. What was most significant was not so much this scene—children have rich imaginations—but the quality of the answers she provided. This little, perky seven-year-old spoke with a profound depth of wisdom that seemed simply extraordinary. Her answers and comments were elegantly simple and deeply insightful, offering the kind of crystal clarity and remarkable depth that I had not heard from her before and rarely hear from the wisest adults I know.

Haley started to wiggle, and it appeared that our conversation was nearing its end. I asked her one more question: "What does your angel do for you?" She said that her angel "lets her know that [she] is loved," and she described being provided guidance and comfort—a kind of centring in love and clarity. She gave me the impression that her angel does not solve problems so much as provide a bigger view of the issues, a vantage point that seems to help Haley centre herself, to calm worry and doubt. The angel does not give her love exactly, but reminds her that she is loved. Our

Angel Stories
SIGHTINGS BY CHILDREN

When my granddaughter was two-and-a-half years old, she woke up from her nap and came into the living room where I was sitting and reading a book. She told me of a dream she had about my deceased son, who had died before she was born. She told me that God and my son asked her if they could lie down beside her. I asked her if she was scared and she told me no; she said it was peaceful. I do believe that this was a sign that my son would always watch over her.

> *Angels from friendship gather half their joy.*
>
> —Edward Young

conversation seemed to be finished as my daughter shifted back into a sleepy seven-year-old. So we said good night, and I left her room dazed.

Does Haley actually receive guidance from an angel? I cannot verify the source of her insight in conventional empirical means; no one can. But I can listen deeply to the quality of the information she offers and watch the impact it has on her life. What I see is that she manages to tap a vein of insight, wisdom and love, intentionally and without any previous training.

I have come to think of her angel as an aspect of her Higher Self, or higher intuition. Wise persons throughout history have named a similar vein:

Socrates called his voice Daimon, Ralph Waldo Emerson called this the Oversoul, Meister Eckhart named it the Inner Man. I don't think it matters whether this is thought of as a guardian angel, a guide, her heart or whatever. What is important is that she can find it on her own and that it serves as a wellspring for love and wisdom.

And as children are often powerful teachers, I have found that watching my daughter listen to her angel has reminded me to listen for my own.

Tobin Hart, Ph.D., serves as associate professor of psychology at the State University of West Georgia. He is a director of ChildSpirit, a nonprofit institute nurturing the spirit of the child.

Frequently Asked Angel Questions

Sightings by Children

With Brad and Sherry Steiger

ARE CHILDREN CLOSER TO THE ANGELS?

Is it true that children can see angels and the spirit world more easily than adults?

Based on reports throughout history, it seems that many children *do* perceive the spirit world and angelic beings more easily than adults. Because of children's sensitivity to such phenomena, it behooves their parents to guide them in a proper manner that neither encourages nor discourages them to report such appearances.

Parents who take a New Age approach to such occurrences would be well-advised not to seek to make their children seers or channels before a certain level of rationality and balance has been achieved. Neither should more conservative and conventionally

Angel Stories

SIGHTINGS BY CHILDREN

I have seen angels on one occasion when I was very young. I must have been one or two years old but I saw about 15 of them all standing together. They had on white robes and they just looked at me. They were in a bright white fog and I could not see their feet or the tops of their heads. I was awake and in the living room, and the sun was shining brightly in my eyes through the upstairs loft windows. The cloud just floated by me all the way across the room and then vanished. I have always felt their presence since and am not scared of anything. I know for a fact I am protected every second of my life.

Sleep, my child, and peace attend thee
All through the night;
Guardian angels God will send thee
All through the night.

—Sir Harold Boulton

religious parents be fearful that their child is possessed.

In our opinion, while we earnestly believe that children should be informed of the reality of guardian angels who watch over them, we also maintain that when they claim that a spirit being has appeared physically to them, it is best to listen sympathetically, neither praising nor scolding them for sharing the experience.

The very sacred relationship between an individual and his spiritual guardian will develop at its own pace and should never be forced. As parents, we may guide our children's spiritual growth, but we cannot force it to flower before its individually appointed time.

Children Talk about Angels

"An angel is a bird with a person in the middle." (Age 4)

"I used to be an angel and watched over my mummy when she was a little girl. I picked her to be my mummy. When it was my turn to come down, I asked my angel friend Lanya to take over for me and then I was born." (Age 5)

"Sophine is a beautiful angel . . . She always comes to my room while I am asleep and makes my flowers grow." (Age 4)

"When I was a baby I used to cry 'waa, waa, waa,' until my angel came." (Age 3)

—From *Drawing Angels Near: Children Tell of Angels in Words and Pictures* by Mimi Doe and Garland Waller

Angel Stories
SIGHTINGS BY CHILDREN

On a Thursday, a few days before my son died, I met a woman who could have only been an angel. She told me of her daughter's death 14 years ago. She said a child will not leave their mother until they know she will survive it. I said my child is not leaving! She said you have to open your heart and hear what your child is telling you.

I kept watching her eyes. They were different—an angel's. We talked for about 30 minutes. That Thursday, they were going to put the respirator down my son's throat. My husband and I were there with him. Then my son said, "Leave," and he smiled so big and his whole body shook with joy. I was so scared. Was he saying goodbye? Inside my head I was screaming NO! He was pronounced dead on a Saturday afternoon. They pulled all of their machines and tubes off of his beautiful body. My son had been in and out of the hospital his entire life. I was sure he would always be with me because he was born with the gift of seeing angels. He would tell me about the angels only he could see. Then, God sent one that I could see. In my heart, I knew it.

Is there any special connection between angels and the mentally challenged? My fourteen-year-old daughter is very convinced of angels. She says she has many and sends them to others for their protection. She says that they kiss her on the cheeks, especially when she is upset. It is a wonderful thing that she has them watching over her.

Over thirty years ago, during Sherry's nurses' training, it occurred to her that the mentally challenged appeared to have developed "extra" senses in a manner similar to the blind and the deaf. It seemed to her that God compensated

for minuses in some areas by giving pluses in others, such as permitting these individuals to see angels and other spiritual beings. In later years, our research would answer in the affirmative the question about whether a special connection between angels and the mentally challenged existed.

We received a letter from one mother who said that there is often a heavenly glow around the bed of her three-year-old mentally challenged son. She is convinced that she has glimpsed her son's guardian angel hovering over him and that the heavenly being seems to pay attention to his special needs.

Another mother wrote to tell us that her twelve-year-old mentally challenged daughter wandered away from their house and was lost for an entire nerve-wrenching afternoon. Suddenly, at dusk, they found the girl sitting quietly

Watch thou, dear Lord, with those who wake, or watch, or weep tonight, and give thine angels charge over those who sleep.

—Saint Augustine

in her backyard swing. She told them that a "shining lady" had taken her hand and walked her safely back home.

While some may consider it only wishful thinking that angelic beings would pay special attention to children who are mentally challenged, we believe that those parents who have contacted us with such a witness are sincere. And based on the many special children that we have personally observed, it would appear that they may also have been blessed with the power to express an almost angelic kind of unconditional love.

As a teenager, I was physically abused by an alcoholic father. One night when he was beating me, I shouted, "No more!" The room was suddenly filled with a bright light. My father became so frightened that he never put a hand to me again. I believe with all my heart that the light was caused by my guardian angel. Do you know of any other such stories wherein an angel interceded to protect an abused child?

Our files are filled with such wonderful accounts. In one case, a young man told

Angel Stories
SIGHTINGS BY CHILDREN

When I was five years old an angel came to me at my preschool to let me know that my grandmother had passed away. When my mother and uncle came to pick me up from school, I walked up to my mother and told her that grandma had died. She looked at me with a perplexed expression and wanted to know who told me as she had not called the school to let them know. My reply was that God had sent one of his angels to me.

us that when he was a child, he was judged mentally slow by his family. He recalled a childhood of horrible beatings by both his parents and his three brothers, who seemed to delight in tormenting the "dummy". The tortured boy's only solace came in the evening, when an angel of healing would come to him and soothe his bruises and cuts. Later, when a compassionate uncle intervened and took the boy to live with him, it was discovered that he had average intelligence but was hard of hearing. Today, the young man wears a hearing aid and is a successful engineer.

A young woman who today is a respected high school teacher and a mother of two children wrote to tell us that as a child, she had somehow been appointed the role of family scapegoat and was abused by her parents and siblings. Her life was

Angel Stories
SIGHTINGS BY CHILDREN

My mum was driving the car and I was in the passenger seat. My little sister was in the backseat behind me. She was two. We were in a heavy rainstorm and my mum could hardly see the road at all. I asked her to pull over until the rain let up but she wouldn't because we had to be somewhere by a certain time. We drove a little farther and the rain got heavier; the traffic was really bad and all of a sudden my little sister, who had been singing in the backseat, made a noise like a gasp of breath and out of the corner of my eye behind my mum I swear I saw a golden light. The whole backseat lit up with a golden light and the car was full of peace, and then the light was just gone. It happened all at once—pretty fast actually. I didn't say anything because it kind of scared me but it felt peaceful not really scary. Anyway, I sat there for a couple minutes then I said, "Mum did you see that?" And she said, "See what?" So I said, never mind, because I didn't want her to think I was crazy. And my little two-year-old sister said, "The angel, the angel—me see an angel!" So my mum just looked at me and then at her and kept driving.

miserable during the day, but nearly every evening two angels would appear in her room and tell her how important and valuable she was. The ministering angels so maintained her self-esteem against the steady barrage of insults and mistreatment that she learned to focus only on her heavenly mentors, worked hard on her school-work and won a scholarship to a state teachers' college when she graduated from high school.

That angels, in the role of ministers of healing, apply emotional balm to children suffering from physical abuse is well-documented in the numerous letters we receive. We are always eager to hear from others who may have experienced similar angelic intervention as an abused child.

Brad Steiger is the author of 140 books, both fiction and nonfiction, with more than 17 million copies in print. Sherry Hansen Steiger is the cocreator of the Celebrate Life program, the founder of the Butterfly Center of Holistic Education and a founding member of the Holistic Healing Board in Washington, D.C. She is the author or coauthor of more than 20 books, including Seasons of the Soul, The Power of Prayer to Heal and Transform Your Life *and* Angels around the World.

God's Pet Care

Would God Send an Angel to Recover a Beloved Pet Dog?

———

By Joan Wester Anderson

Renee Dotson was running uncharacteristically late as she rounded up her children for their martial arts lessons. Their Plano, Texas, home featured a six-foot-tall privacy fence around the backyard, and Renee had forgotten that the family's miniature Schnauzer, Lucky, was still out there. Usually they brought him in when everyone left at the same time. Worse, one of the children had inadvertently left the back gate open. Unaware, Renee herded the children into the truck

Angels Among Us

Shall we gather at the river
Where bright angel feet have trod:
With its crystal tide forever
Flowing by the throne of God?

—Robert Lowry

and set off. They were gone for over an hour.

"The back gate opens onto an alley, and whenever it's left open, Lucky always runs out of the yard and gets lost," Renee said. "So when we returned home and I pulled up to the curb at the front of the house, I was surprised to see Lucky sitting quietly in front of the house next to the fence." But there was another surprise, too.

A girl about ten years old was standing right next to Lucky, holding a golden leash attached to the dog's collar.

"The girl was dressed in old-fashioned garb—a blue dress with a white pinafore, which hung just below her knees," Renee said. "She wore white stockings and some sort of locket around her neck. The dress was trimmed with white lace at the neck and sleeves. She had long thick blonde hair that hung to her waist, and there

was a white glow about her." Renee stared. She had never seen such a person in her neighborhood. Had the girl found Lucky and brought him home? But how would she know where he lived? And where had the leash come from?

Questions bouncing around in her head, Renee took her eyes off the scene to finish parking. When she looked over again, the girl was gone. "But the dog was still sitting there, with the leash not only still attached to his collar, but still somehow suspended in midair!"

The family got out of the truck and walked toward Lucky. "Usually he would be bounding toward us, but he was still sitting there, watching us approach," said Renee.

The leash had disappeared, but when Renee got within five feet of the dog, she heard a girl's voice. "It's okay, Lucky," the voice said. "You can go now." Instantly, the dog began to jump all over the children.

"The kids never saw the girl," Renee said. "But I did. It couldn't have been my imagination because I had no inkling the dog was even in danger." Renee thanked the girl that night because without her, the family would have lost their beloved pet. "She didn't have wings or a halo, but I've never been able to think of her without feeling that she was an angel."

Would God care about the loss of a pet? Enough to send an angel to prevent it? This is the same God who tells us that "every hair on your head is numbered." A God of details. A God who cares.

Since then, Lucky had to be put down. He was eight years old at the time. "He had gotten into a scuffle with a toad and began developing weird neurological symptoms, eventually resulting in seizures," Renee said. "We went into the vet as a family. I had my hand on Lucky when the injection was given, and I physically felt his spirit, as soft and warm as a cloud, lift from his body through my hand and part of my arm, toward the ceiling. Because of this, I knew he was gone before the vet did, and it really hit home with me that our souls have physical substance."

Joan Wester Anderson is the author of seven books on angels and miracles. Her first book, Where Angels Walk, *has sold more than two million copies and has been translated into fifteen languages. For more angel stories, visit her* WhereAngelsWalk *Web site at* http://joanwanderson.com.

Janet and the Angel Musicians

From age six to eleven, a little girl was comforted by heavenly music.

———◦◦◦———

By Joan Wester Anderson

Six-year-old Janet had always had a certain memory, something she couldn't quite get hold of, like a little wisp of smoke that lingered just outside her reach. Her memory involved a sunny, wonderful place where she had somehow been before she came to Earth. And joyful sounds there . . .

Once or twice Janet had tried to describe this vague echo, but those who listened felt it might have been a dream, or a recollection from when she was a baby. Perhaps they were right. But still . . .

One night, Janet was sent to her room because she had been arguing with her sister. "It's almost bedtime, sweetheart," her mother said, "so put on your pajamas, and say your night prayers. Ask God to help you have a happier day tomorrow."

Slowly Janet undressed, feeling a little sad. She knew her mother was disappointed in her. Was God? She got on her knees. "Well, God," she began, "I haven't been very good today . . ."

All of a sudden, Janet heard a sound. Why, it sounded like people singing, far away. As she listened intently, the voices grew louder, closer. Was a radio playing nearby? No, the whole family was downstairs. Janet could hear her older sisters teasing one another as they did the dinner dishes. Bewildered, she got up, looked around her room, then went to check the outside hallway, just in case. Oddly, when she left her room, the music stopped.

Quickly Janet returned, knelt down and resumed her prayers. And the singing started again!

Janet listened intently. She didn't recognize the song and she couldn't hear any instruments. But for some reason, she felt she had heard this choir before. The concert was rich

We are like children, who stand in need of masters
to enlighten us and direct us;
and God has provided for this, by appointing his angels
to be our teachers and guides.

—Saint Thomas Aquinas

and full and beautiful, as if a vast crowd were rejoicing. The song made her heart swell, tears prick her eyes.

Suddenly she knew—they were angels! And they had sung that way to her, long ago in a warm and loving place, when she had no remembrance of anything but Light and Beauty . . .

Oh, how elated the harmony made her feel! As if God Himself were giving her a tender hug. Somehow Janet knew that He wasn't disappointed in her at all.

For the next few years, Janet heard music whenever she prayed in her room. And she'd pray as long as she could, so the glorious melody wouldn't stop. "I thought this happened to everyone," she says today. "Perhaps angels sing to all of us on Earth, but most of us just don't remember."

But she didn't tell anyone—just in case people would laugh. Until the singing episodes ended when she was about eleven, they remained her secret, hers and that choir of angels, who had frequently reminded her just how much she—and all of us—are loved.

Why don't all of us hear heavenly music, as Janet did? Who knows? God's ways are not our ways. But He has given us a precious promise, that He will send angels to guard us in all our ways (Psalm 91), and for that, we too can rejoice!

Joan Wester Anderson is the author of seven books on angels and miracles. Her first book, Where Angels Walk, *has sold more than two million copies and has been translated into fifteen languages. For more angel stories, visit her WhereAngelsWalk Web site at http://joanwanderson.com.*

Dream Angels

Do angels sometimes send us a wake-up call while we're asleep?

By Robert L. Van de Castle, Ph.D.

We're all familiar with stories about angelic appearances to people at critical times in their lives. Often they come in dreams. The Bible describes Jacob's nocturnal vision of angels ascending and descending a ladder that connected him with God as well as messages from the Angel of the Lord to Joseph in his dreams. Religious traditions also tell us that through dream encounters with angels, Muhammad was given instructions to found Islam, and the Book of Mormon was revealed to Joseph Smith.

But while dream messengers are found in the sacred texts of major religions, a most intriguing line of inquiry is whether these types of dreams are experienced today.

To answer this question, I began collecting dream accounts from several sources, and what I found is that angels do appear in contemporary dreams and that their visitations follow several patterns. Just as in waking accounts of angels, dreamers describe angelic beings as "shape shifters", beings that take on a form that makes the perceiver comfortable. Thus, in only a few accounts did dreamers experience anxiety or discomfort when encountering an angelic presence.

Generally, the feelings are extremely positive and remain so for years afterward. One man recalled his angelic dream encounter very clearly even after fifty-two years:

"At the foot of my bed was a golden staircase, which I started to climb, and I came out on soft clouds. Big stars were all around and beautiful angels were everywhere. The angels had wings, but I don't remember halos. The angels picked me up, hugged me and passed me around. They were laughing, very happy and very beautiful. I had a feeling of love and warmth that I have never experienced since.

I am the Angel of the Sun

Whose flaming wheels began to run

When God's almighty breath

Said to the darkness and the Night,

Let there be light! And there was light

I bring the gift of Faith.

—Henry Wadsworth Longfellow,
"Raphael" from *The Nativity*

Finally, I had to go back down the stairs and return to my bed."

Comforting dreams are not limited to children. A fifty-year-old Swiss carpenter dreamed that he was looking out the window:

"It was late evening and very dark. I saw two little rainbows lightly bouncing around outside. I went to the door and opened it. An angel was standing there. The rainbows turned out to be on the tips of the angel's wings. The angel gave me a big hug, and that was probably the most

Angel Stories
DREAM ENCOUNTERS

I have been having some dreams about angels recently. The first dream was vivid and detailed. It involved me and my girlfriend walking in an alley. The left side of the alley was very clean and organized. The right side was blocked by a chain-link fence, but on the other side of the fence there was disarray. (It was dark and shadowed.) There was a figure on the right side behind the fence walking along with us and calling my name. I can't distinguish whether the figure was male or female. I think the figure was an Angel. The voice was very calm and almost whispered. It just kept repeating my name. Then it was like I was awoken from my dream by this same voice calling my name louder, but in the same calm manner. At this point, still dreaming, it was like I was awake but I was not. I heard my door open, and I looked at my door and the door was surrounded by bright light. Then one last time my name was called quite loudly.

The next dream/vision I had was of the Garden of Eden. It was a very short vision. I clearly saw a picture in my mind of beautiful scenery with lots of flowers and plants and animals. Many shapes. Birds were singing, crickets chirping—it was a symphony of sounds and colours, very cheerful and happy. I couldn't help but feel like I was looking at the Garden of Eden. Then I saw an Angel. The Angel came out of a shelter and started flying in the air.

Everyone entrusted with a mission is an angel.

—Maimonides

beautiful experience I have ever had in my whole life."

But not all angels are huggers. Sometimes the angel is simply present or floating in space. In one dream, a person was flying when he suddenly encountered two radiant aerial angels. He felt great joy in their company and decided to join them. But despite great mental effort, he couldn't ascend to the same height.

Since most dreams are visual in nature, it's not surprising that images of angels are the most predominant form of representation. But other sensory channels can also be employed by angelic presences, as in the dream of a woman who reported that she heard a band of angels singing the "Hallelujah Chorus".

When contact is made with angelic energy, the dreamer sometimes experiences increased somatic sensitivity. A Florida woman dreamed she was in a bright room— the brightest she had ever seen in her life—and a man with jet-black hair,

wearing solid white clothing as bright as the room, approached her. He gently shook her and repeatedly called her name, telling her to wake up. When she suddenly awakened, she realized she had been in a diabetic coma and might have died had this angelic Good Samaritan not roused her. After her dramatic dream encounter, the woman was convinced that angels were "real."

According to a dream of a Canadian television producer, angels themselves seem to want to communicate not only that they are real but also that they have messages to deliver: heavenly "public service announcements". This man's dream was their "promotional ad":

"There are some creatures holding a large sign in front of me who seem very animated. Their activity is keeping me lucid; they seem to want my full attention. Finally, I say, 'What is it?' The creatures then clarify into angels holding a huge postcard in front of me. They announce that I must begin letting people know that angels often place messages in people's dreams. They explain that they borrow someone's dream for an instant and place their message within the plot and action so that it is encoded in the dream. They do this often, they say. They want me to be sure to tell people that their dreams often include these 'postcards from their angels.'"

While many dream accounts describe positive experiences, people wonder whether misleading "postcards" can be delivered by dream figures who falsely represent themselves as angels. A useful criterion is whether the figure takes on a judgmental or critical role toward the dreamer or anyone else, appears threatening or seems connected with dark energy. If so, you can be quite sure that the "messenger" was not sent from a higher spiritual source.

If you do receive the gift of a genuine angelic encounter in one of your dreams, I strongly encourage you to write it down in a journal so that you can return to it and contemplate its full significance. If you haven't previously kept a journal, let the meeting serve as your wake-up call, nudging you to begin to record the steps of the spiritual journey that you have been called to follow.

Robert L. Van de Castle, Ph.D. is a clinical psychologist and author of Our Dreaming Mind. *He has been studying dreams for more than thirty-five years.*

Frequently Asked Angel Questions

Dream Encounters

With Brad and Sherry Steiger

NIGHT SCHOOL

I had a dream recently with angels in it. Do you think the angels can actually enter our dream space?

We not only believe that angels can enter dream space, but we feel strongly that they can provide important and meaningful teachings while we are in the dream state.

There may be occasions when you awaken in the night and feel certain that you have been receiving teachings from your angel guide. But you might feel distressed when you're unable to retain the full meaning of the dream.

Don't become angry or frustrated with yourself for losing the message. Call out to your angel guide to help you recover whatever information the heavenly realm wishes you to know. Ask that, when you return to sleep, you'll receive the full knowledge of the dream-vision that has just been entrusted to you.

If you should not be able to recall the lesson or communication on that particular evening, get up the next morning with the resolve that you will reclaim it that evening. To prepare, quiet yourself for a moment or two from time to time throughout the day, and transmit love to the Supreme Being and to your angel guide.

Your motive for requesting an angelic dream teaching must always be the result of a balanced desire. Your goal should never be frivolous or based upon mere ego gratification.

When you retire that evening, take three comfortably deep breaths, holding each one for the count of three. Visualize a golden flame of love within your heart chakra, and in your mind see a ray of golden light travel from your heart to the Source of All That Is. Feel your spirit essence becoming closer to the Source. Begin to sense strongly a

All night, all day,
angels watchin' over me, my Lord.
All night, all day,
angels watchin' over me.

—African-American spiritual

unity with the love within the heavenly dimension. Feel your consciousness becoming one with the energy of love that emanates from the heavenly realm, then request an angelic dream teaching.

Just before falling asleep, call upon the loving energy of your angel guide to send its heightened awareness into your mind. Charge yourself with the task of bringing back the substance of the dream teaching. Ask your guide to stand watch over you so that only good

may enter along with the angelic dream teachings. You might use the following affirmation:

"Source of All That Is, Father-Mother-Creator Spirit, if it is thy will and if it is for my good and my gaining, allow my angelic guide to give unto me a dream teaching. Grant that the teaching will bring me higher awareness. Grant that my angel guide will protect me from all negative entities here on Earth and between dimen-

Angel Stories
DREAM ENCOUNTERS

Yesterday I had a dream wherein I was approaching a room that had about 10 people in it. The people were focused on the centre of the room where there were two very beautiful angels. They were twin angels—both a brilliant white with beautiful wings. They seemed to be working on something in front of them. I was in complete awe of their beauty. They didn't seem to be male or female. What a blessing it was to see them. When I woke up it gave me a sense of being blessed and a knowing that the angels are working with me.

sions while I lie asleep and in the dream state." When you awaken after receiving an angelic dream teaching, hold the images in your mind as long as you can.

Sometimes you may feel a compulsion to share the message of your angelic dream teachings with others. Your angel guide will advise you in this matter, and you will clearly know when a dream teaching is intended as your own message and when it may be shared with another. If you are

given to understand that your dream teaching may be shared, you are likely to discover that each time you share it with another, you will receive even more details of the communication.

Brad Steiger is the author of 140 books, both fiction and nonfiction, with more than 17 million copies in print. Sherry Hansen Steiger is the cocreator of the Celebrate Life program, the founder of the Butterfly Center of Holistic Education and a founding member of the Holistic Healing Board in Washington, D.C. She is the author or coauthor of more than 20 books, including Seasons of the Soul, The Power of Prayer to Heal and Transform Your Life *and* Angels around the World.

An Otherwise Gray Day

A woman is comforted by a mysterious yardman after her mother's death.

By Joan Wester Anderson

Mary Olson had had a mild heart attack over the weekend, so her grown children and her sisters all arrived within hours at the local hospital, except for her daughter Lisa. "Since Mum was expected to recover completely, I decided to wait until she was ready to leave, then drive down and help settle her at home," Lisa said. On Thursday afternoon, Lisa arrived at the hospital to find her mother sitting up in bed working a crossword puzzle, her usual perky self.

The two, with other relatives, spent the rest of the day together. "Mum seemed fine and was due to be released on Saturday," Lisa said. "When I left right after dinner, she was asleep, so I told the nurse to call me during the evening if she wanted company."

At 8:45 P.M., the nurse phoned Lisa and said that Mary was awake and wanted company. But by the time Lisa arrived at the hospital, some fifteen minutes later, her mother had died from a massive heart attack.

The family, of course, was devastated. But they made all the necessary arrangements that families do. A few days after the funeral, Lisa and one of her sisters finished closing up Mary's house and began loading the trunk of Lisa's car. The women were terribly sad and perhaps still in a state of shock as well. Their mother was gone! Was she with God? Was she happy?

"It was a grey day, both emotionally and weather-wise," Lisa recalled. "Suddenly, as we turned around, we saw a man standing behind us." He was about forty years old, slight in build, rather nondescript, without a coat on this raw day. It seemed strange. Although the driveway was gravel, neither of the women had heard approaching footsteps. "Who are you?" Lisa asked.

Speak ye who best can tell, ye sons of light angels, for ye behold him and with songs and choral symphonies, day without night circling his throne rejoicing.

—John Milton

"I'm your mother's yardman," the man explained. "I cut her grass and do small jobs for her. She sits at the picnic table and visits with me. Perhaps there's a job I can do?"

"Our mother has died," Lisa told him.

"Yes, I know," he said calmly.

The women looked at each other. They had never met their mother's yardman, but he seemed capable and pleasant, and the gutters did need cleaning. The yardman agreed, so the women went back into the house. As

Angel Stories
DREAM ENCOUNTERS

I was visited by an angel, and feel so blessed by this. I was very sick. I had been suffering from depression after losing my sister and I was becoming physically ill from it. I felt like I had the flu for months. Then one night I was so fed up with being sick and sad that I said to God that I was angry and I was not going to turn to him for help anymore.

I fell asleep that night in tears because I had leaned on the Lord throughout my life and I felt as though he let me down. That night I had this dream, but it was more than a dream. It seemed real.

In my dream I was walking down a street and suddenly a tornado picked me up. I thought I was going to die, but in the distance I saw a flickering light. The closer it got, the more it looked like an angel. She took me out of the tornado and placed me safely on the ground. She was in a beautiful blue dress and she was so beautiful it took my breath away. She told me that my troubles would ease up and I would start to feel better if I kept my faith in the Lord. I woke up and felt at peace.

When at night I go to sleep

Fourteen angels watch do keep

Two my head are guarding

Two my feet are guiding

Two are on my right hand

Two are on my left hand

Two who warmly cover

Two who o'er me hover

Two to guide my steps to Paradise.

—Engelbert Humperdinck,
from the opera *Hansel and Gretel*

they were sitting in the living room, they heard a sound, like someone singing. It was the yardman. "Listen!" Lisa said. "He's singing 'Sweet Hour of Prayer.'" The women looked at each other again. It had been their mother's favourite hymn.

"I think he also sang 'Amazing

Angel Stories
DREAM ENCOUNTERS

I had a dream about an angel that was so vivid, I actually believe it really happened.

In the middle of the night, I felt hands cupping my face—very gently and lovingly. In my dream state I was not startled or afraid, but sensed that it was an angel. I raised my hands up to put them over the hands on my face and awoke suddenly to the sensation of my own hands on my cheeks. I thought it was strange, but went back to sleep. The same thing happened again. In my sleep, I felt hands cupping my face; I put my own hands up to touch the hands and woke myself up with my own touch. Back to sleep. It happened a third time. This time, after I woke up, I saw in my "mind's eye" the Scripture verse Acts 12:8–9 written in red digital letters, like the numbers on my alarm clock.

I was so dazed, I simply thought, "Hmmmm—I'll have to remember to look that up in the morning," but then a statement cut through my thoughts—"No, you're asleep now and won't remember in the morning. Get up now." So I did. I padded downstairs, opened my Bible and found the verses. It is the point where an angel of the Lord visits Peter in prison: "He did not realize that what was happening with the angel's help was real; he thought he was seeing a vision." Reading on a few verses past that in verse 11 it says, "Peter came to himself and said, 'Now I am sure that the Lord has sent his angel . . .'"

So—that's my angel dream just as it happened. I believe that it was an angel touching my face and that God used that experience to confirm the existence of angels.

Angel Stories

DREAM ENCOUNTERS

One evening I was very stressed and upset about a friend. That night I dreamed that there were angels floating over me in bed. It was as if there was a skylight over my head that was lit up with a warm light and filled with beautiful angels floating around. I had such a feeling of being comforted and at peace. When I woke up, I was crying tears of joy. I truly believe these angels were there to make me feel good and to give me a beautiful experience to share.

Grace,' but I cannot be sure of that," Lisa said. "At some point I went to the mailbox at the front of the property. While walking back to the house, I looked at the roof and saw a light all around the yardman. It wasn't exactly a halo because it was around his entire body. The day was still dreary, but it could have been a small break in the clouds." Yet the light did not appear to be coming from the sun.

Listening to the stranger's joyful singing, Lisa and her sister felt strangely contented and peaceful, as if there were happiness in this situation as well as sorrow. How coincidental that the yardman would drop by on the very day they needed consolation.

When the yardman finished cleaning the gutters, Lisa paid him. The women were leaving and, concerned that he had no jacket, they offered him a ride into town. "No," he said. "I walk everywhere." And with that comment, he was gone. "I don't mean that he walked away," Lisa said. "I mean he was *gone*. He just disappeared. We looked up and down the road, and he was nowhere to be seen."

Another strange happening in this most unusual day. Or were they imagining the significance of these events? Lisa spotted the next-door neighbors on their porch, so she and her sister walked over to say goodbye. "Wasn't it fortunate that Mother's yardman came by just now and cleaned out the gutters?" Lisa asked.

The neighbors both had a strange look on their faces. "That was not your

mother's yardman," one said. "We have never seen him before today." Lisa's aunt, who had the same yardman as her mother, later agreed. "Our man has never walked anywhere in his life," she concurred. "Everyone knows it."

Then who was the mysterious man? For a while, Lisa ignored her own instincts. "I paid him," she pointed out, "and I've never heard of an angel taking money, so how could he be one?" That's a point. But as in the Bible, angels often come disguised and must take on all human attributes or needs in order to be believable. "Now I think he was an angel and not the regular yardman," Lisa says today. "I think he was there to comfort both my sister and me because we were so very sad about our mother's death." She has never seen the man again, but suspects that he—and her mother— watch over her always.

Joan Wester Anderson is the author of seven books on angels and miracles. Her first book, Where Angels Walk, *has sold more than two million copies and has been translated into fifteen languages. For more angel stories, visit her WhereAngelsWalk Web site at http://joanwanderson.com.*

Frequently Asked Angel Questions
Angels and Love

―――◦≈◦―――

With Brad and Sherry Steiger

CAN ANGELS ACT AS MATCHMAKERS?

I yearn for a loving relationship with someone who truly understands me. Is it possible for my guardian angel to connect me with my soul mate?

We have received a number of such queries after individuals have read our book, *Love Is a Miracle*, which explores how angels brought together men and women who were meant to be life partners, including us.

Years ago, Brad was sitting in a lecture audience when a woman sat down beside him, introduced herself and, after a few moments, told him that she had been asked to bring him greetings from a mutual friend, Sherry Hansen, with whom she was attending a class.

Brad had met Sherry some years before but didn't have any idea where she was living. The stranger informed him that Sherry lived in the same city. Because Brad was so pleased that Sherry would remember him, the whole illogic of the situation didn't occur to him: How could either Sherry or this woman know that he would be attending the lecture that night so that greetings could be extended to him?

Additionally, he had decided at the very last minute to attend the lecture; no one knew for certain that he would be there.

Later that night, Brad checked the telephone book and saw that the Reverend Sherry Hansen was listed. Many days later, he summoned the courage to call her, and a warm friendship grew into a working relationship that led to a very happy marriage between true soul mates.

As time passed, Brad learned that Sherry and the stranger did not know each other and certainly had never

Angel Stories
ANGELS AND LOVE

Our first date ended up being on Sept. 29—the feast of the archangels. We had tried for other days but something kept going wrong. There have been a lot of other little angel signs along the way and we both felt almost right away that this was the one we had been searching for all our lives. It is a very calm feeling, and it sustains itself. It's wonderful. They say when a feeling comes from a good source it's very calm, not urgent. All I can tell you is we are getting married next spring! It will be the first marriage for us both.

Goodnight, sweet prince
And flights of angels sing thee to thy rest.

—William Shakespeare, *Hamlet*

attended a class together. The woman, who has since become a dear friend, is a very spiritual individual, who apparently served as a conduit for angelic intelligence to bring two people together who may never have found each other without such intervention.

The concept of finding one's soul mate can easily become a kind of romantic conceit and lead the hasty heart down the path of self-deceit, disillusionment and a rationale for moving from one relationship to another in desperate search for the perfect mate.

A cautious approach that allows romance to grow to true friendship and progress to deep love seems more likely to receive angelic blessings than a transitory attraction to a likely soul mate. But while we issue cautions against the manner in which some people play the "searching for their soul mate" game, it does appear that when two people are supposed to

Angel Stories
ANGELS AND LOVE

One night I got fed up with dating all the Mr. Wrongs and prayed. I prayed for the type of man that I wanted, and I described everything. A few weeks later, a friend at a club told me that a certain man was looking for me. I was about to leave when he walked in. I told him I guess he didn't want to meet me because he was late, and he said he never told anyone that he wanted to meet me but now that he had he did want to see me again. And it took off from there. We were married 2 years after that date. He was exactly what I had prayed for, every detail that I had asked for.

come together to complete their earthly mission, the angels will intervene to see that the relationship does happen.

There are a number of such accounts in biblical and apocryphal literature of angels serving as matchmakers, such as the fascinating story of the angel Raphael posing as one of Tobit's kinsman in order to make certain that the marriage between his son Tobias and Sarah, the woman chosen to be his bride, was not interrupted by demonic interference.

It was Raphael's earthly assignment to see to it that these two children of "holy ancestors" should be brought together as one flesh to fulfill a heavenly decree beyond the understanding of mortals. As humans, we may not always understand the motives or the long-range goals of this higher intelligence, but once Raphael revealed his true identity, he urged them all to pray for guidance so that their union might continue to be blessed. If you believe such a destined love is to be yours, test your emotions with prayer for guidance and a sincere, meaningful contemplation of the sacred.

Is Cupid an Angel?

I've seen representations of Cupid, or Eros, with wings and arrows of love. Is he an angel?

In our opinion, Eros originates in a cosmology quite removed from the

Angel Stories
Angels and Love

I have always had this dream that came to me when I was younger, and as I got older it came with more frequency. I always thought it was my mother's way of telling me who I was to marry. She had died when I was 3 . . . I always knew I would find him because in my dream he was wearing a blue flannel shirt. I knew the minute this man showed up in that same shirt he was the one! The dreams have stopped, and we have been married 7 years now.

The imagery of dazzling, often blinding, light also symbolizes the spirituality of angels. Pure spirits, totally incorporeal beings, cannot be painted, nor can they be described in words that call images to mind. Only by using the symbolism of light, which makes the invisible visible, can painters and poets try to prevent an egregious misunderstanding of the imagery they are compelled to employ. The bodily forms and features that they depict angels as having must be recognized as pictorial metaphors, not as literal representations of what angels are like.

—Mortimer J. Adler, *The Angels and Us*

Vast chain of being! Which from God began,
Natures aethereal, human, angel, man,
Beast, bird, fish, insect, what no eye can see,
No glass can reach.

—Alexander Pope, *Essay on Man*

angelic realm. In the ancient world, he is first depicted as either the consort or the son of Aphrodite, Greek goddess of love. While he may have been considered a minor member of the Olympian pantheon of gods and goddesses, the Greeks never placed any great esteem on Eros, regarding him as the epitome of unbridled sexual passion and therefore a danger to manners and morals in the social order.

Later poets delighted in his trickery, passion and infidelity, portraying him as a handsome youth and a good lover, but irresponsible and superficial.

When the Romans transmuted Eros into Cupid, he still did not become the chubby, winged cherub with his arrows of love as he has been depicted in modern times. The Romans portrayed him as charming, but sadistic, gracious, but malicious, tormenting whomever he chose with his love darts, regardless of the pain or awkwardness that such random shooting might create. That doesn't sound like an angel to us.

Brad Steiger is the author of 140 books, both fiction and nonfiction, with more than 17 million copies in print. Sherry Hansen Steiger is the cocreator of the Celebrate Life program, the founder of the Butterfly Center of Holistic Education and a founding member of the Holistic Healing Board in Washington, D.C. She is the author or coauthor of more than 20 books, including Seasons of the Soul, The Power of Prayer to Heal and Transform Your Life *and* Angels around the World.

Heaven Sent

Who made the mysterious call that brought us together?

By Azriela Jaffe

In 1992, I advertised for a husband in the personals section of a local newspaper in Boston. After several months of trying to find "the one," I gave up and cancelled my ad. It turns out, the man of my dreams, Stephen, was married at the time my ad was running, and he was not a subscriber to the paper. When Stephen's marriage fell apart, he reluctantly reentered the singles scene. He visited an aunt in another town who gave him her

Angel Stories
ANGELS AND LOVE

At the University of Oslo, I arrived late and sat down in the last row with 3 guys. One of them wanted to know my name and where I was from. I wasn't in the mood to explain so I told them I was kind of homeless. One of them had the most beautiful blue eyes and blond curls. His name was Christian. Over the next six weeks, we became incredibly good friends. By the end, we were going our separate ways—I to New York and Christian to Russia and China. We were not sure that we would ever see each other again. But Christian and I felt spiritually linked. Later, I remembered he mentioned his return flight. I reserved a ticket and left a message for an announcement to be made when the flight would arrive. Within 4 hours, I was looking into those blue eyes. We will soon be celebrating our 10th wedding anniversary. I never have to worry about "losing" him—this planet is our home and there is no corner that will keep us apart.

Angels Among Us

current copy of a newspaper, suggesting that he check out the personals ads.

When Stephen glanced at the personals column, he noticed an ad that immediately grabbed his attention. He responded to the mystery ad that night. It was my ad. How was that possible? I had cancelled my ad months earlier. It should not have been running in the newspaper at all. Stephen knew on our first date that we were going to be married—he felt me to be his soul mate. I knew shortly afterward. I had to get over my cold feet about being a stepparent and marrying a man much more religiously observant than I was at that time. A few weeks after our meeting, I called the newspaper to inquire about why and how my cancelled ad had been rerun on Labor Day weekend.

Courtney answered the phone. She replied, "This is strange. I remember you calling me, Azriela. You asked that I specifically rerun your ad in the Labor Day weekend edition."

I hadn't called her. Who or what did? It was the *only* time my husband ever looked at the personals in that paper. We were engaged only a few weeks after meeting and married one year later. We've been together almost ten years and have three beautiful children together. It was our guardian angels who made it happen—we're sure of it!

Azriela Jaffe is author of Create Your Own Luck: 8 Principles of Attracting Good Fortune in Life, Love, and Work.

Frequently Asked Angel Questions

Angels of Darkness

—————

With Brad and Sherry Steiger

HOW DO YOU TELL THE GOOD ANGELS FROM THE BAD, OR FALLEN, ANGELS?

When an alleged heavenly being appears, how can you tell whether it is good or evil?

"Beloved, do not believe every spirit, but test the spirits to see whether they are of God" (1 John 4:1).

While this familiar New Testament passage is easily quoted, it's more difficult to put into practice when you have encountered what appears to be an angelic being of light. It would be so much easier to identify fallen angels if they appeared as grotesque monsters. But as we are warned in 2 Corinthians 11:14, "Even Satan disguises himself as an angel of light."

Scriptures of different spiritual paths advise that faith, purity, adherence to

Angel Stories
ANGELS OF DARKNESS

As a child I acted as a child, but now that I have begun my unfoldment, I put this one away right after I tried it. Playing with voodoo—my neighbor was from the Islands and showed me a thing or two—I put a little effigy in the bushes of a friend's adversary. I thought I'd help her out a bit. The next day the dog at the delivery site was found dead. Curiously, the word on the street was it died after it had been rummaging around in the very bushes! I stopped and turned my quest around completely.

The devil often transforms himself into an angel to tempt men, some for their instruction and some for their ruin.

—Saint Augustine

revealed truth and the performance of good deeds are the best way to ensure fellowship with spiritual beings of the highest levels. At the same time, we know that the greatest and most devout saints were not immune from contact with alleged heavenly beings who sought to lead them astray.

Our physical Earth plane world is closer to the realm of the lower, more chaotic, spiritual frequencies than it is to the dimension of the most harmonious—so efforts to communicate with heavenly or enlightened beings will always contain more of the lower vibratory realm than of the higher. Thus, we attract more astral masqueraders who seek to deceive us to achieve their own selfish goals.

A "test", that is, an evaluation, of alleged heavenly beings might contain these elements for serious consideration:

✧ Did the being tell you that it has appeared because you are a chosen person from a special group of evolved humans?

✧ Does the being encourage you to pray to it or to worship it?

✧ Does it promise to reward you with material wealth in exchange for your devotion?

✧ Does it perform apparent miracles for your benefit?

✧ Does it issue short-term prophecies that all come true?

✧ Does it issue revelations that upon closer scrutiny are filled with half-truths, lies and bigotry?

Various scriptures advise us that angels are not to be worshipped and that true heavenly beings will discourage humans who attempt to bow down to them.

The fallen angels delight in corrupting humans. They encourage us to express greed and the acquisition of material, rather than spiritual, treasures. A litany of alleged revelations are

Angel Stories

ANGELS OF DARKNESS

Of course I've been tempted by the dark side, and more often than I like to admit I've succumbed. But it doesn't require a dark angel to explain all the self-destructive acts that plague the species. We're quite capable of inflicting harm on ourselves without the assistance of infernal agencies.

designed to rival our genuine faith in God, and a belief in miracles for their own sake may also lead us astray.

As a general spiritual law, these negative entities cannot achieve power over humans unless they are invited into a person's private space—or unless they are attracted to a human aura by that person's negativity or vulnerability.

A general guideline is never to enter meditation or prayer with the thought of aggrandizing one's ego or acquiring material gain. Selfish motivation may put you at risk of becoming easily affected by those spirit beings who rebelled against the Light and became ensnared in their own selfish lust for power.

CAN ANGELS FALL?

According to tradition, at the beginning of the world angels who rebelled against God "fell" and became demons, or "fallen angels". Can angels today "fall" by going against the will of God?

Time and time again the scriptures of various faiths advise that the angels are not omnipresent, omnipotent or omniscient—and neither are they immune to falling into temptation or error. "Even in his servants he puts no trust, and his angels he charges with error" (Job 4:18).

Perhaps the greatest area of angelic weakness lies in their unique relationship to humans, earthly creations to whom the Creator gave free will. In the biblical and Qur'anic traditions, we find references to the jealousy that afflicts certain angels regarding the attention God displays toward his human creations.

Truth will I speak, repeat it to the living;
God's Angel took me up,
and he of hell Shouted:
"O thou from heaven, why dost thou
rob me?"

—Dante Alighieri, *The Purgatorio*, Canto V

In the Qur'an (17:61–64), Iblis (Satan), the leader of the rebellious angels, refuses to bow to a creature that God has created of clay, and he threatens to make existence miserable for human beings.

Because of the fallen angels' animosity toward those heavenly beings faithful to the Creator, and toward those who seek higher truth, we should not only engage in spiritual warfare with those of flesh and blood who serve the dark side but also "against the spiritual hosts of wicked-ness in the heavenly places" (Ephesians 6:12).

DISCERNING THE DARK SIDE

How do you tell the good angels from the bad or fallen angels?

Through discernment. But sometimes that's easier said than done, especially because some of those dark side beings can make themselves so darned attractive.

Native American medicine men and women instruct their people that

Angel Stories
ANGELS OF DARKNESS

We are all tempted by the dark side. Take comfort in the words that Jesus said in John 10:27–28: "My sheep listen to my voice; I know them, and they follow me. I give them eternal life, and they shall never perish; no one can snatch them out of my hand."

a spirit who is called or summoned and asked to do the bidding of supplicant will always want something in return. All too often that seemingly innocent process of barter will turn out to be something far from benign.

Spirit guides and angels have, as a considerable portion of their earthly mission, the task of guiding us toward ever- expanding spiritual awareness. In addition to their having been assigned to be there on certain occasions to give us a helping hand, we believe that it is also an integral part of their task to lead us to a clearer understanding of our true role in the cosmic scheme of things. Judging from our own interaction with these beings, they seem to cast themselves in the role of tutor, far preferring to teach us by example and inspiration rather than by intervening in our learning process. It is in this very crucial area of noninterference that the benevolent angels and guides differ markedly from the negative beings, the spiritual parasites, that emanate from the dark side. The shadowy entities that masquerade as benign angels have no compunction about interfering with humankind's spiritual evolution. Quite the contrary, they appear to delight in manipulating our spiritual destiny, exploiting our physical bodies and enslaving our souls.

A number of religious traditions maintain that individuals have a good and a bad angel that remain with them throughout their lives. While it may be one's professed belief that "all things work together for good for those who love God", we have also been given free will. Because of our God-given gift to

Angel Stories
ANGELS OF DARKNESS

The Earth is a school and we are here to learn lessons from its curriculum (called experiences). Once lessons are learned, we garner an understanding about whom we are, why we are and where we are going—our spiritual nature. Yes, I am presently experiencing the ignorance (dark side). But once I have mastered the challenges of the darkness, I will be on my way to my spiritual heritage.

Angel Stories
ANGELS OF DARKNESS

Many, many times I have felt the presence of angels and demons. I have not always recognized the evidence of their presence, but I have felt them. There is a constant spiritual war being fought between these beings of light and darkness. At the same time, they are involved in the lives of mankind. We must remember that we do not share the same timetable in which God or these beings operate. We cannot understand how angels can do more than one thing at a time. We are limited to time and space, but they are not. How do we know if it is an angel or a demon? My Mother explained it like this: You have a little voice inside you that tells you about things. Listen to that voice; it's there to guide you. The feeling in the pit of your stomach will give you the insight of what entity is about you. There is not an in-between; it is good or it is evil.

be able to make choices, we must work extra hard on developing discernment, the ability to judge truly the difference between the good and the bad in all things. For a very good reason, the Bible reminds us to "test and try" the spirits. The holy books of many spiritual traditions teach that there are millions of angels with different assignments, capacities and missions.

There are also many levels of angels, from those that are just a little higher than us to those majestic beings that surround the throne of God. If we truly are just "a little lower than the angels", then it stands to reason that there may be countless members among the "powers and principalities" that don't know a great deal more than we finite creatures on Earth. When an alleged heavenly being appears, test it and practice discernment.

Am I utterly cursed? An angel of light was sent to me twenty-one years ago and forbade me to deal with the element with which I was becoming involved. I never forgot the message, but I didn't believe it. Later, I had an encounter with an

Everything that seems empty is full of the angels of God.

—Saint Hilary

angel from the dark side, and today I am in financial ruin and in emotional purgatory. Can anything be done to thwart the ill effects of encounters with dark angels? Will God ever forgive me?

If it weren't for the scriptural promise that God loves a contrite heart, who among us could hope for release from the entanglements in which we have become ensnared while travelling our earthly path? Many of us have at one

Angel Stories
ANGELS OF DARKNESS

We are told in the Qur'an that angels are not given a free will. They do as they are commanded and glorify God without being able to disobey him. However, the nation of the Jinn, to which Lucifer belongs, was created with a free will like mankind. We know that the angels and jinn existed before man and that Satan is man's extreme enemy. But God told us that Satan was not from among the angels; he existed before man at the time when the angels also existed.

We also know that he was ardent in his glorification of God until he became prideful, disobeyed God and was condemned to hell. We are told that Gabriel (Jibra'il) is the angel with the highest rank and he is in charge of revelation. Michael (Mika'il) has been entrusted with the bringing forth the rain from the skies. He and his helpers make the wind and the clouds move by the commands of God. Israfil will blow the trumpet with three blasts signaling the beginning of the Day of Judgment. Angels are the custodians of the Garden of Paradise and their overseer is Ridwan. Malik is the overseer of the guardians of Hellfire. Belief in the angels is an essential part of faith in Islam. Not many people know the nature and essence of belief for a Muslim.

Angels Among Us

O passing Angel, speed me with a song,
A melody of heaven to reach my heart
And rouse me to the race and make me strong.

—Christina Rossetti

time or another believed we could boldly walk where angels feared to tread and have come to pay dearly for our ignoring the warnings issued by our own guiding angels of light. We can say with great confidence that forgiveness is found by approaching God on bended knee with penitent heart. No curse of the dark side can withstand the full force of God's love and light.

Here is a prayer of protection that you may use whenever you sense the presence of that dark angel who has caused you so much anguish:

O beloved [say here the name of your angelic guardian or a revered holy figure], send your protective energies of light and love around me at once.

Erect a mighty shield of love and light around me that is invincible, all powerful and unable to be penetrated by an evil force.

Keep me protected from all things that are not of the Light or of God.

Keep me immune from all negative and hostile beings, from all seductive and deceitful entities. Banish at once the dark spirit that I see [feel] near me.

Amen.

Angel Stories
ANGELS OF DARKNESS

God loves you and is not looking for a way to trip you up. Fall and he will lift you back up. The despair, doubt, worry all come from Satan's last trick to keep you from getting back to God.

Hold your child in your arms, console a friend, help someone get a job, remember your parents when they get old and lonely, and you will get an idea about true life. The reward starts in the living of it.

Angels are bright still, though the brightest fell.

—William Shakespeare, *Macbeth*

You've written about good angels and bad or fallen angels. Are there any angels somewhere in between?

As we heard someone say recently, there are only three kinds of angels: the good, the bad and the evil deceivers pretending to be good.

It is our understanding that there can be no undecided angels. An angel is either a messenger of God or a disciple of Lucifer. They are either on the side of good or of evil.

As a point of interest, certain medieval Christian theologians suggested that fairies were entities between humans and angels—in essence, demoted angels, working their way back to full heavenly status, although many take great delight in performing mischievous deeds against humans.

In the teachings of Islam, there are three distinct species of intelligent beings in the universe: the *malak*, a high order of light beings; the *jinn*, ethereal, perhaps multidimensional, beings; and humans, fashioned of the stuff of Earth and born into physical bodies. The Qur'an tells us that while a certain number of the jinn act benevolently toward humans and may even serve as guardians and guides, the great majority of these "in-between" entities are dedicated to performing devilish acts against humankind.

Brad Steiger is the author of 140 books, both fiction and nonfiction, with more than 17 million copies in print. Sherry Hansen Steiger is the cocreator of the Celebrate Life program, the founder of the Butterfly Center of Holistic Education and a founding member of the Holistic Healing Board in Washington, D.C. She is the author or coauthor of more than 20 books, including Seasons of the Soul, The Power of Prayer to Heal and Transform Your Life *and* Angels around the World.

Four Angels Dressed in Black

A timely message of healing arrives from an unexpected source.

By Marilynn Carlson Webber

Four angels came to me in a dream, but they were not the glorious, shining angels I had always pictured in my mind's eye. I was startled to see that they were dressed in black. Their body language spoke volumes. They were in mourning. Summoning up my courage, I asked, "Why are you in mourning?"

One angel replied, "Because you are dying. If something is not done soon, you will die."

Angel Stories
ANGELS THAT HEAL

My youngest son had trouble breathing from birth and needed to be awoken many times during the night. They call it sleep apnea. At age 1½ he was particularly sick one night. I was sick also and after a couple of sleepless nights shaking him whenever he would stop breathing, I was too weak to stay awake. I prayed, "God, I can't do this anymore. Please give me the strength to stay awake and take care of him."

At that instant, the room felt calm. I looked up with tears flowing down my face and saw a young woman and an elderly bald man sitting on the bed with us. I don't remember anything else except saying, "Thank you, God; he is safe." I fell asleep on my knees and woke the next morning (from the best night's sleep in years) to see the angels still sitting there brushing the hair off his face and smiling. As I stood up I could no longer see them, but I knew everything would be fine.

Songs of praise the angels sang,
Heaven with hallelujahs rang,
When creation was begun,
When God spake, and it was done.

—James Montgomery

Suddenly I was wide awake. I was frightened by the vividness of my dream. I was trembling because of the encounter. For the first time, I also felt pain—severe pain. I woke my husband. "I need to tell you my dream," I insisted to my sleepy spouse. "It's so real. I know that God sent his angels with a message."

I described the black-robed angels in mourning and their message that I was dying unless something was done . . . soon.

"First thing in the morning," Bill told me, "we will find a doctor."

I had not seen a doctor for a few years. I had my excuses. My internist had retired. I had gone to two other doctors, but although they were comparatively young, both had stopped practising medicine. The last physician warned me that I needed to be monitored for cancer and had recommended a specialist, but when I called for an appointment I was told that he was taking no new patients. I had meant to find another doctor but for two years had put it off.

The morning after my dream, my husband urgently called the doctor that had been recommended. The receptionist told him the doctor was still taking no new patients. Bill asked to talk to the doctor himself but was transferred to his nurse. He told the nurse that his wife needed to see the doctor immediately. When she asked why it was so urgent, he told her of the dream.

"It's impossible for you to see Dr. King," the nurse replied, "but let me see if I can work you in to see one of his colleagues."

In a minute she came back on the line. "I have an appointment for your wife with Dr. Keeney," she said. "He is one of the best oncologists in the area."

With fear and trembling I kept my appointment with Dr. Keeney. As he took my medical history, he asked what had brought me to see him. I poured out my dream about four angels dressed in black and watched as he wrote it in my file.

A biopsy was taken, then almost every known medical test—or at least it seemed to be that way to me. They found cancer and a tumor that needed to be removed. Dr. Keeney explained that pain was not a symptom of this type of cancer.

Angel Stories
ANGELS THAT HEAL

In June of 1979, I had a son who died at birth. As the years passed, I somehow knew when he is with me. In 1994, I went to my doctor for a check up, and they found a lump in my breast. As time got close for me to go to the hospital, I just kept busy, not talking to my husband, daughter, sister or mother about it.

One Saturday, I walked up to my husband in the yard and was talking of something else when he turned and looked at me and asked if I was afraid. I just smiled and said, "No." Then he looked at me, with tears in his eyes, and said, "I am," and that really hit me hard.

The next day, I got more upset knowing that come Monday morning I would be going to the hospital. I just kept working around the house and telling everyone that it was going to be all right, but the whole time I was so scared of having cancer. That Sunday night as I lay in bed, I couldn't sleep worrying about the morning, then all of a sudden, there was a warm breeze on my face—there were no windows open. I opened my eyes to see a round white glowing light coming to our bedroom. It came in the room and there was a calm that came over me. A small whisper said, "It's going to be all right." And it was. I know that it was my son and he has watched over me many times and spared my life.

Why, then, had I felt pain on the night of my dream? I believe that God knew that I was a reluctant patient and to get my attention, he needed not only to send his angels in a dream but also to underscore their message with pain.

As a part of the routine preoperative procedure, I was seen by a resident. He began taking a complete medical history. I asked why it was necessary, inasmuch as I had answered the same questions for Dr. Keeney. He replied that Dr. Keeney was the best in his field, he could remember everything about all his patients, but that no one could read his handwriting. "All I can make out in your medical history is that four angels in mourning came to you in a dream and told you that you were dying if nothing was done."

Surgery was set for September 2 at the Loma Linda University Medical

Angel Stories

ANGELS THAT HEAL

I was 13 years old. I was going to make dinner for my sister before my father got home from work. But when I tried to start our gas stove, the flame burst out at me and my clothes caught fire. I ran into the bathroom screaming and my sister (then 11 years old) and I put the fire out in the bathtub. She called 911. It wasn't until weeks later after three surgeries, being unconscious and unable to breathe on my own for about a week, that I felt anything. I was an open wound.

My body would stick to the sheets and the orderlies would have to peel them off my raw body and change them. One time, I couldn't bear it and I cried out to Jesus. I never believed in God until that day. Outside I heard the sound of rain and I also heard soft music playing, and there was no pain. I asked the orderly who was holding me to turn up the radio and open the window so I could see the rain. But the sun was shining and there was no radio. Still, I could hear it.

I was protected from death by these angels that worked around me daily. They brought me comfort and eased my pain. The rain never ended nor did the music end until I was recovered enough to walk on my own. I believe they were angels sent by God to give me hope. Others believe that I was delusional. But I think that in the condition I was in, I was more open. I did not rationalize it. I did not try to dissect it. And now, as a believer, I do not doubt it.

Center. The doctor told me I was considered to be a high-risk patient. I believe in prayer and began to ask my friends to pray for me. I asked to be put on every prayer chain I knew.

The day of surgery came. The doctor told my husband that he could expect me to be in intensive care for two days. Surgery took four hours, but after a few hours' stay in the recovery room, I was placed in a regular hospital room. Five days later I returned home. Prayers are answered!

When they count my sins in heaven,
then I'll get to know my luck.
Is it furnace number seven
or a harp for me to pluck?

—Bertolt Brecht, "Happy End"

The doctor explained they had caught the cancer in time and were able to remove it completely. I did not need chemotherapy or any follow-up treatments, but if the cancer had not been discovered, it would have spread and been life threatening.

I knew I would have put it off, as I

Angel Stories
ANGELS THAT HEAL

I think there are people on Earth that are angels. For years I battled with clinical depression. I lost everything I had in life—my career, my family, my friends—everything. There was one psychiatrist and one therapist who would not give up on me. Even when I had no insurance and should have/could have been sent to overcrowded, understaffed state-run facilities, they kept me on as their patient. They both had separate practices and bore the expense of my treatment themselves. Once they took a $10,000 hospital bill out of my hand and I never saw it again.

Had it not been for these "angels", I don't think it would have been possible for me to survive all that I have been through. Now, I am stable, healthy, happy and peaceful. They had hope when I had none. They carried me when I could not go on, and now I have come through the fire and into the Light. I truly believe that God put these people in my life, as my guardian angels, to help see me through.

Angel Stories
ANGELS THAT HEAL

When I gave birth to my second son, I had a C-section. I was very afraid to have the surgery so I closed my eyes and asked Jesus to be with me. I know he was there with me because when I woke up all I kept saying was, "Don't go; don't leave me." But he left me with the warmest feeling of unconditional love. I will never forget it. Ever since then I see these little twinkles of light out of the corner of my eyes. Sometimes it happens right before my eyes and disappears in less than a second. It's really weird but I know it's angels that I see. It comforts me to know that these spirits follow me around.

had done for years, but God, in his mercy, sent four angels in mourning, dressed in black, to impress me with the urgency of seeing the doctor. I continue to praise God for his goodness and my health!

Marilynn Carlson Webber, with her husband, the Reverend Dr. William D. Webber, is the author of A Rustle of Angels: Stories about Angels in Real Life and Scripture *and* Tea with the Angel Lady. *The Webbers have been frequent guests on radio and television programs about angels.*

The Doctor Was an Angel

After a difficult surgery, a woman is comforted by a heavenly physician.

By Joan Wester Anderson

It was May 1995, and forty-four-year-old Denise lay in the recovery room at Yale University Hospital in New Haven, Connecticut. She had been very ill with throat cancer for over a year. Radiation hadn't worked and surgery had been her only option. Now her voice box and lymph nodes had been removed to halt the disease's progress. But her chance for life seemed even less than the doctor had anticipated.

Now, as Denise slowly awakened, many people in white coats surrounded her. They seemed grim, and Denise was seized with a sudden terror. What was wrong? She looked up and noticed one very young doctor. He was looking down at her, his expression kind, and he seemed to glow. She must be dreaming, she thought.

When Denise got back to her room, her worried brother, Ron, was waiting. Although she could no longer speak, she gestured to Ron. "I wanted to see what they had cut and what they had done to me. Ron hesitated but handed me my compact." Denise gasped. Her head looked at least three times its normal size. Her throat had been cut past both ears, and she couldn't raise her head. She began to sob. Ron ran for a doctor.

Instead, the young man Denise had seen in the recovery room came in. "It's all right," he told her soothingly. "Your head won't stay like this. The scar is bad, yes, but you're alive and you're going to get better." He picked up her hand and held it. Peace seemed to flow through Denise. She fell asleep.

The next time Denise awakened, it was 4:00 A.M. When she rang for a nurse, the same doctor came in. He was smiling, and he spoke so softly she could barely hear him. "You're going to be all right. I want you to know that. I'm here. I'll never leave you," he said, leaning over her. This time Denise was awake enough to study him. His features seemed flawless. His hair was short and blond, cut in an old-fashioned way with longish bangs and parted on the left. He had bright blue-green eyes. His hand was warm, soft and strong. Again, Denise fell asleep with him telling her she would be fine. From that point on, every day at 4:00 A.M. she would wake up and he would be there, holding her hand and talking softly.

"The next time Ron came in to see me, I wrote to him on my tablet about this doctor," Denise says. "I wanted

Angel Stories
ANGELS THAT HEAL

I had what I felt to be an angelic encounter when I was 32 years old. I was shopping with my mother-in-law, my sister-in-law, niece and two-year-old son. It was Saturday afternoon and we went into an extremely crowded and loud McDonald's for lunch. When we were starting to eat, I heard a loud voice above the din say, "Touch your breast."

I just did as I was told and put my hand into my t-shirt and felt a lump the size of a cherry tomato. As soon as I felt this lump, I also felt as if a veil was thrown over me and my son, who was sitting next to me. This veil was like a sparkling mist and the noise of the place sounded as if it were very far away. I felt incredible peace and love and when my boy and I looked at each other, he leaned over and gave me a kiss. I felt as if he and I were in a special bubble by ourselves and that the people around us could not see it.

When the mist lifted I told my mother-in-law that I had felt a lump and she said that it was probably nothing, but to go see a doctor. I did and it turned out to be an extremely aggressive form of breast cancer. I had to have my breast removed and to undergo nine months of chemo, but I have recovered and am now fine. I believe an angel came to tell me so that I would go to the doctor right away.

Ron to find out his name. I wanted to thank him for being so kind to stay with me when I was too afraid to be alone. I suggested Ron check the interns because I thought he must be an intern. What doctor would have this much time to spend with just one patient?"

Ron went out to talk to the nurses, but when he returned, he looked at her strangely. "You must have been dreaming," he said.

"NO!" Denise scribbled on the pad.

"He doesn't exist, Dee. I asked all the nurses. And they checked. No one has seen anyone like him. No one knows him, either."

Denise knew better than to argue with Ron. It was only later, when she

I believe in one God, Father Almighty,
Maker of heaven and earth,
And of all things visible and invisible.

—Nicene Creed

got home, that she learned her brother had continued to look for the unknown doctor. Ron had stopped only when several nurses assured him that it wasn't at all unusual for a hospital patient to see her guardian angel.

Denise recovered from cancer, and she knows she suffered less because God allowed her angel to be very visible to her. "Maybe someday," she says, "I can tell him face to face once again, 'Thank you so much.'"

Joan Wester Anderson is the author of seven books on angels and miracles. Her first book, Where Angels Walk, *has sold more than two million copies and has been translated into fifteen languages. For more angel stories, visit her* WhereAngelsWalk *Web site at* http://joanwanderson.com.

We Are Not Alone

The harvest truly is great—and all we have to do is ask.

———◆———

By Joan Wester Anderson

It was the end of harvest. Twenty-three-year-old Joanie had just come home from a job interview in town when her sister met her. "Dad needs you out in the field to help bale the rest of the hay," Joanie's sister told her. So Joanie hurried into the house to exchange her business clothes for jeans.

When she met her dad, he had almost finished, but the wagon was full—225 bales. "We decided to take the wagon back to the barn to unload," Joanie said. "But as I drove the tractor, the baler and the full wagon of hay toward the barn, I started to get nervous. It was a huge load and I didn't want to damage anything. I asked my father to take over."

Joanie and her father exchanged places, and she went around the front of the tractor to say "hello" to her father's girlfriend, Ann, who was standing near the fence. "I started to trip and Ann tried to grasp me, but she lost her grip," Joanie said. "I grabbed the corner of the wagon and the next thing I knew, I was under it!"

Ann screamed, but Joanie's father couldn't stop in time. Before anyone could react, the wagon—all one-and-a-half tons—rolled over Joanie.

Joanie lay on the hard ground as her father bent down to touch and reassure her. "Keep calm, honey. Ann went to call the doctor." He sounded like he was crying.

She was bleeding from the mouth and could hardly breathe. What parts of her had the wheels crushed? "God," she whispered, "please don't let me be disabled." Weakly, she turned her head to the side and saw her sister running across the fields toward her, in bare feet. Right behind was the doctor. He must have gotten here very fast. Or

I gazed intently down, my master said,
"Within the flames are spirits; each one here
Enfolds himself in what burns him."

—Dante Alighieri, *The Inferno*, Canto XXVI

perhaps she had been lying here for a long time. Ann was running too. And suddenly there was another woman, standing right next to Joanie. Joanie looked up. She must be hallucinating, probably dying—for the woman was her mother, who had died almost twenty years ago, when Joanie was just a small girl.

"Everything is going to be fine, Joanie," her mother said quietly. "You will not be hurt."

Oh, Mama, I do hurt. Please don't go away. But now the doctor was here and people were beginning to reach toward her, to move her out from under the wagon. The vision of her mother was gone.

Despite the exhausting day,

Joanie's father went to church that evening and lit a candle in thanksgiving. For although the massive wagon had rolled over her chest, his daughter had no broken bones, no damaged organs, no injuries at all. The doctor could not believe it. But to this day, Joanie knows that she was given a gift from heaven.

"We are not alone in this world," she said. "Angels and saints are out there to help us, and all we have to do is ask."

Joan Wester Anderson is the author of seven books on angels and miracles. Her first book, Where Angels Walk, *has sold more than two million copies and has been translated into fifteen languages. For more angel stories, visit her WhereAngelsWalk Web site at http://joanwanderson.com.*

Frequently Asked Angel Questions

Lending Comfort in Death

————

With Brad and Sherry Steiger

WHY DON'T THE ANGELS ALWAYS SAVE US?

If angels are meant to protect us, then why do people die in airplane crashes and car crashes?

Perhaps the concept of a "guardian angel" is understood by far too many people as a kind of comic book superhero that will appear like magic whenever they are in danger, saving them from injury or death, just the way Superman always rescued Lois Lane or Jimmy Olson. Those who refer to their angels as teachers or guides may be closer to defining the actual role that these heavenly benefactors fulfill.

People die in airplane and car crashes because humans are not immortal. Each one of us is fashioned of mortal clay and will be called home to the spirit realm when it is our appointed time. At that time, we may expect a loving angel at our side to guide us homeward. But we must all face the reality that even if we were previously blessed by being saved from an accident or tragedy, our years on this planet are numbered. One of these times, our encounter will be with the Angel of Death.

It becomes confusing to many when, for example, a few people survive a major airline tragedy and most of the other passengers perish. None of us mortals have access to the cosmic timetable that decrees who does or doesn't walk way from a burning building or a twisted mass of metal wreckage. When survivors testify that angels guided them to safety, many who hear such testimony wonder why the heavenly beings chose this or that person and none of the others.

Angels are primarily messengers, mentors and examples of God's glorious powers of creation. They are not

Angel Stories
LENDING COMFORT IN DEATH

A year ago my mother was going into the hospital for heart surgery. She was 84, but in good condition and the doctor said there should be no problem. The night before surgery, she and I had a long talk. One of the subjects was angels.

I told her that since I couldn't be in intensive care all the time, an angel would be there in my place. All she had to do was look to him (I knew it was a "him" because I saw him at her left shoulder) for peace and comfort until I could come to her. I started to tell her that he was at her left side when she jumped and said, "Something just touched my left shoulder." He had made his presence known. He was small and had an iridescent green colour. I told her that this was a comforting/healing angel and not the one who could take her home to God. I said that if that type angel was what she needed, she would have to make that decision between herself, God and another angel.

Two days later at 3 A.M., I got a call from the hospital to come quickly. I got there before the rest of the family, and saw my mother lying on the bed with the most beautiful, large, reddish-orange-hued angel hovering about 3 feet above her. I took my mother's hand and said, "I see you, God, and this angel must have decided it's time for you to go home. I don't want you to go, but if you are too wounded to get well, and if God agreed to send the angel, then I understand." I kissed her and said goodbye, said I love you, and immediately the angel opened her wings and lowered herself over my mother. She wrapped her wings around her in the most gentle, loving manner I had ever seen and started to rise. As she rose and began to fade away, the monitor on my mother's EKG machine went off and my mother was pronounced dead. I don't know why I have been given this gift of seeing. I only know my prayer was answered, and I am surrounded by true peace and love always.

If a man is called to be a street-sweeper,

he should sweep streets even as Michelangelo painted,

or Beethoven played music,

or Shakespeare wrote poetry. He should sweep

streets so well that all the hosts of heaven

and earth will pause to say, here lived

a great street-sweeper who did his job well.

—Martin Luther King Jr.

privileged to serve on any panels that decide who does or doesn't survive accidents, hurricanes, volcanic eruptions or earthquakes. It is not their role to determine when they intercede in the flow of natural events or when they deliver an individual human from harm's way and truly become a "guardian" angel.

Rather than relying on our guardian angel to save us from a burning building or a crashing automobile, it behooves us to strive to live each day in a manner pleasing to God so that when we are called home, we take our guiding angel's hand with an attitude of loving acceptance, rather than regret.

Why do angels rescue or deliver some people from harm and seemingly allow others to suffer or even perish?

When we asked this question as children in Sunday school class, we were silenced with the response: "It's God's will". In other words—or so it seemed to our youthful minds—God apparently had it in for some people, so it was best to stay in His good graces. The more positive Sunday school teachers would emphasize "God calling His beloved home" when "it was their time". Then we would be advised not to question such matters, but to trust in God's overall plan.

A good many of those Sunday school puzzlers became easier to answer as we matured: how Eve, the mother of us all, came out of a man; where Cain got his wife; how Noah managed to collect all those animals in one boat. All of these biblical mysteries more or less answered themselves as we

Angel Stories
LENDING COMFORT IN DEATH

Before my nine-year-old niece Karen died, she told her mother that an angel was sitting in a tree outside her room and visited her frequently. She told her mother that she was going to die, that the angel had told her so. The angel told her to say goodbye and she did. She died in a tragic car accident the next day.

progressed through school and as we explored the universe through prayers and visionary experiences.

However, the question of why the angels—or God—rescued some people from harm and seemingly allowed others to suffer never became easier to answer. Why does God allow bad things to happen to good people?

While some conservative Christians are uncomfortable when we bring up karma, Jesus' admonition that what one sows, one will someday reap expresses essentially the same concept. Karma is not synonymous with punishment but is the result of previous actions, a balancing of the energies—positive or negative—that we expend. What appears to be the negligence or indifference of angelic beings may simply be the spiritual laws of compensation. Indeed, the person suffering harm may actually require the unpleasant experience for the good and the education of his or her soul.

We believe that all of us live in "Schoolhouse Earth" and that sometimes the greatest lessons are learned through our struggles, pain and suffering. While our guardian angels may shed a tear or two as they witness our angst and agony, they know that they must not interfere when we are taking our bumps and bruises. We seem to acquire wisdom best when we have endured the skinned knees, black eyes and bloody noses suffered while walking our own outrageous and individual life paths.

Angel Stories
LENDING COMFORT IN DEATH

When I was 16, I wanted to commit suicide. I began taking pills when I heard an angel's voice in my ear. He told me that I had to go through the pain because I was learning something and had things to do later in life. He told me that if I killed myself, I would only have to go through everything I'd gone through all over again. It kept me alive to hear that.

They are celestial visitants, flying on spiritual, not material, pinions. Angels are pure thoughts of God, winged with Truth and Love, no matter what their individualism may be.

—Mary Baker Eddy

It's also true that we are limited from appreciating or understanding the implications of our actions—good and bad, painful or joyful—because we are trapped in linear time. Haven't we all experienced a terrible ordeal that later proved to have been a blessing in disguise?

We look back with shame at the times when we thought our angels had deserted us. With hindsight, we see that we were not being shunned, but saved and blessed for a much more productive future.

Yet as much as we trust "all things to work for good for those who love God", it is inevitable that one day, the bell will toll for us. When it does, we hope that benevolent heavenly beings will escort us to our true home beyond the stars.

Prior to my cousin's death, she told me that she had seen her angel. Might angels foretell our impending death?

Angel Stories
LENDING COMFORT IN DEATH

When my mother passed away after being in the hospital for 30 days, my daughter was in her hospital room holding her hand. As I walked in, it was as though I walked into the Light that is always talked about. It was like a glowing halo. The brightness was so intense that you could see nothing but a bright glow. At that very moment, I knew that the angels were in this room taking my mother to heaven. This is one of many reasons why I know angels are real.

Angel Stories

LENDING COMFORT IN DEATH

In November 1995, my mother was diagnosed with stage 5 cancer. On December 22, 1996, she passed away. About a week before, my two sisters and I felt that this was going to be "the night" so we stayed up talking while my mother slept, then one by one, we went into her room and fell asleep with her—one sister in the bed next to her and the other one and myself on the floor. I could not fall asleep. It was about 6:00 A.M. when all of a sudden I felt this warm presence or someone right next to the right side of my cheek. When I turned to look I saw this cherub-like figure with red curly hair staring right at me. As soon as I saw it, it disappeared in a flash and I fell asleep. I was scared, but in a way relieved because I felt that this was my mother's angel watching us watch over her.

We have received many reports of those who have seen angels days or weeks before their deaths, and the literature in the field contains hundreds of such accounts. According to the testimony of vast numbers of men and women, many individuals have also witnessed the appearance of angels at the bedside of a dying friend or relative.

We ourselves recently had that experience. Brad's brother-in-law was told by his doctors that he had several months to live, but it seems as if he received angelic messages preparing him for his death. Only days before an unexpected relapse, he said that he was having vivid dreams of angels and was aware of angelic presences around him.

While the desire to hold on to life may have made him interpret these encounters as an uplifting sign, inspire him to plan specific exercises to strengthen his muscles and acquire an electric wheelchair that would permit him greater mobility, he suddenly took a turn for the worse.

Family members were called and, throughout the day, they arrived from all parts of the country. Then the doctors informed the tearful circle in the hospital room that there was no hope of keeping him alive. Sherry sensed the moment, and the family gathered around his bedside to pray for God to send His angels to surround us all in spiritual comfort and strength and to take the spirit of our beloved brother, father, husband "home".

All of us who so loved this man felt that we had participated in the most holy of moments: As he took his last breath, we palpably sensed his soul soaring to heaven on the wings of angels.

Brad Steiger is the author of 140 books, both fiction and nonfiction, with more than 17 million copies in print. Sherry Hansen Steiger is the cocreator of the Celebrate Life program, the founder of the Butterfly Center of Holistic Education and a founding member of the Holistic Healing Board in Washington, D.C. She is the author or coauthor of more than 20 books, including Seasons of the Soul, The Power of Prayer to Heal and Transform Your Life *and* Angels around the World.

Caught by an Angel

A young boy somehow avoids disabling injury in a dangerous fall.

By Joan Wester Anderson

Krisellen Lang had lost her first three babies at early stages in her pregnancies. So when she found herself expecting yet again, it was hard to work up any enthusiasm. Why should she begin to love this child when it might never live long enough to be born?

But Krisellen's pregnancy was a result of in vitro fertilization, with four embryos transferred—and the hope that one would implant. When she went to her obstetrician for her first checkup and ultrasound, she discovered that all four embryos had implanted! "It was as if God was giving me all my lost children back," she said. The pregnancy proceeded normally, and her quadruplets, two boys and two girls, were born robust and healthy.

Once, as we dashed onward like a hurricane, there was a flutter of wings and the bright appearance of an angel in the air, speeding forth on some heavenly mission.

—Nathaniel Hawthorne, *The Celestial Railroad*

It was a hectic time, and eventually Krisellen's marriage faltered. "Our divorce was mutual and amicable, and David is, and always has been, a wonderful father," Krisellen said. But she was understandably fearful. How would she raise four children alone? Krisellen prayed as she never had before. God had heard her once, she knew, and brought her joy after suffering. Could He, would He, do so again?

She found a part-time job at a construction company, and her family pitched in to help care for the quads. It seemed as if she might just make it— until one morning when she stopped at a job site to measure the rooms in a house. Her four three-year-olds were with her, so she brought them into the house to "help".

One of the rooms had a hole in the centre of the floor, so Krisellen directed the children to stand at the edge of the room, all except for Addi-

son, who was holding one end of the tape measure. Krisellen took the other end and started for the far corner. When she looked back, Addison was dancing on her tippy toes, a recently acquired skill. "Addison, stop, you're going to trip," Krisellen said and then screamed. Addison had stumbled and was falling backward through the hole!

Krisellen ran to the hole and looked down. Her daughter had fallen eight feet and was lying face down on the concrete basement floor. Addison was completely still. The other children burst into tears. "Hurry!" Krisellen told them. "We have to get down there!" They rushed out of the house and around to the basement stairs. When they reached Addison, she seemed lifeless. But as Krisellen gently lifted her head, the little girl began to vomit. "Her eyes were staring off to the side, and I couldn't bear to look at them," Krisellen recalled. "So I closed them

Angels Among Us

and held her head so she wouldn't choke."

Krisellen called for the paramedics on her cell phone and sent the other children outside to wait for them. When they arrived, they fitted Addison with a cervical collar and sped away, as Krisellen herded the children into her car to follow. Later, the paramedics told her that her daughter was completely unresponsive all the way to the hospital. In the emergency room, Addison was examined then whisked off for tests. "It's lucky that she landed on her face," the emergency room physician tried to reassure Krisellen. "She might be spared brain damage."

"I don't know how that could be," Krisellen told him, "because she fell backwards into the hole."

The doctor shrugged. "That's odd, because there are no bruises on her face."

Something else was odd too. When the radiologist came out to give Krisellen the results of Addison's CAT scan and X rays, he was baffled. "There are no signs of any injuries," he told her. "No concussion, no internal injuries. She may have some bruising later, even a few little facial fractures, and you can give her Tylenol for that. Otherwise, she's fine. You can take her home now."

Home? Krisellen was stunned. How could her daughter have sustained such a terrible fall with no injuries? But here she was, walking down the hall with a nurse, smiling and completely herself. How could this be?

It wasn't until that evening that Krisellen learned the answer. She and the four children were saying their night prayers together, and they all thanked God for keeping Addison safe. Krisellen started to get up off her knees. "Mummy," Addison looked up. "Aren't we going to thank the angel too?"

"The angel?" Krisellen asked.

"Uh huh. She was with me in the hole," Addison said matter-of-factly. Krisellen started to cry. "Don't cry, Mummy, she was very happy. She was all sparkly!"

Addison never did develop any bruises, but she did make sure that everyone she loved heard about her beautiful angel. And when she eventually moved into another bedroom, Addison asked for angel wallpaper.

Today, Krisellen still recalls the event with awe. "I never should have exposed the children to such danger," she said. "But I think everything happens for a reason. Perhaps God wanted me to know that I would never raise the children alone—that He would send all the help I needed."

Joan Wester Anderson is the author of seven books on angels and miracles. Her first book, Where Angels Walk, *has sold more than two million copies and has been translated into fifteen languages. For more angel stories, visit her WhereAngelsWalk Web site at http:// joanwanderson.com.*

Angel on the Highway

A defiant young man begins to take life seriously after a motorcycle crash.

By Joan Wester Anderson

John Mustain is a popular radio talk show host on WNWS-FM in Jackson, Tennessee. He's also a devoted husband and father, a writer, security director and a minister in the Church of Christ. Given all these accomplishments, we could assume John had always followed a straight path of good behavior. But we would be wrong!

John was a teenager in the '70s, raised in a very religious family. But he was more interested in hot cars and pretty girls. "My faith was very superficial," he said, "consisting mostly of a strict adherence to the rules—except when my parents weren't looking." Shortly after getting his driver's license, John landed a well-paying job at a local grocery store chain. It wasn't long before he talked his dad into letting him buy a motorcycle. "Now, my independence was complete," John explained. "I earned my own money. I was buying my own vehicle. I felt like an adult." So one morning, when John's mother forbade him to visit his girlfriend after school that day, he was immediately rebellious. "I'm going, and nothing you can say or do will change my mind!" he shouted. His mother, stunned, began to cry. John had never openly defied her. But now her son was storming out the back door. "I'll be home by ten!" he shouted over his shoulder.

After school, John went to his girl-friend's house in a nearby town about thirty minutes away. The teens spent the evening together watching televi-sion, "and trying to stay as far away from her parents as possible," John said. "I was so wrapped up in her that I paid no attention to the time. Finally at 9:45, I headed for home."

Home was, of course, thirty min-utes away, not fifteen. But John decided he could arrive by 10:00 P.M. if he rode fast. He decided to take a "shortcut" across a highway closed for construction. Veering around the yellow-and-black striped barricades, John increased his speed to about

seventy miles per hour. Just a few moments later, he lost control and the motorcycle began to flip.

"Everything slowed to a crawl," John said. "I hit the pavement, head first, and tumbled down the highway, head over heels. I remember seeing the moon pass my knees! And as I rolled to a stop, I remember the extreme silence of the night." John's clothes had been torn off, he was bleeding from head to toe, and he could barely move. He was also in the middle of nowhere, on a detoured highway, with no hope of traffic coming by. Would he die, he wondered hazily, before the road crews discovered him the next morning?

"As I lay there drifting in and out of consciousness, I saw two very bright lights approaching," John said. "It was a vehicle and I needed to stop it." Shakily, John stumbled to his feet, stood sway-ing in the middle of the road, and waved his arms for a moment, then fell again onto the pavement. But the driver had apparently seen him, for the car slowed, then stopped. It was a recreational vehicle.

A man stepped out of the RV and quickly assessed the situation. He lifted John's huge motorcycle to the side of the road, then walked over to John. He leaned over and easily picked John up in his arms, then carried him to the RV and gently laid him in the back. Was the man old, young? John couldn't concentrate. Everything seemed to be happening a million miles away. It was the last thing he remembered until they reached his girlfriend's house. "Her surprised mother opened the door, and the man carried me inside and laid me down on their couch," John said. He passed out again.

Later at the hospital, John and his mother heard an amazing story. His girlfriend's mother explained that, with hardly a word of explanation, the stranger had deposited John on their couch, and while the women were caring for John had simply disappeared, never to be seen again.

The incident was a turning point for John; he became far more serious about his behavior, his respect for his mother and especially his faith in God. But today, despite his role in his church, John is a major sceptic when it comes to miracles. "Yet I have thought about these events over the years and have found several things that I cannot explain."

For example, how did John escape a seventy-mile-per-hour crash with only minor cuts and abrasions? Why was the stranger driving on a barricaded road? How could he be strong enough to move the motorcycle off the road and carry John in his arms? How did he know where John's girlfriend lived? ("While it is possible I could have awakened in the RV and told him, I don't remember doing that.") How did he leave without the women noticing his departure?

Finally, why didn't the man stick around and see how John was doing? Unless he already knew . . . "I believe in angelic beings, although I am sceptical as to the popular view of their interventions," John said. "But I can't help but wonder if my rescuer that night wasn't an angel."

Who else?

Joan Wester Anderson is the author of seven books on angels and miracles. Her first book, Where Angels Walk, *has sold more than two million copies and has been translated into fifteen languages. For more angel stories, visit her WhereAngelsWalk Web site at http://joanwanderson.com.*

The Warrior Angels

By Marilynn Carlson Webber and Dr. William D. Webber

Joyce Story is a frail woman, weighing only eighty-five pounds. She is a scant five-foot-one. Severely handicapped with rheumatoid arthritis, she walks with a noticeable limp.

She was the treasurer of her Sunday school class, and every Tuesday morning it was her routine to go to the Security Pacific Bank on the corner of Van Buren and Arlington in Riverside, California, to deposit the offering from the class. It was already hot at 10:00 one day in June 1985 as she went with her niece to the bank. The deposit was quickly made.

As Joyce and her niece left the bank they heard a woman scream, "Please don't! No! No! Help, help!" There in the bank parking lot was a huge man, well over six feet tall, weighing about 250 pounds, wearing a ski mask. He was beating the shouting woman as he tried to steal her moneybag. She had the handle of the bag wrapped around her arm, and the more the mugger pulled, the tighter it became. Then with a mighty blow, he knocked the woman to the ground.

As tiny Joyce saw this, something welled up deep within her spirit. There were many emotions, but the one she remembers feeling the most was grief—not just grief for the victim but grief for the assailant. Grief that one person would treat another so brutally.

In a moment, the grief was replaced by an urgent feeling that God would have her take action. A small, handicapped woman confronting a large and violent criminal? Obediently, she limped toward the mugger. Raising a gnarled index finger and pointing at him, Joyce said softly, "No! In the name of Jesus, no!"

Joyce's niece, La Shell, watched fearfully at the strange encounter. Intent on stealing the moneybag, the man continued to beat his victim while she was on the ground. Joyce kept limping slowly toward him, repeating calmly, "No! In the name of

Jesus, no!" As she advanced, the handicapped woman became aware of a strong presence with her. Knowing she wasn't alone, all fear left her.

The man in the ski mask paused in his assault of the woman on the ground. He looked contemptuously at little Joyce, but then he looked up, over her head. He became startled; his eyes filled with terror. He began to back up as if in shock, saying, "Oh, oh, oh!" Then he turned and ran for his life.

What did he see? Joyce has no doubt. She knows she would not frighten anyone, but she was aware of an angel behind her. From the way the mugger looked, the warrior angel must have been at least nine feet tall.

Joyce helped the woman get up from the pavement and into the bank for first aid. The police were called and responded quickly. The officer making the report was sceptical about the angel. He did recognize the description of the mugger, however. The man had assaulted several people at different banks in the area, and the police said that he was not afraid of anyone—certainly not of a handicapped little woman. Joyce said, "There is no human explanation why this mugger was

frightened of me. He could have snapped me like a pretzel. Praise the Lord, he was frightened of my angel."

The story came to us from Joyce Story's point of view. How interesting it would be if we were able to find the criminal with the ski mask and hear his account of the angel that struck fear in his heart. Was it enough to make him "scared straight"? Was his life changed by this awesome encounter? In this case, we do not know.

Mighty Warriors Dressed for Battle

There have been times when lives were changed by an encounter with warrior angels. The best-documented case of this happening occurred in the life of John Patton.

John Patton and his wife were pioneer missionaries to the New Hebrides Islands. Faithfully, they tried to live out the Christian gospel and model a Christian lifestyle. They were met with hostility. They returned insults with kindness, hatred with love.

It soon became apparent that even their lives were in danger. There were threats that their home would be burned and the missionary couple murdered, but the Pattons felt called by God. Praying for divine protection, they continued to minister in a spirit of love.

Then one night they heard noises outside their small missionary compound. Looking out, they saw they were completely surrounded by the chief and his men with torches and spears. They were being true to their word. They had come to burn their home and kill the missionaries. The Pattons had no weapons. There was no earthly means of protection, but they could pray, and pray they did! Throughout the terror-filled night they prayed for God to send his angels to protect them. They prayed that this warlike tribe would someday find peace with God.

When the morning came, the tribe silently left. The Pattons were elated but very surprised. There seemed to be no reason for the war party to leave.

Others of fainter heart would have sailed away from the island looking for more hospitable mission territory, but the Pattons felt called by God to stay. Fearlessly, yet gently and lovingly,

they continued to witness but without any noticeable results.

A full year later, the chief became a Christian. Finally, John Patton was able to ask the question that had puzzled him for so long: "Chief, remember that night you came and surrounded our house? Your men all had spears and torches. What had you planned to do?"

The chief replied, "We came to kill you and burn everything you have."

"What kept you from doing it?" the missionary asked.

"We were afraid of all those men who were guarding your house," the chief replied.

"But there were no men," Patton responded. "We were alone, my wife and I."

"No, no," the chief insisted. "There were many men around your house. Big men. Giants. They were awesome. They had no torches but they glowed with a strange light, and each had a drawn sword in his hand. Who were they?"

Instinctively the missionary knew. He and his wife had prayed for protection, and God had sent His angels. The missionary also recognized that this

Outside the open window the air is all awash with angels.

—Richard Wilbur

was a teachable moment for the new convert. "Let me explain what you saw," Patton said as he opened his Bible to 2 Kings, chapter 6. He read the biblical account of the time that the king of Aram sent his army to capture the prophet Elisha. During the night, the army surrounded the place where Elisha was. In the morning, Elisha's helper saw that they were surrounded by an army with horses and chariots.

"'What shall we do?' the man asked in fear. 'Don't be afraid,' the prophet answered. 'Those who are with us are more than those who are with them.' And Elisha prayed, 'O Lord, open his eyes so he may see.' Then the Lord opened the servant's eyes, and he looked and saw the hills full of horses and chariots of fire all around Elisha" (2 Kings 6:16–17).

Nightly Camping in Haiti

The voodoo drums began softly. Each hour their incessant throbbing became louder and more insistent. There was an almost hypnotic power in the compelling beat.

Kay Kallander had come as a missionary nurse, working in a clinic outside of Port-au-Prince, Haiti. She shared a small house with another woman missionary. A low fence surrounded their home, marking the property boundaries. It certainly was not high enough to be a deterrent to anyone who might want to break into the house.

Every night the drums would serve notice that the voodoo rituals were taking place. In the morning as Kay made her way to the clinic, she would see evidence of the nightly ceremonies: blood, fragments of animal parts and cult objects. It was unpleasant at best; at times it was gruesome.

There was trouble every night. Kay tried not to think of it when she went to bed at the end of a long day. As the drums began, she would pray for those caught in the spell of voodoo. And she would pray for her own safety.

During the day at the clinic, Kay

often treated wounds and injuries that resulted from the hysteria of the nightly rituals. Before dark she would return to her home. It was a scary place to be, but Kay had told God she would go where He wanted her to go—and she was convinced God wanted her to use her nursing skills here where they were so needed.

Poverty was everywhere. In desperation, the poor would break into houses and steal anything of value.

According to U.S. standards, the two women missionaries had only modest belongings, but in that area of Haiti, what they had was worth stealing. And far worse things often happened to women living alone.

Yet the two missionaries had no problems, and their home was never broken into. Night after night the drums would beat, and Kay was aware that violence was taking place all around where they lived.

One day a middle-aged Haitian man suffering with pain came to the dental clinic. The dentist did oral surgery and extensive repair work on his mouth. Because of the amount of work, the man stayed quite a while. On this day, Kay was working with pain management and had time to talk with the patient. Finding him to be friendly and open, she asked a question that had been troubling her. "Why is it that with all the problems in our neighborhood and the break-ins that happen nightly, there has never been any theft at our house? It would seem that we would be a natural target."

"No one would ever enter your yard," the Haitian replied. "Everyone knows about the guards you have."

"The guards?" Kay asked incredulously. "What guards?"

"The guards you have on duty every night. There are four of them. Big, big men. Dark, very dark men. One stands on each corner of your property. They are very frightening. No one would dare to come into your house. Everyone knows about them. Lady, nobody will cause you any trouble."

Who were these guards? The missionary had not hired any guards. Often they looked out of their windows at night. Never had they seen a guard—or any other person—on their property.

Kay is certain that they were angels of God, unseen to the missionaries but clearly visible to potential troublemakers.

"The angel of the Lord encamps around those who fear Him, and He delivers them," Kay quoted from Psalm 34:7. "At our house in Haiti, we had four angels who camped out every night."

Angels Are Not Always Described in the Same Way

These warrior angels are awesome! Ask a person what an angel looks like and chances are that he or she may describe a beautiful blonde woman with wings—sometimes angels do appear that way. Ask what a cherub looks like, and you will be told that it is a little childlike angel—but not in the Bible. The cherubim (the plural of cherub) in the Bible are warrior angels. They are the first to appear in the Bible, in

Genesis 3:24, where they guard the Garden of Eden so that no one can enter. In Solomon's temple there were carved cherubim that were thirty feet high with wings that were each fifteen feet wide—a far cry from the cute cherubs found on greeting cards. Throughout the Bible, the cherubim are not always described in the same way. Perhaps the form in which these spirit beings manifest themselves changes according to the function they serve.

We learn much about angels from the Bible and from experience. Some things about angels remain mysteries to us. We have noted that angels are not usually visible, but when it serves God's purposes they can be seen. It is interesting that there are times when some people who are present see angels and others do not. Our human logic would tell us that angels would be seen by those who were people of faith, while the angels remained unseen by those who did not believe. But as often is the case in spiritual matters, human logic does not always hold the answer. For example, Missionary Patton did not see angels, but the tribesmen coming to murder him and his wife did. One principle seems clear: Angels are seen by those who have a need to see them. How is this done? Some things remain a mystery. There is a range of evidence found even in this book. Some who've experienced angelic encounters have been very aware of the presence of angels but have not seen them. Others have seen the angels. It's interesting that all appearances of angels are not alike. The descriptions that people give of angels vary from what appears to be an ordinary person to a moving sphere of light. And yes, some do see angels that look like our traditional image of the heavenly host.

How do we account for this difference of form that angels take when they materialize? Do angels simply choose in what form they will appear? Or do differing orders or ranks of angels manifest themselves each in their own way? The Bible nowhere answers this question. Professors of theology may speculate when they teach angelology, but your speculation is as good as theirs. We simply do not know.

Nick Stoia's Story

"The flat had seemed to be just right for our family. It was a two-story, yellow brick building with the upstairs identical to the downstairs on the west side of Detroit. When we moved in, we had the ground floor. My wife's cousin, who owned the building, lived with her family on the second floor.

"Later the flat above us was rented to a couple who seemed nice enough when they moved in. To our consternation, the man became increasingly irritable.

"We learned that he was suffering from Graves' disease, caused by overactivity of the thyroid. When his medication wasn't right, his eyes would bulge or seem to pop. He would become very nervous and irritable.

"One day he was very stressed out. He stood on our front porch, threatening to come in and kill us. It was frightening. Seeing him with his face red, his eyes bulging—and watching his constant activity—made us realize he was far from normal. We knew that his threats were not to be taken lightly. He was dangerous in this condition.

"We stayed on our guard through-out the evening. Before going to bed, my wife, Sandy, and I prayed for God's protection over us. We prayed for God to set a hedge of angels around us to protect us. My wife fell asleep, while I stayed awake, continuing to pray for our safety.

"I became aware that we were not alone in the room. An angel was standing guard. He was tall, about six-foot-four and with a very muscular build. His entire being was radiating a light, something I had not seen before. If I had to name a colour, the closest I could come to it would be a very deep cobalt blue. The look on his face reminded me of the special Marine guards stationed around important places like the White House: extremely proud of the duty they are performing and not somebody you'd want to mess with.

"I was filled with a feeling of safety. God had sent His angel. I was allowed to see this angel so that I would know that my prayers were being answered and that God would keep us safe and protect us. Since the

All day I have been tossed and whirled

in a preposterous happiness:

Was it an elf in the blood?

or a bird in the brain? or even part

Of the cloudily crested, fifty-league-long,

loud uplifted wave

Of a journeying angel's transit roaring

over and through my heart?

—C. S. Lewis

angel was standing guard, there was no reason for me to stay awake. Free of worry, I fell sound asleep.

"The next day we rented a truck and moved out. What's neat, as I think back about this experience, is that it illustrates how God cares about the day-to-day affairs of just common people. God doesn't send his angels just to the leaders, the king of Israel or the head of a church. He cares for all His children—even me."

The Reverend Dr. William D. Webber has been the pastor of American Baptist churches. He and his wife, Marilynn Carlson, are the authors of A Rustle of Angels: Stories about Angels in Real Life and Scripture *and* Tea with the Angel Lady. *The Webbers have been frequent guests on radio and television programs about angels.*

An Angel in a Hurry

A business "guru" gets a little help from a guardian angel when she desperately needs it.

By Joan Wester Anderson

Barbara Brabec is the acknowledged "guru" of the home-based business crowd, a popular author and Internet expert. She is smart and organized, but like many busy women, she is also in a hurry most of the time. One Saturday, Barbara headed for the garage to run a few errands. "I had a large cheque and a couple of other small cheques for deposit, so I'd written the deposit slip and endorsed the cheques at home," she said. "In the garage, with my hands full, I laid the three paper-clipped cheques on the roof of the car so I could get my keys out and put other stuff down on the seat." Barbara got in the car, tore out of the driveway and was almost at the bank before she realized that she had left the cheques on the roof of her car!

Racing home again, Barbara cried and prayed. "God, I really need you now!" But all had to be lost because

At the round earth's imagined corners, blow your trumpets, angels.

—John Donne

the wind was strong, blowing old leaves and papers around, whipping flags on their poles. "Logic told me I didn't have a chance of finding those cheques," Barbara said, "but fools always have hope." As she turned onto her street, she began looking at lawns for bits and pieces of paper.

Then Barbara realized something else. She had endorsed the cheques because she was just going to hand them to the bank teller. Any unscrupulous person could find the cheques and cash them. Since it was Saturday, there was no way to notify the company that issued her the cheques to stop payment on them. She really needed this money. She feared it was as good as gone.

Barbara swerved into her driveway, and her heart almost stopped. Lying on the sidewalk at the end of the driveway were her three paper-clipped cheques. Barbara screeched to a halt, leaped out of the car, and grabbed them. "I knew God had sent my guardian angel to put his foot on them and hold them there," she said, "because there was no way they wouldn't have blown away otherwise."

It had been a while since Barbara had a miracle, but this was a big one. She cried tears of thanks and gratitude to God as she drove back to the bank, a little more slowly this time. And today she wants "to shout to the world that God is good, and He does watch out for us, especially when we do stupid things!" All busy people agree.

Joan Wester Anderson is the author of seven books on angels and miracles. Her first book, Where Angels Walk, *has sold more than two million copies and has been translated into fifteen languages. For more angel stories, visit her WhereAngelsWalk Web site at* http://joanwanderson.com.

PART THREE

ANGEL COMMUNICATION

Famous Encounters with Angels and Ways to Bring Them into Your Life

Angels Affect History or Inspire Beautiful Work

By Johanna Skilling

In every era, there are people who seem to rise above the norm, lighting up the world with their powers of creativity in art, music, philosophy, writing, even statesmanship. These are not only the people who inspire those in their own historical era, but they also survive as icons in our shared history; we look back to their lives and work to guide us in our own decisions and illuminate our own spiritual paths.

We know they inspire us. But who inspired them?

Many of our most revered artists, musicians and leaders believe they were inspired directly by heaven. Visions of angels, prophetic dreams, even conversations with visitors from the spiritual world all figure in their life stories. In the coldest, darkest days of the American Revolution, George Washington encountered in his study an angel who offered him a vision of the Union he was to help create. In the midst of a financial and professional crisis, George Frideric Handel heard the angelic voices

The Angels' Bread is made
The Bread of man today.

—Saint Thomas Aquinas

that he recreated in his masterwork *Messiah*.

But angels don't always come at times of crisis. William Blake saw angels and spiritual visitors in treetops and on sidewalks. He lived his life among the angels as naturally as among his human family. A teenage Joan of Arc was guided by angelic voices to succeed where generations of French leaders had failed. And Saint Francis of Assisi was lifted to an ecstatic state by an angel playing the violin.

Sometimes a single visit was enough to shape the life and career of painters as diverse as Marc Chagall and Howard Finster; another lone encounter between author J. R. R. Tolkien and an angelic messenger assured him that his beloved son would return safely from the war— and that his work would thus be completed and survive far past his own lifetime.

Even those who didn't necessarily believe in angelic visitors or heavenly

Angel Stories
ENCOUNTERS AND SIGHTINGS

My family was going through a tough time. My father lost his job during my senior year in high school. I felt like my life was going to end because my parents could not help me pay for a college education. I was crying and asking God why this was happening to me. I went to sleep in my bedroom and woke up in the middle of the night. A beautiful angel that looked like a young woman whispered to me not to worry; God would take care of me. She had a white glow around her and I felt a peace that I never felt before.

intervention may in fact have been the recipients of such guidance. It may well be that Charles Lindbergh guided his aircraft, *Spirit of Saint Louis*, safely over the Atlantic with the help of heavenly guides.

In his epic poem, *Paradise Lost*, John Milton tells us that

Millions of spiritual creatures walk the earth

Unseen, both when we wake and when we sleep.

Read on to see how some of these "spiritual creatures" entered the lives of these beloved figures, and in inspiring them, opened a glimpse of heaven to the rest of us as well.

Johanna Skilling is a freelance writer based in New York City.

George Frideric Handel

Inspired by Heaven

———❦———

By Johanna Skilling

Who has not thrilled to the strains of the classic example of holiday music, *Messiah*? But how many know that George Frideric Handel, its composer, felt that he was divinely inspired to compose this masterpiece?

By the time he wrote *Messiah*, Handel was an accomplished composer, known throughout Europe for his operas, oratorios and church music. He was barely thirty years old when he wrote *Water Music* to serenade King George I at a party for the monarch on the Thames River in London. Yet despite his access to rulers and church leaders, Handel's musical career was often artistically and financially uncertain.

At the age of fifty-two, Handel suffered a stroke that paralyzed his right arm. Alone, debt ridden and crippled, he went to a convent in

France to try to recover. It was there that Handel sat down at the harpsichord one day, wondering if he could still play. To his astonishment, and that of the nuns caring for him, the music that flowed from the instrument was perfect, almost as if angels were at the keys instead of the recovering patient.

Handel returned to London only to produce two oratorio performances that were spectacular failures. Afterward, he was left with just one request to compose new music—from a charity in Dublin, Ireland. The proceeds would be used to help those in debtors' prison—a fate that Handel himself was very close to experiencing. Handel had more than thirty-five years of composing experience behind him when he sat down to write *Messiah*. But this work was to affect him like no other. For three weeks, Handel worked tirelessly, inspired by the angels whose voices he was attempting to capture in his music. On finishing the "Hallelujah Chorus", Handel is said to have exclaimed, "I think I did see all Heaven open before me and the great God Himself." Later, he would compare his experience to that of Saint Paul, saying, "Whether I was in my body or out of my body when I wrote it, I know not. God knows."

Messiah was first performed in Dublin in April of 1742. Although Handel himself earned very little from this first performance, the concert

Angel Stories
GUARDIAN ANGELS

I have been meditating for 28 years. During that time I have received many messages from my guardian angel. Unfortunately, there have been too many times where I overanalyzed what I heard. Instead of listening to the "knowing" and wisdom of my guardian angel, I followed logic. What terrible decisions they turned out to be. I am now in the process of disciplining myself to follow the wisdom of my guardian angel.

Their faces had they all of living flame,
And wings of gold, and all the rest so white,
No snow unto that limit doth attain.

—Dante Alighieri, *Paradiso*, Canto XXX

raised enough money to free 142 men from debtors' prison. During Handel's lifetime, many more performances of *Messiah* were devoted to raising funds for charity. When he died, at the age of seventy-four, he left *Messiah* to the Foundling Hospital of London. Despite his German birth, Handel was buried in Westminster Abbey, the resting place of many of Britain's greatest artists and statesmen, recognizing his tremendous contribution to Western music.

SOURCES: "Georg Friederich Handel (1685–1759)", from The Grove Concise Dictionary of Music, edited by Stanley Sadie © Macmillan Press Ltd., London, as found at http://w3.rz-berlin.mpg.de; http://gfhandel.org; www.geocities.com; http:// herbalmusings.com; and Rick Hamlin's "Voices of the Heavens" in Angels on Earth magazine (Sept./Oct. 1995), pages 43–46.

Angel Communication

George Washington

A Vision of His Country's Future

By Johanna Skilling

In the darkest, most difficult days of the Revolutionary War, Anthony Sherman, an aide to General George Washington, was standing outside the home of his commander-in-chief. It was the winter of 1777 at Valley Forge, where Washington had retreated with his ragged troops after several defeats by the British army.

Sherman saw Washington leave his house that chilly afternoon, looking pale and distracted. When the General returned, he fell into conversation with his aides and told them an incredible story. He had been working in his study earlier that day, when a brilliant light shone into the room. According to Sherman's account, this is what the General said:

"I do not know whether it is owing to anxiety of my mind or what, but this afternoon, as I was sitting at this table engaged in preparing a dispatch, something seemed to disturb me. Looking up, I beheld standing opposite me a singularly beautiful female. So astonished was I, for I had given strict orders not to be disturbed, that it was some moments before I found language to inquire the cause of her presence. A second, a third and even a fourth time did I repeat my question, but received no answer from my mysterious visitor except a slight raising of her eyes.

"By this time I felt strange sensations spreading through me. I would have risen but the riveted gaze of the being before me rendered volition impossible. I assayed once more to address her, but my tongue had become useless, as though it had become paralyzed.

"A new influence, mysterious, potent, irresistible, took possession of me. All I could do was to gaze steadily, vacantly at my unknown visitor. Gradually the surrounding atmosphere seemed as if it had become filled with sensations, and luminous. Everything about me seemed to rarify, the mysterious visitor herself becoming more airy and yet more distinct to my sight than before. I now began to feel as one dying, or rather to experience the sensations which I have sometimes imagined accompany dissolution. I did not think, I did not reason, I did not move; all were alike impossible. I was only conscious of gazing fixedly, vacantly at my companion."

The woman stood before him, silently, in a silvery blue dress. Finally she spoke. "Son of the Republic," she said, "look and learn!"

Washington continued: "I now beheld a heavy white vapor at some distance, rising fold upon fold. This gradually dissipated, and I looked upon a strange scene. Before me lay spread out in one vast plain all the countries of the world: Europe, Asia, Africa and America. I saw rolling and tossing between Europe and America the billows of the Atlantic, and between Asia and America lay the Pacific."

"'Son of the Republic' said the same mysterious voice as before, 'look and learn.' At that moment I beheld a dark, shadowy being, like an angel, standing, or rather floating in mid-air, between Europe and America. Dipping water out of the ocean in the hollow of each hand, he sprinkled some upon America with his right hand, while with his left hand he cast some on Europe.

"Immediately a cloud raised from these countries and joined in mid-ocean. For a while it remained stationary, and then moved slowly westward, until it enveloped America in its murky folds. Sharp flashes of lightning gleamed through it at intervals, and I heard the smothered groans and cries of the American people.

"A second time the angel dipped water from the ocean and sprinkled it out as before. The dark cloud was then drawn back to the ocean, in whose heaving billows it sank from view.

"A third time I heard the mysterious voice saying, 'Son of the Republic, look and learn.' I cast my eyes upon America and beheld villages and towns and cities

springing up one after another until the whole land from the Atlantic to the Pacific was dotted with them.

"Again, I heard the mysterious voice say, 'Son of the Republic, the end of the century cometh, look and learn.' At this, the dark shadowy angel turned his face southward, and from Africa I saw an ill-omened spectre approach our land. It flitted slowly over every town and city of the latter. The inhabitants presently set themselves in battle array against each other. As I continued looking I saw a bright angel, on whose brow rested a crown of light, on which was traced the word *Union*, bearing the American flag which he placed between the divided nation, and said, 'Remember ye are brethren.' Instantly, the inhabitants, casting from them their weapons, became friends once more, and united around the National Standard.

"And again I heard the mysterious voice saying, 'Son of the Republic, look and learn.' At this the dark, shadowy angel placed a trumpet to his mouth and blew three distinct blasts; and taking water from the ocean, he sprinkled it upon Europe, Asia and Africa. Then my eyes beheld a fearful scene: from each of these countries arose thick, black clouds that were soon joined into one. Throughout this mass there gleamed a dark red light by which I saw hordes of armed men, who, moving with the cloud, marched by land and sailed by sea to America. Our country was enveloped in this volume of cloud, and I saw these vast armies devastate the whole country and burn the villages, towns and cities that I beheld springing up. As my ears listened to the thundering of the cannon, clashing of swords, and the shouts and cries of millions in mortal combat, I heard again the mysterious voice saying, 'Son of the Republic, look and learn.' When the voice had ceased, the dark shadowy angel placed his trumpet once more to his mouth, and blew a long and fearful blast.

"Instantly a light as of a thousand suns shone down from above me, and pierced and broke into fragments the dark cloud which enveloped America. At the same moment the angel upon whose head still shone the word *Union*, and who bore our national flag in one hand and a sword in the other, descended from the heavens attended by legions of white spirits. These immediately joined the inhabitants of America, who I perceived were well nigh overcome, but who immediately taking courage again, closed up their broken ranks and renewed the battle.

"Again, amid the fearful noise of the conflict, I heard the mysterious voice saying, 'Son of the Republic, look and learn.' As the voice ceased, the shadowy angel for the last time dipped water from the ocean and sprinkled it upon America. Instantly the dark cloud rolled back, together with the armies it had brought, leaving the inhabitants of the land victorious!

"Then once more I beheld the villages, towns and cities springing up where I had seen them before, while the bright angel, planting the azure

Angel Stories
DREAM ENCOUNTERS

Angel visions have been therapeutic for me. In most visions where angels were involved, I usually was transported in a beam or shaft of light. In one vision, I was instructed to "stay in the light", after observing the "churning of darkness". In another vision, being apprehensive regarding an upcoming eye surgery, I was told in the vision or dream to "climb the backs of the angels", a string of light beams, that formed in the form of human light forms. Most of my visions were angels guiding me down a beam or shaft of light to something. In the vision, one of the issues was that of "forgiveness". A conversation took place between the angel and myself, of which the angel took the position that he was a messenger and served merely as a guide for me in my vision.

In my earlier visions, light did not play a prominent role as it did in my later visions or dreams. Angels or light beings were humanoid forms that were incandescent. The light flowed out, and provided a peace and a sense of serenity.

*It is not known precisely where angels dwell—whether in the air,
the void, or the planets.
It has not been God's pleasure that we should be informed of their abode.*

—Voltaire, *Philosophical Dictionary*

standard he had brought in the midst of them, cried with a loud voice, 'While the stars remain, and the heavens send down dew upon the earth, so long shall the Union last.' And taking from his brow the crown on which blazoned the word *UNION*, he placed it upon the Standard while the people, kneeling down, said, 'Amen.'

"The scene instantly began to fade and dissolve, and I at last saw nothing but the rising, curling vapor I at first beheld. This also disappearing, I found myself once more gazing upon the mysterious visitor, who, in the same voice I had heard before, said, 'Son of the Republic, what you have seen is thus interpreted: three great perils will come upon the Republic. The most fearful is the third, but in this greatest conflict the whole world united shall not prevail against her. Let every child of the Republic learn to live for his God, his land and the Union.'

"With these words the vision van-

ished, and I started from my seat and felt that I had seen a vision wherein had been shown to me the birth, progress and destiny of the United States."

Washington was a devoutly religious man, who prayed even in the harsh outdoor conditions in which his army camped. If Sherman's story is true, perhaps Washington received a vision not only of the Revolution, but of the Civil War and a later conflict that imperiled the Republic. Was it the First or Second World War? Vietnam? Or the more recent terrorist attacks on America?

Whatever the answer, it's clear that, like Moses on Sinai, Washington may have been granted a vision of the nation that even now reveres him as the "father of our country".

SOURCES: *Tom Slemen, "George Washington's Vision of the Future", as found at www.geocities.com; Luke Stevens, "George Washington's Remarkable Vision" (originally published by Wesley Bradshaw in the* National Review *Vol. 4, No. 12, December 1880), as found at www.geocities.com; "George Washington's Visions/Prophecies", as found at www.crystalinks.com.*

Angel Communication   295

Joan of Arc

Moving Armies with Angels

By Johanna Skilling

Think of a thirteen-year-old girl you know or have known. If she's like most young girls, she is alternately naive and wise, giddy and sulky, vulnerable and just starting to chafe at the boundaries of childhood. And yet you wouldn't expect her to leave home, travel hundreds of miles and lead an army against an enemy force. Particularly if this thirteen-year-old had no education, couldn't read or write, and had never so much as picked up a weapon.

And yet Jeanne d'Arc did just that. Did she see an angel? Was it the archangel Michael who became her advisor and led her to become commander-in-chief of the French army? Because with no military background, this young girl did what generations of French generals had been unable to achieve: beat back the English invaders and liberate much of her homeland.

Joan was the youngest of five children, a girl who was good at sewing and spinning. From a young age, she was

Angel Stories

LENDING COMFORT IN DEATH

On the morning of the day that my father died from cancer, I could not go to sleep at all. I felt no fear, but peace. On the balcony of the apartment that I live in appeared the brightest light that I have ever seen. The most glorious angel was standing there, as if to let me know that this was to be the day that my father would be taken home. Although it still hurts that my father died, I feel as if I have been given a clear message from God that He is taking very good care of my father.

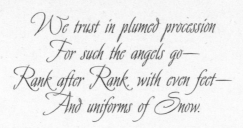

We trust in plumed procession
For such the angels go—
Rank after Rank with even feet—
And uniforms of Snow.

—Emily Dickinson, "To Fight Aloud, Is Very Brave"

often in church, kneeling for hours in prayer. At age thirteen, Joan heard a voice. It sounded quite close, as if someone were speaking in her ear; a blaze of light accompanied the sound. Joan continued to receive these heavenly messages; as time went on she recognized her angelic counsellors to be St. Michael, St. Margaret, St. Catherine and others.

By the time she was sixteen, the voices had begun to urge her to find the French Dauphin, Charles, whose armies were waging a losing war against the English for control of the country. She actually tried to meet one of Charles's generals, but after she was rudely sent away, Joan's voices became even more insistent.

"I am a poor girl," Joan replied. "I do not know how to ride or fight." And yet the voices told her, "It is God who commands it." So once again, Joan made the trip to see the general. While trying to gain access to him, she

received a vision: The French would suffer a terrible defeat by the English in the Battle of the Herrings in the town of Orléans. When her prediction proved true several days later, the general arranged for her to have an audience with Charles himself.

The Dauphin, of course, was sceptical of this young woman who claimed to hear the voices of angels. He had her brought into a room where he was in disguise, surrounded by many other men and women of his court. Joan knew him right away—this in an age before photography or other technology existed to transmit pictures of leaders throughout the country. Joan's voices had not only helped her recognize Charles, but had given her a sign to show him that she indeed had heavenly guidance. This sign was never publicly revealed, but we know that Charles accepted it as proof of Joan's powers.

Angel Stories

It is sobering and touching that each one of us has an angel appointed especially for us. He (or she, if you prefer) is not a genie who grants our every wish, but rather protects us from the snares of Satan. Sometimes, if it suits God's will, they will grant us temporal help as well. Know your angel and give him a name, and if you never leave him he will never leave you.

Joan herself never doubted her angels. "I saw them with my bodily eyes as clearly as I see you," she once said. "And when they departed, I used to weep and wish they would take me with them."

With Charles's permission, Joan returned to the battlefield. Although he had given her a weapon, she wanted to find an ancient sword that, she had been told, was buried behind the altar in the small chapel of Ste-Catherine-de-Fierbois. A search was made, and the sword was found precisely where Joan's voices had predicted.

Before going into battle, Joan made a series of startling predictions. According to a letter of the time, she said "that she would save Orléans and would compel the English to raise the siege, that she herself, in a battle before Orléans, would be wounded by a shaft but would not die of it, and that the King, in the course of the coming summer, would be crowned at Reims." All of these events came to pass.

A year later, her voices warned her that she would be taken prisoner by the English within weeks, and once again, this proved true. Even so, she remained unbowed. She told her captors that "within seven years' space, the English would have to forfeit a bigger prize." Six years and eight months later, the English indeed lost Paris back to the French army.

Sadly, Joan wouldn't live to see that day. Not long after her capture, and only a few months after her nineteenth birthday, she was burned at the stake for heresy. "Until the last," the recorder

Angel Communication   299

of her trial said, "she declared that her voices came from God and had not deceived her." Legend has it that her heart would not burn. After her death, her ashes were thrown into the River Seine.

Almost five hundred years later, in 1920, Joan, the Maid of Orléans, was recognized as we know her today—Saint Joan of Arc.

SOURCES: *www.everythingaboutangels.com*; *Rebecca Arrington, "Author's Vision of Joan of Arc Realized in Newly Published Novel on Saint's Life", as found at www.virginia.edu; Herbert Thurston, transcribed by Mark Dittman, "St. Joan of Arc", The Catholic Encyclopedia, Vol. VIII, as found at www.newadvent.org.*

Emanuel Swedenborg
A Sober Scientist's Detailed Vision of God

By Johanna Skilling

Two-thirds of the way through his long life, Emanuel Swedenborg experienced a change of heart—and of soul.

Born in Stockholm in the winter of 1688, Swedenborg lived a life of privilege. His father, a prominent Lutheran bishop, had ties that later allowed young Emanuel to develop a close association with Charles XII, King of Sweden. For more than thirty years, from the time he was twenty-seven until he was fifty-eight, Swedenborg was Special Assessor to the Royal College of Mines, a sober and scientific pursuit.

But while he might have stayed in this respected position until he retired, in 1746 Swedenborg suddenly resigned. "My sole object in tendering my resignation," he wrote, "was that I might have more leisure to devote to the new office to which the Lord had called me."

Three years earlier, Swedenborg had been in Amsterdam on an October morning when "such dizziness . . . overcame me that I felt close to death."

He felt a roaring wind pick him up; a hand clutched his, and he saw Christ.

"He showed me the face of my spirit," he wrote toward the end of his life, "and thus led me into the world of the spirits and allowed me to see heaven and its wonders, and at the same time to see hell as well, and also to speak with angels and spirits, and this has gone on continually for twenty-seven years."

Swedenborg's connection with the spiritual world gave him the gift of clairvoyance. One night he was at a party in the town of Göteborg when he "saw" a raging fire burning in Stockholm, almost three hundred miles away. The next day, he was able to confirm that his vision of the fire had indeed been true.

(Not all of Swedenborg's predictions turned out to be accurate, including his assertion that a race of people lives on the moon, speaking through their stomachs, making a sound like belching.)

Angel Stories
DREAM ENCOUNTERS

While battling colon cancer, a series of events lead me to the care and guidance of a tender and loving group of vegetarian fellows who all claim to have once been monks.

After being in the care of the group for several months, while going through a total physical, mental and spiritual cleansing, I was meditating one night and fell asleep. I dreamed of pulling myself up the side of a steep mountain. Using a thin, luminous white cord, I pulled and pulled until I pulled myself over the top of the mountain. As I did so I heard a voice saying, "Congratulations John, you've reached the top of God's holy mountain." I turned to find a radiant body of white light smiling broadly. At the same time I was hearing what I can only describe as the sound of every angel in Heaven singing, rejoicing at once. The being, which I feel was an Angel, told me, "From this day forward your name shall be known in Heaven as John."

Angel Communication

Swedenborg came to define his entire life as one lived among the angels. And yet he also continued to find acceptance among his peers.

"I am a Fellow and Member, by invitation, of the Royal Academy of Sciences in Stockholm," Swedenborg wrote, "but I have never sought admission into any literary society in any other place, because I am in an angelic society, where such things as relate to heaven and the soul are the only subjects of discourse, while in literary societies the world and the body form the only subjects of discussion . . .

"Moreover, all the bishops of my native country, who are ten in number, and also that sixteen senators and the rest of those highest in office, entertain feelings of affection for me; from their affection they honour me, and I live with them on terms of familiarity, as a friend among friends; the reason of which is that they know I am in company with angels. Even the King and the Queen, and three princes, their sons, show me great favour . . .

"But all I have thus far related I consider of comparatively little importance, for it is far exceeded by the circumstance that I have been called to a holy office by the Lord Himself, who most mercifully appeared before me, His servant, in the year 1743, when He opened my sight into the spiritual world and enabled me to converse with spirits and angels, in which state I have continued up to the present day.

"From that time I began to print and publish the various arcana that were seen by me or revealed to me, concerning heaven and hell, the state of man after death, the true worship of God, the spiritual sense of the Word, besides other most important matters conducive to salvation and wisdom. The only reason of my journeys abroad has been the desire of making myself useful and of making known the arcana that were entrusted to me. Moreover, I have as much of this world's wealth as I need, and I neither seek nor wish for more."

Swedenborg believed that God can only be revealed through man's humanity, and that both men and women are totally free to create their own lives. They can choose lives devoted to doing good and loving God or lives of selfishness and evil. By doing so, however, they are choosing either heaven or hell after death, and that choice is final.

O, speak again, bright angel, for thou art

As glorious to this night, being o'er my head,

As is a winged messenger or heaven

Unto the white-upturned wond'ring eyes

Of mortals that fall back to gaze on him,

When he bestrides the lazy puffing clouds,

And sails upon the bosom of the air.

—William Shakespeare, *Romeo and Juliet*

Swedenborg's view of heaven is of a rather earthly place populated by angels, who are former humans complete with bodies, clothing and homes. They even marry and have occupations. They have no sense of time, however, only of states of faith, love and intelligence. There they progress to higher states of consciousness. All people, not just Christians, are accepted into heaven, where the angels instruct them in the ways of the Lord. Interestingly, for a lifelong bachelor, Swedenborg had an idealized vision of marriage in heaven. Married love, he believed, bonds two minds into one, and each couple becomes one angel.

Swedenborg's vision of hell is equally fascinating—much like the evil Gotham City in a *Batman* movie, with bestial lairs, filthy streets, tumbledown homes and brothels. The residents of hell continue their evil, selfish ways, burning in a fire of their own hatred. There is no devil in charge.

For all these revelations, Swedenborg gave credit to his angelic visitors. "I have seen a thousand times that angels are human forms, or men, for I have conversed with them as man to man, sometimes with one alone, sometimes with many in company." Like the scientist he was, Swedenborg recorded his visions down to the last detail in numerous books, including the most famous, *On Heaven and Its Wonders and on Hell*.

Swedenborg's vision influenced millions. His spiritual writing exerted tremendous influence on writers and artists, including Emerson, Goethe, Dostoyevsky and William Blake. His thinking also had an impact on religious leaders like Joseph Smith, founder of the Mormon Church. Not long after his death, a group of Swedenborg's devoted followers founded the New Jerusalem Church, and later, the Swedenborg Society, which still exists today. The author of more than fifty works, Swedenborg's books have been translated into thirty languages.

SOURCES: "Emanuel Swedenborg (1688–1772)", as found at www.swedenborg.net; Antony Gormley, "Angel of the North", as found at www.kirjasto. sci.fi; Robert H. Kirven, "Angels in Action", as found at www.swedenborg.net; and Rosemary Ellen Guiley, The Encyclopedia of Angels (Facts on File, 1996).

Saint Francis of Assisi

A Friend to Man, Beast and Angels

By Johanna Skilling

Almost a thousand years ago, a young man named Francesco Bernardone was born in the small Italian town of Assisi. He eventually underwent a transformation that led him from being a spoiled "rich kid" to the patron saint of peace, the animals and the poor.

What happened?

Francesco's father was a wealthy merchant; his mother came from a noble French family. As a boy, Francesco lived a life of ease. As he became a teenager, he and his friends loved nothing more than to spend the nights drinking and singing, not going home to sleep until dawn.

Francis was not very studious, nor was he interested in his father's business. But like many young men before and since, Francis changed when he was called to war at the age of nineteen. Francesco was taken prisoner and held captive for more than a year.

When he was released, he decided to continue his military career. The night before he was to leave on his first mission, he had a dream.

He was in a huge hall; there were suits of armor hanging everywhere, all marked with the cross. "These," said a voice, "are for you and your soldiers." Francis's reaction to the dream was excited: "I know I shall be a great prince," he said.

But not long afterward, midway through his travels, he had another dream in which the same voice told him to return to Assisi. This he did at once.

His friends saw that Francis had somehow changed. He was no longer the free spirit he had been before. He began to embrace a new life of poverty and fasting. Not long after his return to Assisi, Francesco was praying in the forsaken, tumbledown chapel of St. Damian's, when he heard a voice saying,

The angels of the inmost heaven are naked, because they are in innocence, and nakedness corresponds to innocence. It is because garments represent states of wisdom that they are so much spoken of in the Word, in relation to the Church and good men.

—Emanuel Swendenborg

"Go, Francis, and repair my house, which is falling into ruin."

He took this request literally. He went to his father's shop and helped himself to an armful of expensive cloth; he sold both the cloth and his own horse to raise money to repair the little chapel. The effort did not go well: The priest refused to accept the money, and Francis's father became so angry that Francis hid in a cave for a month. When he emerged, he was dragged home by his father, beaten, bound and locked in a dark closet.

His father got his money back but remained so angry that he tried to disinherit his son. Francis was taken before the bishop, but instead of pleading for his inheritance, he took off all the clothes he was wearing and handed them to his father, saying, "Hitherto I have called you my father

Angel Stories
ENCOUNTERS AND SIGHTINGS

I am currently about three months pregnant. I have been feeling like I have an angel watching over me, especially lately. For example, I was out walking my dog one day not really looking at my feet in front of me. My dog took off after a squirrel down a really steep hill. When the dog pulled, she jerked me forward and I lost my footing and began to fall backwards. All of a sudden it felt like something was all around me and lifted me forward enough to get my footing back. I feel like there was an angel around me that day, and lots of other times I feel like there is a spirit watching over me. It's a very peaceful feeling.

Silent night! Holy night! Wondrous star, lend thy light;
with the angels let us sing, Alleluia to our King.

—Joseph Mohr, *Silent Night, Holy Night*

on earth; henceforth I desire to say only 'Our Father who art in Heaven.'"

Francis left Assisi to wander the countryside praising God. He was beaten and robbed, left hungry and cold, and worked in menial jobs. Eventually, he came back and began to beg for stones to restore the little chapel of St. Damian's. Doing all the work himself, he eventually rebuilt it. Francis, afterward, restored two other chapels, St. Peter's and St. Mary of the Angels.

The humble chapel of St. Mary became the cradle of the Franciscan Order (*Caput et Mater Ordinis*) and the central spot in the life of Francis.

One morning in February, Francis was hearing mass at St. Mary; the Gospel that day told how the disciples of Christ were to have few possessions and no money and that they were to declare the Kingdom of God and bring sinners to repentance. As soon as mass was over, Francis threw away his shoes, cloak, pilgrim staff and wallet. He put on a coarse brown tunic, the same type worn by the poorest peasants, and tied it with a piece of rope.

Angel Stories
GUARDIAN ANGELS

Whether we believe it or not, angels guide us every day of our lives. Have you ever taken a different way home only to discover that there was a horrible accident on the route you usually take? That was your guardian angel, pushing you to safety. Have you ever spoken to a stranger, someone you would usually not speak to, and discovered that the person has something, some knowledge or gift that you need? Your angel guided you to that person.

Angel Communication   309

Still searching for signs from heaven, Francis decided to confirm God's will by opening the book of the Gospels at random three times in a row. Each time it opened at passages where Christ told His disciples to leave all things and follow Him. "This shall be our rule of life," exclaimed Francis. He led his companions to the public square, where they gave away all their belongings to the poor and began to preach penance, brotherly love and peace.

Even the Pope received heavenly wisdom about Francis. While other princes of the church rejected Francis's vow of poverty, Pope Innocent III had a dream in which he beheld the "Poor Man of Assisi" bearing up the papal basilica. Moved by his dream, the Pope gave Francis and his fellow monks permission to preach everywhere.

And so he did. Francis travelled tirelessly, going to Syria and to Spain, as well as throughout Italy, preaching his message of love. He usually preached outdoors where admiring crowds met him with music and singing; they brought the sick for him to bless and even kissed the ground he walked on.

Francis did not just believe in brotherly love; he believed in love for all creation, including the animals, birds, flowers, and even the sun and moon. Early legends tell us how half-frozen bees crawled toward him in the winter to be fed; how the wild falcon fluttered around him; and how his "little brethren the birds" listened devoutly to his sermon.

In his forty-fourth year, Francis and three of his many followers climbed a mountain behind Assisi to prepare for Michaelmas with a forty-day fast. During this long vigil, an

Angel Stories
ANGELS OF DARKNESS

I can tell the difference between an angel and a demon in disguise of an "angel". Real angels always come with good messages or messages with things you have to do because you or someone else is in danger.

A perfect woman, nobly planned,
To warn, to Comfort, and command:
And yet a Spirit still, and bright
With something of angelic light.

—William Wordsworth, "She Was a Phantom of Delight"

angel with a violin appeared to him, playing one note so beautifully that Francis's joy was "boundless and unbearable". One night not long afterward, the villagers living below the mountain saw a light as bright as day, high up, near where Francis and his companions were praying. That same night, Francis received a glorious vision of a seraph who appeared from heaven and hovered over him as he prayed.

The next day, the stigmata appeared on Francis's body. Brother Leo, one of Francis's companions, described the saint's right side as bearing an open wound, which looked as if it were made by a lance, and black nails of flesh through his hands and feet.

After the reception of the stigmata, Francis suffered increasing pain. Exhausted by years of travel and toil, his strength gave way and he became almost wholly blind. Despite this, Francis paid a last visit to the little chapel of St. Damian's, and it was in a little hut of reeds, made for him in the garden there, that he composed the "Canticle of the Sun", one of the most beautiful poems in the Italian language.

Not long afterward, Francis was carried to his beloved St. Mary of the Angels to leave this world where his true calling had been revealed, and where his order had first come into being. Francis died on October 3, 1226. Less than two years later, he was canonized by Pope Gregory IX.

SOURCES: M. A. O'Roark's "Francis of Assisi" in Angels on Earth *magazine (Sept./Oct. 2000), pages 40–45; Paschal Robinson, "St. Francis of Assisi", The Catholic Encyclopedia, Volume VI © 1909 by Robert Appleton Company Online Edition Copyright © 1999 by Kevin Knight.*

J. R. R. Tolkien

Love Individualized

By Johanna Skilling

If anyone in the world hadn't heard of Frodo the hobbit or Gandalf the wizard, *The Lord of the Rings* movie surely changed all that. For more than fifty years prior to the movie, J. R. R. Tolkien's original books, *The Hobbit* and *The Lord of the Rings*, have delighted and inspired millions of children, teens and adults around the world.

One of the most striking aspects of Tolkien's books is the characters' feelings of family love, loyalty, courage and endurance. These were subjects very close to the heart of John Ronald Reuel Tolkien—known as Ronald—because of the deprivations of his childhood.

Like Frodo the hobbit, Ronald found himself on his own at a tender age. His father died when he was still a very young child. Born in South Africa in 1892, Ronald moved with his mother and his younger brother,

Hilary, to England, where she had been born and still had family. As a poor widow with two small children, Ronald's mother, Mabel, found solace in the Catholic Church.

A few years passed in relative harmony, but by the time Tolkien was twelve, disaster struck. In 1904, the two boys came down with the measles, followed by whooping cough and pneumonia. When Mabel went to the doctor herself, she learned she had diabetes. Before the year was over, Mabel died. First placed in the care of a Catholic priest, Ronald and Hilary were sent to live with an aunt, then later with a foster parent.

Young manhood held no immediate peace for Tolkien either. Like all of the young men he knew, he was sent to the battlefields of World War I. Sent home with "trench fever" after fighting in the infamous Battle of the Somme, Tolkien was once again on

Angel Communication 313

his own. "By the time I was twenty-one," he would later write, "all but one of my friends were dead."

And yet Tolkien moved on to create his own family. He married another orphan, Edith Bratt, whom he had met in foster care, and went on to have four children with her: John, Michael, Christopher and Priscilla. Tolkien enjoyed making up stories to tell the children, who helped him invent new characters and adventures.

One day, Tolkien was working in his study when he suddenly thought of these words: "In a hole in the ground lived a hobbit." To entertain his children, he began to invent the story of this odd creature, and together Tolkien and the four children continued to make up new tales

Angel Stories
ENCOUNTERS AND SIGHTINGS

When my granddaughter got her driver's license, I gave her a heart-shaped ornament and engraved on it: "Never Drive Faster Than Your Angel Can Fly". She put this on the mirror in her car.

My husband had been very sick for years and was getting worse. He had been having pain in his back and was to go into the hospital the next day for a biopsy. He called me at work and said the pain was unbearable. He couldn't get up from his chair to get his pain medicine. I told him I would be right home. I had a 35-mile drive, winding roads etc.

I drove faster than I should have, but I made it home, got him his pills and settled him down. I went out on the porch to pull myself together. While I was calming myself down and thanking God for getting me home safely to help my husband, I thought about the heart I had given my granddaughter and that I must have a fast angel. As I looked out toward the sky I saw my guardian angel, no face but these huge wings. I just sat there and watched and shortly my angel disappeared. I knew that this was my guardian angel keeping up with me and protecting me on my way home.

If you pray truly, you will feel within yourself a great assurance;
and the angels will be your companions.

—Evagrius of Pontus

about hobbits, wizards, elves and all the strange lands of Middle Earth. Tolkien wrote down the stories as they developed, until the day when that one strange phrase had grown into his first book on Middle Earth, *The Hobbit*, published in 1937.

When World War II broke out, Christopher, the youngest of the four Tolkien children, joined the Royal Air Force. Christopher had always been close to his father, but the war offered an unusual opportunity for them to begin writing to one another. They wrote of spiritual things, including their beliefs about heaven and guardian angels. Tolkien was very concerned for his son's well-being—not just because Christopher was a fighter pilot, but because he had a dangerous heart condition. Like his mother years before, Tolkien found solace in religion and prayed for Christopher often.

One day in late 1944, not long before the end of the war, Tolkien was praying as usual for his son's safety when something extraordinary happened. As Tolkien later wrote his son, he received a vision of divine light, which connected every human soul directly to God. He became aware that every soul had its own individual guardian angel. "Not a thing interposed between God and each creature," Tolkien wrote to Christopher, "but God's very attention itself, personalized . . . I received comfort . . . I have with me now a definite awareness of you poised and shining in the Light."

Tolkien's vision of his own family held in the light of the family of man—and the family of angels—sustained him until Christopher's safe return from the war. Father and son continued their exploration of Middle Earth, and in the 1950s, *The Lord of the Rings* was published to international acclaim. After his father's death in 1973, Christopher completed Tolkien's last book, *The Silmarillion.*

Tolkien would never forget the sweet comfort he received that November day. The inspiration he received from the angelic realm concerning his son, and indeed, all living souls, remained to help him bring joy and entertainment to millions of his readers today and in the future.

SOURCES: *Edward Hoffman, "Tolkien's Angel", www.beliefnet.com, reprinted with permission from* Angels on Earth *magazine; Theresa Carson, "Remembering J.R.R. Tolkien",* Catholic Heritage, *pages 26–27, Our Sunday Visitor, Inc., Sept./Oct. 1998, as found at www.petersnet.net.*

Marc Chagall

Painter of Angels

By Johanna Skilling

For close to a century, Marc Chagall painted luminous, beautiful angels in fantasy landscapes of fiddlers, lovers, cows and flowers. Famous for his depiction of biblical scenes as well as nostalgic images of his Russian childhood, Chagall's work continues to amaze, delight and inspire us. But what inspired this visionary painter?

Born Mark Zakharovich Shagal in the small Jewish ghetto of Vitebsk, Russia, Chagall was one of ten children. His father packed herring for a living; his mother ran a small store. While they didn't have much money, the family was able to give young Marc violin and singing lessons. From an early age, Marc also drew and wrote poetry.

Angel Stories
ENCOUNTERS AND SIGHTINGS

I was a young mother with three small girls. One was just beginning to walk. We lived out in the country and were burning some trash in a barrel. Somehow the yard caught on fire and the fire was going up the walls of our small house. The fire just skipped around and was heading for the propane tank and my car. I ran outside and tried to fight the fire with a quilt but I saw it was out of hand. I cried out for help from the Lord and all of a sudden a man appeared from nowhere and began fighting the fire for me, then another man. I went inside to call the fire department but when I ran back outside the fire was out and the men had vanished. I believe these men were angels.

And the angel said, "I have learned that every man lives, not through care of himself, but by love."

—Leo Tolstoy

Becoming an artist was an unlikely goal for a boy growing up in rural Russia, and it was not an idea that Marc's parents supported. Marc and his father fought frequently about his future. One day, after a particularly furious argument, Mark ran away from home to the imperial capital of St. Petersburg. He wasn't yet twenty years old.

Far away from home, living in a small, furnished room, Marc faced many challenges. As a Jew, he was forbidden to live in St. Petersburg. Without a permit to live in the city, he was continually forced to evade the authorities. Marc was jailed once but still managed to study at two of St. Petersburg's great art schools.

At that time, an amazing vision had a cataclysmic effect on his life and art. One night, drifting into sleep in his small room, Chagall thought he heard the rustle of wings. He opened his eyes and immediately felt pins and needles of pain in his forehead. The room was filled with an unearthly, brilliant blue light. An angel hovered above him. As Chagall watched, the angel slowly floated up through the ceiling; the light and the beautiful blue air vanished with him.

After this vision, Chagall began a lifetime of work to portray the wonder of the angel and the colour of the beautiful blue air. Later, he would describe his work by saying, "My art is an extravagant art, a flaming vermilion, a blue soul flooding over my paintings."

The miracle of blue also figured in Chagall's long love story with his wife, Bella. When she met him, she thought that his eyes, piercingly blue, must have come from heaven. For his part, Chagall felt that Bella brought "blue air, love and flowers" into the room every time he saw her. The angel that blesses the young couple in his painting *The Marriage* expresses the sense of divine joy he found with his wife.

In 1910, the Chagalls moved to Paris. Living and working as a poor

Angel Communication

artist, he moved back and forth between Paris and Moscow. Slowly, his reputation grew. By 1930, Chagall was world famous.

Chagall's beloved Bella died suddenly in 1944, but Chagall's work sustained him. Not long after Bella died, he painted one of his greatest pictures, *Blue Concert*, a blend of his early angelic vision with the faces of Bella and their daughter, Ida.

Marc Chagall continued to work until his death at age ninety-seven. He created paintings, tapestries, theater costumes and stained glass windows. His work illuminates museums and other public buildings throughout the world. Many of his works show images from the Hebrew Bible. "I have been fascinated by the Bible since I was very young," Chagall once said. "It always seemed to me, and it still does, that the Bible is the greatest source of poetry that has ever existed. Since that time, I have been seeking to express this philosophy in life and art."

One of his most emotional works

Angel Stories
DREAM ENCOUNTERS

When I was 6 years old, I awoke because I felt the most loving and calming feeling. Someone had been caressing my cheek. I felt so much love and peace. I asked my mother again about this, and she said that it was my guardian angel. I fell asleep with a smile on my face. As an adult, I have often fallen asleep and sensed a presence. It comes into my room and sits on my bed. I feel the bed leaning or yielding. I am in that realm of sleep of not being quite awake or asleep. I reach out my arm and try to feel for who's there, and there's nothing. I am not afraid when this happens. It almost feels as if someone is coming in to check on me and to see if I am all right. I don't sense it to be male or female. I don't feel like it wants to communicate with me, but more like he/she is my guardian. I realize that this happens when I am at the most stressed in my life.

later in life was a series of stained glass windows on Jewish folk themes for the Hadassah University Medical Centre in Jerusalem. This work brought him a very different type of vision. "All the time I was working," he said, "I felt my father and my mother were looking over my shoulder, and behind them were Jews, millions of other vanished Jews of yesterday and a thousand years ago."

Chagall died on March 28, 1985, shortly after an exhibition of his work in Russia, his mother country. He remained active, creating art until the end of his extraordinary life. Pablo Picasso once said, "When Chagall paints, you do not know if he is asleep or awake. Somewhere or other inside his head there must be an angel."

SOURCES: T. Fleming's "Marc Chagall's Angelic Inspiration" in Angels on Earth magazine (July/Aug1998), pages 40–44; www.angel-art.com; Gad Nahshon, "The Great Tapestries of Marc Chagall", as found at www.jewishpost.com; The Worldwide Art Gallergy, found at www.theartgallery.com.

William Blake
A Life among the Angels

By Johanna Skilling

Almost two hundred years after William Blake died and was buried in a pauper's grave in London, thousands of people flocked to exhibits of his work in major museums on both sides of the Atlantic. Although his talent was largely unrecognized in his own lifetime, Blake eventually achieved fame as a poet, a painter and a pioneer engraver, exerting a lasting influence in both literature and graphic arts.

Blake believed much of his inspiration came from his lifetime encounters with angels. Born in London in November 1757, young William was only ten years old when he saw a vision of angels clustered in the branches of a tree near his home. From then on, wherever he went,

Blake saw visions from the other world—from angels in a hayfield to apparitions of monks in Westminster Abbey. He talked with the angel Gabriel and the Virgin Mary, as well as other historical figures.

Far from scoffing, Blake's parents believed in his visions. Even though they were not well off, they offered to help him become a painter so that he could portray his otherworldly companions. But William decided instead to train as an engraver, a profession that was not only less-expensive to learn, but more likely to give him an income faster.

Although Blake's experience as an engraving student was not particularly happy, in his adult years he went on to revolutionize the art. When William was thirty, his brother, Robert, died. William believed he saw his brother's spirit rise from his lifeless body. Later, Robert appeared to William in a vision, describing an invention that would forever change the art of engraving. By the time a year had passed, William had invented a new technique he had seen in this vision called "illuminated printing".

This new method of engraving allowed Blake to etch both drawings and handwritten poems on a single metal plate, reducing the cost of printing while heightening the effect of the illustrated work. For the first time since the hand-illuminated manuscripts created by monks in the Middle Ages, words and images became inseparable on the page. Blake hand-coloured the illustrations and bound the resulting pages between paper covers.

Blake was also a poet. His first poems were collected by friends in hand-printed editions when he was only twelve years old. Blake went on to write some of the most memorable lines in the English language in his two books, *Songs of Innocence* and *Songs of Experience*. Blake's engraving method allowed him to illustrate his own poems as well as the classics, bringing to vibrant life works including the Book of Job and Dante's *The Divine Comedy*.

As a young man, Blake married Catherine Boucher, who became his partner and lifetime love. Illiterate when they met, Catherine learned from Blake to read and write. Eventually they worked side by side, she printing and colouring the engravings he produced. Together, they created the extraordinary work that resulted from Blake's visions and spiritual experiences.

Blake was a poor man when he died in August 1827. Catherine was forced to borrow the money for his small funeral and buried him in a common grave in Bunhill Cemetery, London.

In his poem "The Angel That Presided", Blake wrote what might be his own epitaph:

The Angel that presided o'er my birth

Said, "Little creature, formed of joy and mirth,

Go love without the help of any thing on earth."

Abou Ben Adhem

Abou Ben Adhem (may his tribe increase!)
Awoke one night from a deep dream of peace,
And saw, within the moonlight in his room,
Making it rich, and like a lily in bloom,
An Angel writing in a book of gold:
Exceeding peace had made Ben Adhem bold,
And to the Presence in the room he said,
"What writest thou?" The Vision raised its head,
And with a look made of all sweet accord
Answered, "The names of those who love the Lord."
"And is mine one?" said Abou. "Nay, not so,"
Replied the Angel. Abou spoke more low,
But cheerly still; and said, "I pray thee, then,
Write me as one that loves his fellow men."
The Angel wrote, and vanished. The next night
It came again with a great wakening light,
And showed the names whom love of God had blessed,
And, lo! Ben Adhem's name led all the rest!

—James Leigh Hunt

Apart from his wife and family, Blake might not have had help—or recognition—from many people on Earth. But his legacy in art and poetry had the help of angels.

SOURCES: *"Visions Fired the Imagination of Eccentric Artist Blake"*, from the Associated Press, as found at www.geocities.com; www.beliefnet.com; www.themystica.com; Brain Candy Quotations Collection, as found at www.corsinet.com.

Charles Lindbergh

A Messenger from the Sky

By Johanna Skilling

On a warm May night in 1927, a crowd of one hundred thousand people stood on a Paris airfield waiting for a sign from the heavens. Shortly after 10:00 P.M., they saw the messenger descend from the dark skies and touch land. The crowd roared. Charles Lindbergh had completed his historic trip across the Atlantic, flying alone 3,610 miles from New York to Paris in thirty-three-and-a-half hours.

Lindbergh became an international hero, winning a twenty-five thousand dollar prize and the admiration of millions for his daring feat.

But is it possible that heaven intervened to sustain him on his trip and bring him safely back to earth?

Just before 8:00 A.M. on the morning of May 20, 1927, Lindbergh took off from Roosevelt Field, Long Island. The ground was wet; the takeoff was sluggish. Lindbergh had carefully supervised the building of his plane, *Spirit of St. Louis*, but had equipped himself with only four sandwiches and two canteens of water for the long flight.

Lindbergh flew northeast along the New England coast until he reached St. Johns, Newfoundland. In

*He heard an odd voice, as though of a whirring...
and when he strained for a wider view, could have sworn
he saw a dark figure born aloft of a pair of strong black wings.*

—Bernard Malamud, "The Angel Levine"

an era before air travel, people all along the route scanned the sky, waiting for a sight of the small plane. Others waited by their radios for news of the flight. At Newfoundland, Lindbergh headed east across the Atlantic as the sky darkened. He was alone, with only a compass, an air-speed indicator and luck to navigate toward Paris.

Writing in his memoirs, Lindbergh remembered watching darkness descend and a thick fog form over the ocean: "Darkness set in about 8:15 and a thin, low fog formed over the sea. This fog became thicker and increased in height until within two hours I was just skimming the top of storm clouds at about ten thousand feet. Even at this altitude there was a thick haze through which only the stars directly overhead could be seen. There was no moon and it was very dark."

Hours passed. Though cold, lonely and tired, Lindbergh had to stay alert.

Angel Stories
DREAM ENCOUNTERS

As I was falling asleep, in that state between awake and sleep, I heard a noise outside my window and then saw a bright light. I saw several angels fly by the window. I wasn't sure if I was dreaming it or if it was for real. I told some close friends about it, and I felt it was a sign that a man I knew who had leukemia and was quite ill was going to get better and live. In my heart, I really felt it was true. Sure enough, after many months and a bone marrow transplant, he did get better and is alive and well.

Angel Communication

Hearing the air cleft by their verdant wings,
The serpent fled, and round the Angels wheeled,
Up to their stations flying back alike.

—Dante Alighieri, *The Purgatorio*, Canto VIII

To doze off would mean certain death in the icy Atlantic. The isolation and weariness made Lindbergh meditate on the nearness of death as he piloted his small plane across the dark ocean. But as the miles rolled on, Lindbergh increasingly felt that he was not alone. Behind him, in the fog, he saw human forms, transparent and weightless.

Surprisingly, Lindbergh didn't feel afraid. In his book, *The Spirit of St. Louis*, he recalls his experience as if it were happening all over again: "Without turning my head, I see them as clearly as though in my normal field of vision. There's no limit to my sight—my skull is one great eye, seeing everywhere at once."

"These phantoms speak with human voices—friendly, vaporlike shapes, without substance, able to vanish or appear at will, to pass in and out through the walls of the fuselage as though no walls were there. Now, many are crowded behind me. Now, only a few remain. First one and then another presses forward to my shoulder to speak above the engine's noise, and then draws back among the group behind. At times, voices come out of the air itself, clear yet far away, travelling through distances that can't be measured by the scale of human miles, familiar voices, conversing and advising on my flight, discussing problems of my navigation, reassuring me, giving me messages of importance unattainable in ordinary life."

It was some time before Lindbergh saw his first sign of human life. Far below, he saw a fishing boat, and then several more. Within an hour land appeared—the coast of southern Ireland. Shortly afterward, Lindbergh was circling the Eiffel Tower and then heading toward the lights and runway of Le Bourget, the Paris airfield.

The roads around the field were jammed with cars. As Lindbergh landed, he had to stop the engine quickly to avoid hurting anyone as the crowd came rushing forward. He opened the door of the cockpit and was immediately hoisted onto the shoulders of the local gendarmes, who carried him through the cheering crowd.

It was over a quarter-century later that Lindbergh first publicly acknowl-edged his vision that remarkable night. It didn't take away from the worldwide acclaim and lasting fame that he had earned. If anything, perhaps, his brush with angels made it stronger.

SOURCES: *www.charleslindbergh.com; Rose-mary Guiley,* The Encyclopedia of Angels *(Facts on File, 1996); Charles A. Lindbergh,* The Spirit of St. Louis *(Scribner Classics).*

Howard Finster

Painter of Sermons

By Johanna Skilling

Howard Finster was an American folk artist whose life spanned most of the twentieth century. He didn't start out as an artist, though. For much of his life, he was an itinerant Baptist preacher. Finster was born on a small farm in DeKalb County, Alabama, and began to preach at the age of sixteen. For more than thirty years, he travelled through Alabama, Georgia and Ten-nessee, preaching at tent revivals and earning extra money with odd jobs like plumbing and bicycle repair.

So how did this back-country preacher become a world-famous artist, with work appearing everywhere from the Smithsonian Institution to album cover art for bands such as R.E.M. and Talking Heads? Finster's work in both his ministry and his art were inspired by visions.

"God called me into the minister work," Finster told an interviewer. "I got crowds of mixed-up people in my tent meetings—Catholics, Methodists, Church of God, all kinds. I pastored churches for close to forty years and I thought I'd run a survey one day on the members of my church. I asked them in the night service what I had preached on in the morning service, and they wasn't anybody there that remembered. And I said to myself, they're not paying much attention to me, what am I gonna do? Lord, I want to preach all over the world and reach more people. Then God called me unto sacred art, got to putting messages on it."

Finster's creations used a common touch to create what he called "sermons in paint". His paintings are full of childlike, colourful images and religious messages like "Hell is a hell of a place" scrawled in crooked block letters. He often included pop images in his work, like the Coca-Cola bottle, Cadillacs and Elvis Presley.

"When Christ called his disciples, he called fishermen," Finster said in a 1990 magazine interview. "He didn't call nobody from a qualified university. He used common people to reveal parables. That's what I do. I use Elvis because I'm a fan of Elvis. Elvis was a great guy. By using him, I get people's attention and they read my messages."

In 1961, Finster began creating his three-acre Paradise Garden, which he described as a "folk-art haven", built on filled swampland behind his home in northwestern Georgia. Eventually, Paradise Garden included such diverse

Angel Stories
GUARDIAN ANGELS

I am Catholic and I very much believe in my Guardian Angel and angels in general. I find them fascinating to learn all about. It just so happens that my son's Guardian Angel is connected to St. Florine. Now who would have ever known when he was born that he would grow up to become a fireman—and St. Florine is the Patron Saint of firefighters. I call that fate and God's plan for my son's path in life. Others may say it is just a coincidence, but I believe otherwise.

Angel Stories
ENCOUNTERS AND SIGHTINGS

Anyone who lives in the East remembers the blizzard of 1997. Snow was as high as the telephone poles, higher in some places. I had just moved into a very old "fixer upper" house I'd purchased in November. There was a small stove in the kitchen and a meager supply of wood. This house was located on top of a mountain with 1,000 acres of state land all around it. My two children and I moved into this rustic home with great joy in our hearts. I quickly found out that one of our greatest needs was wood for the stove.

I closed the upstairs off and we "played" camping, always staying near the small stove. The day the blizzard was to come started bright and sunny, with me scared to death watching my two babies playing with their snowsuits on in the house. I could see their breath from the cold.

I remember looking out a window and watching the light dance over the snow. I had put the last of the wood in the stove early that morning and prayed, asking for guidance, strength and a way to get dry wood. It seemed obvious that we were going to freeze to death without it. Every time I checked that fire throughout the day it was burning exactly the same as it did the last time I checked it. Warmth was beginning to spread through our "camp".

As I watched out the window, from nowhere came a large truck. It stopped in our driveway. That was when I noticed it was full of cords of seasoned wood. I answered the knock on our door. There was a man and his son. He said they were just passing through and thought we could use some wood.

Not saying another word, he and his son unloaded every bit of that wood into the cellar to keep it dry. Then they climbed into the truck and drove away. By then it was snowing so hard we could barely see them.

That small stove required wood cut in an unusual size. Every piece of that wood was the exact right size, and we weathered the storm warm and well. While our house was covered with snow, food had to be flown in for us, our neighbors, the deer. We never saw that man and his son again, nor did anyone down in town know of such a pair. I have absolutely no doubt in my mind that they were angels, sent to answer a frantic mother's prayers. I will be eternally grateful.

"Pass in, pass in," the angels say,
"In to the upper doors,
Nor count compartments of the floors,
But mount to paradise
By the stairway of surprise."

—Ralph Waldo Emerson

work as mosaic cement paths, a giant cement boot, the Tomb of the Unknown Body and Finster's folk-art chapel.

But creating art was not to be an end in itself for Finster. "The Lord had to show me to sell my art," he said. "He give me a vision that the art was to support me and to build the garden."

"One day I had a vision to go full-time on my art and lay everything else aside. I was out on the porch looking down toward the road, and there was a man standing at the gate about fifteen feet tall, and his head was big as a refrigerator. He was familiar to me, I'd met him before, but I couldn't think of his name to save my life. I didn't know what to say to him, so I finally said what I say to the other customers, 'What can I do for you, sir?' And he said, 'You can get on the altar.'

"And that surprised me. I been preaching forty years, what does he mean? I asked him, 'Did you say, "Get on the altar?"' And he said, 'Yeah, get on the altar.' And when he said that he went down to a normal man, just looking over the top of the gate.

"And after that went away I said, 'Lord, what does this mean?' The Lord said, 'If you want to be pretty big in the art world, just reach on out there and go full-time. If you just want to go on and do art part-time, you can be a little guy like you are.'"

Finster's vision proved true: He became a pretty big guy in the art world. But even after becoming a darling of the high-flying New York art scene, with work in many popular galleries both in the United States and abroad, Finster remained modest about his achievements.

"I don't really know what I've accomplished," he said. "Sometimes I get uneasy about myself and wonder if I'm ready, and wonder does God love me, would I go to heaven if I die now. I know God has been with me many times, and the spirit of Jesus has been with me, and I seen angels. I think about meeting Matthew, Mark and Luke and all the apostles. I'm gonna see them some day."

The Reverend Howard Finster died October 23, 2001. He completed over forty-six thousand pieces of original art works. The remaining pieces of his art have been stored until they can be displayed to the world one day and continue to spread his messages.

SOURCES: *Frederica Mathewes-Green, "Matthew, Mark, and Luke—I'm Gonna See Them Someday", and Chad Roedemeier, "'Sermons in Paint': Baptist Artist Howard Finster", as found at www. beliefnet.com.*

Saint John Bosco's Four-Legged Angel

A mysterious dog often came to the rescue of an Italian priest.

———————

By Joan Wester Anderson

As Catholics know, everyone who is in heaven is called a saint. But there are also "official" saints, those recognized for all the good they did here on Earth. One who couldn't have succeeded without a particular heavenly helper was Saint John Bosco, whose feast day is observed January 31.

John was born in Becchi, Italy, in 1815, and although he grew up in poverty, he had a determined mother who saw that he received an education. Before John reached his teens, he was already having wonderful dreams about his future. It seemed clear to him that he was destined to become a priest and work with homeless boys, saving them from the streets, educating them and teaching them about God. Just how this was all to come about was not explained in his dreams. John set out to accomplish the task anyway.

The street kids whom he dealt with

Angel Communication   333

Everything we call a trial,
a sorrow or a duty,
believe me, that angel's hand is there.

—Fra Giovanni Giocondo

were rough, angry and not all that interested in reforming their lives. Often they would rob John when he approached them. Gradually, he won over the younger ones and established group homes for them. But the assaults continued. And because many of John's rescued boys were hard to handle, the citizenry was not exactly thrilled with his mission. Often, they too attempted to drive him out of the area.

One autumn evening in 1852, John Bosco was making his way across the most broken part of the slum district. He was alone and depressed. "Lord," he prayed, "I know you want me to care for the least of your children, but I can't go on being mugged and robbed and still do the work you've assigned me. How about a little help?"

Suddenly, John noticed a dog behind him. Or was it a wolf? The creature was huge and grey but friendly. Timidly, John called it, and

the dog trotted up and took his place alongside him as if he had been trained to do so. "I'll call you Grigio," John told the dog (*grigio* means grey in Italian). The two strolled along in silent companionship until John reached his house. Then the dog left, as if his job was done. But it wasn't. A few days later, John had to travel through a dangerous area where he had once been beaten by street thugs. He was apprehensive, but then Grigio appeared. Again, the canine body-guard stayed next to John until he reached his home. How had he known?

Thus began a tender pattern— John walking alone, the dog suddenly appearing and escorting him to safety. On one occasion, someone behind a tree fired two shots at John. They missed, and the shooter aimed again. But Grigio raced at him, teeth bared, and the man fled. Another time, as John was walking down a dark and

Angel Communication

unfamiliar street, two men threw a sack over his head, obviously intending to kill him. Suddenly John heard barking. Although he hadn't seen his faithful companion, here came Grigio again, growling and driving the men away. A few days later, Grigio saved John's life in an ambush. Several men had surrounded him with their sticks raised to strike when Grigio arrived on the scene, causing the attackers to flee.

The animal became popular as he

Angel Stories
ENCOUNTERS AND SIGHTINGS

On October 9, 2001, about 7:30 p.m., I was having a cup of coffee alone in my office. My co-workers were in the next room playing games with the kids. I work in a juvenile facility. A woman appeared outside the door, looking at me through the window. Sometimes people get lost and ask for directions at this time of night, so I walked to the door thinking she's probably lost.

I opened it and said, "Can I help you?" She looked into my eyes, gave a smile and said, "I have a message for you." I said, "Who are you? Are you lost?" She said, "No, I'm at the right place. You're the one I'm supposed to see. I have three messages for you from God. He sent me to answer your questions."

At this point, I was in shock. I didn't know if what I was hearing was real or, for that matter, if she was real. She folded her hands and said, "Please don't be afraid, but I need to tell you your messages." I said, "Okay, what are they?"

The first was: "You are doing a great job, you're okay, you're doing fine. God is proud of you." The second one was: "It's okay to ask God for blessings." The third was Psalm 138.

At this point I began to cry. I couldn't believe what I was hearing. It was the answer to my questions that I asked just days before. My heart filled my body: I felt at peace. She then reached out and hugged me.

Angel Communication

sometimes came into John's house and allowed the smaller boys to play with him. But the dog's appearances at John's side always had a purpose—to meet John at the door before some journey, to escort John safely home. At least once, Grigio even prevented John from going out. He lay down on the threshold and barred the exit. "Grigio, move aside!" John commanded, but the dog resisted. John eventually gave up and took off his coat. Later, John's neighbor rushed in to warn John that a trap had been set for him. Grigio had saved him again.

By now, John realized that something heavenly was going on. And as if to confirm it, the dog appeared one day as John was on his way to visit a farmer. When they arrived, John brought the dog inside. Grigio lay down quietly in a corner while the family ate. But when they had assembled leftovers for Grigio's dinner, they could not find him. No doors or windows had been open, yet he had vanished.

For more than thirty years, as John Bosco traveled Italy, saving boys and establishing the Salesian Society, a new order of priests, faithful Grigio continued his inexplicable but wondrous mission. To this day, if a Salesian priest is in danger, a large grey dog sometimes appears, just at the right time.

God sends angels in many forms. Even dogs? You decide.

Joan Wester Anderson is the author of seven books on angels and miracles. Her first book, Where Angels Walk, *has sold more than two million copies and has been translated into fifteen languages. For more angel stories, visit her WhereAngelsWalk Web site at* http://joanwanderson.com.

There Are Many Ways to Open a Dialogue with Angels

By Sharon Linnéa

S o if angels are real and powerful and all around us, how should that affect our everyday lives? How can we rise above the mundane tasks that consume our days to live in the presence of mystery and awe? Do we need a special reason for calling on angels, or are we justified in contacting them at any time?

For Estella Vera of Riverside, California, it happened spontaneously in a moment of crisis. It was Easter, and Estella was thrilled when her daughter, son-in-law and grandchildren decided to pay a surprise visit. Estella and her grown son and daughter were on their way to the store for extra food and some eggs for the children to colour. As they were driving, they saw a man with a knife robbing the driver of an ice-cream truck. Estella's son stopped the car and ran to join another passerby in helping to subdue the robber. Her daughter ran to call 911. Estella herself stood in front of her car, hoping help would come quickly.

Suddenly, the robber broke free, jumped aboard the ice-cream truck and gunned the motor. In one terrifying moment, Estella realized he was

Angel Stories
ANGELS OF DARKNESS

Fallen Angels exist, dear heart. Be careful and test the words of everyone who writes to you. If it goes against scripture, it is a spirit meaning you harm. I repeat: If their words do not edify you and make your faith strong, better stay away from those people. Demons use all measure of disguise; they may even appear as an angel of light.

When you are lonely or frightened, talk to your guardian angel.
You can do it out loud or inside your head—your angel can hear you.
Ask your angel to be near you, to put his or her hand on your shoulder,
to give you courage and protect you.

—Joan Wester Anderson, *Where Angels Walk*

purposely driving directly at her. She would be crushed against her own car and killed. She could see his eyes and the deliberate evil of his intent. She cried out to be spared such a horrible death.

It was then she saw the angel. He was very tall and surrounded by a bright light. His clothing was luminous and pink. He had a kind expression on his face and the most compassionate eyes she had ever seen. He reached out to her in love. Instantly Estella knew that her life would be spared. She was at peace. The angel gathered her in his arms and held her.

The ice cream truck did hit her, but Estella felt immense peace and joy even as her severe injuries healed. Once again, God had sent an angel not to free someone from a trial, but to help her through it. The experience of the angel was so overwhelming that

Estella told the story over and over. It changed her priorities, too. Previously, she had been a designer of wedding dresses, but now she made her top priority sewing warm blankets for the poor and making sure her grandchildren knew, without a doubt, the power and mystery of God's angels. She also felt compelled to forgive the robber. She visited him in prison and shared with him the transforming power of love that was available to him as well.

Asking Angels to Help Others

At this point, I'd like to share my own story of angelic protection. I had an elderly friend, Laura Benet, sister of Stephen Vincent Benet, one of America's most prolific poets, novelists and short story writers.

Through the years, Laura and I

340   Angel Communication

became very close. Despite our seventy-four-year age difference, she always called me Little Sister. But as she reached her midnineties, I became concerned about her living by herself. Many times I prayed that God would not let her be alone in time of trouble.

One day, I was supposed to meet Laura at church, but she was not there. Panicked, I ran to Laura's apartment building and learned that my friend had suffered a heart attack the previous night and broken her hip as she fell. She'd been alone and in pain until someone found her in the morning and took her to the hospital.

I rushed to her hospital bedside and told her, "Laura, I'm so sorry you were alone!"

"Oh, but I wasn't alone, Little Sister," replied Laura. "There was a man with me, a young man. He said, 'Laura, when I'm in trouble or afraid, I pray to the Lord.' So we held hands and prayed and sang all night."

I had no doubt that God had answered her prayers by sending an angel to Laura in her time of need. Several months later, at lunch with a friend, I suddenly felt an urgent impulse to go to Laura's nursing home. I arrived just as she was leaving this world for the next. I got to say goodbye to her—and thank you to the angel who had summoned me.

When Is It Okay to Invoke Angels?

One often-asked question is whether we can communicate with angels simply to be in touch with their love and wisdom. Can humans initiate the conversation or must we wait for an angel to make the first move?

Just as different spiritual traditions have a different theology, each has a different answer to this question as well. Some believe that it is desirable to contact your angels on a daily basis, to commune with them regularly and learn from them, to ask them to bless daily activities. Others believe it's best to relax and enjoy the knowledge that you have a guardian angel but to wait until it initiates contact, which it will do only on special missions from God.

Almost all traditions emphatically agree that discernment must be used when dealing with beings of a different realm, as evil spirits can also approach, masquerading as good.

In the remaining sections, writers

of different traditions suggest helpful ways to commune with the angels, including journaling, letter writing, meditating, even gardening and dancing. Brad and Sherry Steiger answer specific questions about whether to contact your angel, what to watch out for and how to find other people who will partner with you in a spiritual way.

You'll also find practical information about how to make your own space more "angelic"—including suggested use of colour, fragrance, music and even the creation of a home altar.

Sharon Linnéa is a writer in New York and was Beliefnet's founding Inspiration Producer. Currently, she serves as head writer for the New Morning Show on the Hallmark Network. She is an editor and coauthor of the Chicken Soup for the Soul series and has been a contributing editor to Angels on Earth magazine.

Frequently Asked Angel Questions

Communicating

───◦◦◦───

With Brad and Sherry Steiger

COMMUNICATING WITH ANGELS

I would like to make contact with the angelic realm on a daily basis. Do you have any suggestions as to how I can achieve this?

The important thing is to know that the angelic realm is in contact with you on a daily basis, whether you are even aware of it.

To help you realize this wonderful truth, we suggest that you set aside some time each day in which to practice meditation or contemplation and quiet the physical senses that distract you from hearing the angelic whispers of love and the teachings of higher awareness. You might play some soothing music in the background as you enter the silence and permit yourself to "stop the world"

The most beautiful and most profound emotion we can

experience is the sensation of the mystical.

It is the dower of all true science. He to whom

this emotion is a stranger, who can no longer wonder

and stand rapt in awe, is as good as dead.

To know what is impenetrable to us really exists,

manifesting itself as the highest wisdom and the most

radiant beauty which our dull faculties can comprehend

only in their most primitive forms—this knowledge, this

feeling is at the centre of true religiousness.

—Albert Einstein

for at least half an hour a day. The reading of sacred texts and inspirational books may also help you achieve an attitude of receptivity from the angelic realm.

Before seeking contact with the angelic realm, you might pray for protection from negative entities:

Beloved Angel Guide, establish your protective light energies around me.

Erect a shield of love about me that is invincible, all powerful and impenetrable.

Keep me absolutely protected from all things that are not of the Light.

Surround me with the perfect love of the Father-Mother-Creator Spirit.

Prepare yourself for communication with the angelic realm by visualizing your angelic guide moving a soft, violet light all over your body in a wave of warmth. See this heavenly light touching every part of your body. Say inwardly or aloud to your angel guide:

Beloved Angel Guide, assist me in calling upon the highest of energies.

Evoke the law of harmony within

me so that I may never stray from the God-Light.

Allow the transforming heavenly Light to purify me and to remove all impure desires, anger, wrongdoing and improper thoughts from my spirit.

Keep this Holy Light bright within me.

Replace all chaotic vibrations around me and within me with the pure Light of the Father-Mother-Creator Spirit.

I recently went to a psychic who told me that angels were waiting to make contact with me. She suggested that I buy a particular book and tape and that I take a class that she was offering. Are there really angels waiting to make contact with me—or was she just trying to promote her business?

We will not be judgmental toward those who offer angelic readings or classes in achieving contact with celestial beings. Indeed, it may be that certain individuals have been blessed with the gift of achieving communication with angels, and they may also have received a particular method of establishing contact that they feel they can share with others. Each individual must use discernment to assess such psychics' abilities to establish a genuine link with the heavenly kingdom.

Our greatest objections are directed toward those who depict angels as magical servants who carry out the bidding of humans who say the proper prayers (read: spells). Some of these people say that angels can reveal winning lottery tickets and the names of the fastest horses at the racetrack. Others imply that the wondrous beings of light can be commanded to carry out acts of personal revenge on enemies.

We feel that those who make such claims know little of the beauty and wonder of human/angel interaction and have been seduced into bargaining with dark-side entities. We cannot imagine a true angel becoming a money machine or a brutish thug, but fallen angels would gleefully obey would-be dark magicians long enough to ensnare their souls.

If you feel that the intentions of those who claim to be able to teach you to make angelic contact are sincere, then cautiously examine the process they prescribe. If you feel that your own motive for attaining such contact is to achieve higher awareness and not simply to feel special, then you should cautiously proceed with the class.

There is nothing improper about a teacher requesting payment for classes, tapes and books. If, however, your teacher makes additional demands, and the extra payments are for the removal of an evil spirit, bad luck or a "dark force" from your psyche, you

Angel Stories
COMMUNICATING

Yes, the spirits are with us. Angels, or whatever those presences are named, are very close. There's just a thin gauze between worlds. Concentrate very hard, and you might be able to see between worlds. I know this because my coma and being pronounced dead by doctors after a severe accident changed my perception of this world, and I can now see these beings more easily.

might seriously begin to reevaluate your teacher's true motives.

It is to be expected that your teacher might share his or her own messages from angels. If your mentor preaches prejudice toward any particular group, the exclusivity and specialness of his or her teachings, or his or her own divinity, then you should consider finding another mentor.

We believe that every sincere seeker who is willing to practice discernment, discipline and devoted study may receive inspiration and guidance from angelic beings. If you feel the need to have a mentor at your side until you have more confidence in your own ability to establish such communication, take some time to observe the motives and the works of any teacher before you make your final decision to take classes in angelic contact.

And if you truly believe that you have made contact with a heavenly being, remember the admonition of scripture to test the spirits. Don't forget that the astral masqueraders who take great delight in deceiving humans are always out there, waiting patiently to ensnare the innocent, the unwary and the unprepared.

COMMUNICATING WITH SPIRIT GUIDES

I've heard that everyone has spirit guides. How does one communicate with them? I've read all kinds of books and discussed this with other people but, for some reason, I can't communicate with my guide. Is there some foolproof way to know for certain whether you've contacted your guide?

If someone claims to offer you a "foolproof" way to contact or communicate with your guide, you would be well-advised to excuse yourself and walk briskly in the opposite direction. Sadly, the universal hunger to establish meaningful contact with divine energy or an intelligence outside of oneself opens many impatient men and women to exploitation by opportunists who claim special powers and supernatural abilities for themselves.

First of all, you should ask yourself: Is it really necessary to communicate with your guardian angel? Isn't it better to live a good life? If you want to experience a sense of partnership with your guardian angel, then live with the knowledge that you are the material aspect of a union created in the

Angel Communication   347

heavenly planes. Rather than attempting to force communication with your angel, seek to create a tranquil, loving attitude that will encourage the manifestation of angelic energy around you.

Authentic communication with a spirit guide is nearly always initiated by the nonmaterial member of the spiritual partnership. We have interviewed many well-known spirit mediums and channels who have established a reciprocal working relationship with a nonphysical spirit being. In each case, the spirit guide first presented itself to the medium. Such a process seems a demonstration of the old adage: When the student is ready, the teacher will appear.

One should never force communication with otherworldly beings. It's too easy for negative spiritual interlopers to masquerade as beautiful heavenly beings or as important historical entities and to deceive the impatient and the hopeful. Rather, practice a lifestyle that emphasizes prayer, proper living, and love of God and all living things—and you will begin to observe evidence of angelic interaction and spiritual guidance in your life.

I firmly believe that I have established a rich and rewarding line of communication with my guardian angel. Why is it that some people seem opposed to people communicating with their angel guides?

We rejoice that you feel that you have been so blessed as to have developed a

Angel Stories
COMMUNICATING

Some people say that since something bad happened to me that my angels must not have been around. Or why won't my angels help my loved ones when they are hurting? I'm learning that it is important to look at bad or difficult experiences as learning experiences. It is so easy to get caught up in our earthly life and forget that there is a much greater plan at work. I figure if you feel the need to have your angels do more, then just ask them to.

Is man an ape or an angel? My lord, I am on the side of the angels.

—Benjamin Disraeli

line of communication with your guardian angel. We are certainly in favour of everyone enjoying such heavenly linkups. What we continually advise is that people exercise discernment and take the time to evaluate the status of the spiritual entity with which they feel they are in contact.

We also strongly suggest to those who wish such contact that they carefully assess the qualifications of those psychics or channels who state that they can establish such angelic communication in exchange for a fee. In our opinion, the contact is always more likely to be genuine if the guardian angel is the one who initiates communication, rather than the connection having been forced. In fact, we are uncertain whether a true angelic contact can be achieved by any intelligence other than that of the heavenly being itself.

We make a distinction between guardian angels and spirit guides. We believe that spirit guides come to us from an "in- between universe", a multidimensional realm between heaven and Earth. Some of these guides were once physically expressed in human form; others are light beings that have never visited Earth in physical bodies. While one always hopes to contact benevolent entities, one must understand that this in-between universe is also home to sometimes mischievous, sometimes negative, astral masqueraders that delight in deceiving gullible and desperate humans.

We hold angels to be messengers of God who receive their heavenly assignments from the Creator of All That Is and are therefore unlikely to be readily responsive to the trivial whims and desires of mundane human enterprises and ambitions. While we may develop attitudes of reverence and respect that may encourage the presence of angels, we are not to pray to them, worship them or expect them to become involved in material matters beneath their dignity.

Can I contact angels through a Ouija board?

Why do people keep thinking that Ouija board's are harmless children's games, fun enterprises at teenage slumber parties or casual tools for instant enlightenment?

You may believe that you have made contact with a wonderful angelic being, but you are more apt to have summoned an astral masquerader by your naive approach to spiritual awareness.

Beware of exploring the occult world of tarot, Ouija and spirit mediumship. Without the proper discipline, study and discrimination, you will likely interact only with those entities that seek to deceive and entrap you. Such tools of the occult should never be utilized by any other person than those who have learned firm mind control and the techniques of surrounding themselves with loving and harmonious vibrations. Instruments of divination are most surely not games for children.

Those who feel disciplined enough to seek contact with otherworldly intelligences must always remember that our physical world is much closer to the realm of the lower, more negative spiritual frequencies than it is to the dimension of the most harmonious and loving beings. Because we exist in a material world, our psyches will always contain more aspects similar to those of the lower vibratory realms than the higher spiritual planes.

Brad Steiger is the author of 140 books, both fiction and nonfiction, with more than 17 million copies in print. Sherry Hansen Steiger is the cocreator of the Celebrate Life program, the founder of the Butterfly Center of Holistic Education and a founding member of the Holistic Healing Board in Washington, D.C. She is the author or coauthor of more than 20 books, including Seasons of the Soul, The Power of Prayer to Heal and Transform Your Life *and* Angels around the World.

Calling All Angels
How to Create an Angel-Friendly Environment

Transforming your everyday surroundings into sacred space.

Although angels cluster around those who believe in them and who ask their blessing, it's often hard to be conscious of them above the noise and frantic atmosphere of modern life. Probably it was

Matthew, Mark, Luke and John,
The bed be blest that I lie on.
Four angels to my bed,
Four angels round my head,
One to watch, and one to pray,
And two to bear my soul away.

—Thomas Ady, "A Candle in the Dark"

easier to commune with angels in the distant past before mobile phones, TV, radio, boom boxes and the ever-present hum of traffic impinged constantly on our minds and senses.

Fortunately, there are also plenty of modern inventions—as well as natural means—that make it possible to create an environment conducive to getting in touch with angels.

Stick around angel lovers for any length of time, and you'll hear a lot about "creating sacred space". Meeting angels takes place on a different plane of consciousness than ordinary life, and the space where that happens is

A Mother's Prayer to the Guardian Angels of her Children

I humbly salute you, O you faithful, heavenly friends of my children! I give you heartfelt thanks for all the love and goodness you show them. At some future day I shall, with thanks more worthy than I can now give, repay your care for them, and before the whole heavenly court acknowledge their indebtedness to your guidance and protection. Continue to watch over them. Provide for all their needs of body and soul. Pray, likewise, for me, for my husband and my whole family, that we may all one day rejoice in your blessed company.
Amen.

Prayer of St. Gertrude

O most Holy Angel of God, appointed by Him to be my guardian, I give you thanks for all the benefits which you have bestowed on me in body and in soul. I praise and glorify you that you did condescend to assist me with such patient fidelity, and to defend me against all the assaults of my enemies. Blessed be the hour in which you were assigned to me as my guardian, my defender and my patron. In acknowledgement and return of all your loving ministries to me since my youth, I offer you the infinitely precious and noble Heart of Jesus, and firmly resolve to obey you henceforth, and most faithfully to serve my God. Amen.

sacred. Sacred space conveys a sense of harmony, peace, love and meaning, and you can bring such a feeling into your surroundings.

Angel intuitive Terry Lynn Taylor, author of many books about angels and spiritual living, doesn't believe in setting down a lot of rules. "It's very individual," she says. "The more we know of ourselves and our likes and dislikes, the better we'll be able to intuitively pick things to put around us that have a higher meaning—and that will give us the connection to the angelic realms."

Elements of Sacred Space

Colours. Choose colours for your clothing and your home décor that make you feel good and celebrate who you are. "When I tuned in to what colours I should wear to attract angels," says Taylor, "I got the image of an abalone shell—iridescent colours like pinks, aquas and lavenders." These connected her to the more ethereal angels. "But if you want to attract the more earthy type of nature angels," she says, "bring in shades of green and brown."

Fragrance. Scents help to lift your mind and spirit to a higher level and make it easier to tune in to angels. That's why burning incense is so often used in spiritual and religious rituals. Taylor likes to light scented candles—but, she warns, be extremely careful with anything involving fire.

We shall be free: th' Almighty hath not built
Here for his envy, will not drive us hence:
Here we may reign secure, and in my choice
To reign is worth ambition though in Hell:
Better to reign in Hell, than serve in Heav'n.

—John Milton, *Paradise Lost*

Blooming plants, fresh flowers and herbs help create an angelic environment. Jasmine, lavender, rose, rosemary and vanilla are especially uplifting. To spread the scent, you can put essential oils into a diffuser (available at candle stores), mix a few drops of oil in a spray bottle filled with water and spray around the house, or crush herbs into potpourri. Taking a bath with a few drops of scented oil is healing on many counts—both the water and the fragrance relax the spirit and make the mind more receptive to the angelic realm.

Music. Sound vibrations naturally resonate with our own vibration. Classical, religious and New Age music help us enter a meditative state. Mozart, Vivaldi and Handel are especially angelic-sounding. "Put some beautiful music on the CD player," says Taylor. Angel favourites are harp, flute and violin music. But any sound that's peaceful and harmonious will be inspiring. The sound of chimes blowing in the breeze can seem like the soft chant of a heavenly chorus.

Home Altars

For many people, creating sacred space involves making a home altar—a special room or even a private little corner that contains the things that bring you spiritual sustenance. Joan Borysenko, Ph.D., writes in *Inner Peace for Busy People*, "Make sure that every object you place there is intensely meaningful so that the power of the place remains undiluted by clutter. Less is definitely more. Once you've created your refuge, use it only for peaceful activities."

A Greek Orthodox friend of Borysenko has a home altar in her living room that holds several precious icons.

"These spiritual paintings," she writes, "are like doorways to divine realms. Each one carries its own unique power to uplift, heal and inspire." She notes that pictures of saints and gurus or family and friends, figurines, comfortable cushions, prayer shawls, special books and journals, music, candles or prayer books can also grace your home altar.

Taylor has "at least three or four altars going" in her home. Her principal one is the little study where she writes her books. Lit with tiny pink Christmas lights, her altar holds a big piece of rose quartz, a bell, candles, a glass angel, a statue of Mary, an angel Christmas card from the musician Carlos Santana ("He's really into angels") and some small four-leaf clover glasses from her mother ("my Irish connection"), among other personal items. "I think it's nice to have the four elements on my altar—earth, air, fire and water— because that's who we are," she says, adding, "and of course the angels are the ether, the fifth element."

Cleanse the Space, Register Your Intention

Cleansing the area is a good way to focus your attention and to keep

To St. Raphael, Angel of Happy Meetings

O Raphael, lead us toward those we are waiting for, those who are waiting for us! Raphael, Angel of Happy Meetings, lead us by the hand toward those we are looking for! May all our movements, all their movements, be guided by your Light and transfigured by your Joy. Angel Guide of Tobias, lay the request we now address to you at the feet of Him on whose unveiled Face you are privileged to gaze. Lonely and tired, crushed by the separations and sorrows of Earth, we feel the need of calling to you and of pleading for the protection of your wings, so that we may not be as strangers in the Province of Joy, all ignorant of the concerns of our country. Remember the weak, you who are strong—you whose home lies beyond the region of thunder, in a land that is always peaceful, always serene and bright with the resplendent glory of God.

Amen.

My good angel, you come from heaven;
God has sent you to take care of me.
Shelter me in this present night;
enfold me under your wings;
lighten my heavy task; direct my steps.
Do not leave me, be near me,
defend me against the spirit of evil.
But above all, come to my aid in the last struggle of my life.
Deliver my soul so that with you it may praise,
love and contemplate the goodness of God forever and ever.
Amen.

vibrations at a high level. You might sprinkle salt or water in the corners of your space or "smudge" the area with sage or cedar. To do this, bundle the herbs, tie them together, then light one end and blow out the fire. Wave the smoldering ends around the room to purify the space. (Be sure to extinguish the bundle with water.)

Or you could simply clean and straighten up the room where your sacred space is located.

Then register your intention to invite your angel in. Angels respond to our intentions, says Taylor. "Make some kind of statement out loud or to yourself that you're going to just be open to [angels'] energy," she advises. Then light a candle, say a prayer, put on music and sit quietly. This opens up a whole energy system to you—and creates a very welcoming environment for angels.

Asking for Angelic Help, with Love and Reverence, Can Bring a Response

Once you create a sacred space for yourself, there are many beautiful ways to keep angels in your life and to call for their help when you are in need. It's essential to treat angels with the same love, respect and gratitude that

To be as God, can be understood in two ways:
first, by equality; secondly, by likeness. An angel
could not seek to be as God in the first way,
because by natural knowledge he knew that this was
impossible....And even supposing it were possible, it
would be against natural desire, because there exists in
everything the natural desire to preserve its own nature
which would not be preserved were it to be changed into
another nature. Consequently, no creature of a lower
nature can ever covet the grade of a higher nature, just
as an ass does not desire to be a horse.

—Saint Thomas Aquinas

Prayer of the Church Concerning St. Gabriel

May the offering of our service and the prayer of the blessed Archangel Gabriel be acceptable in Thy sight, O Lord; that he whom we venerate on Earth, may be our advocate before Thee in heaven. Through Our Lord, Amen.

you would any beloved friend. It is important, however, to never worship them. This is an honour that rightly belongs only to God.

The channels through which angels are most likely to communicate with us are via intuition and dreams. But angel messages also come through other people, who may appear at just the right time with a helpful thought or much-needed assistance. At times we may find an unexpected answer to a problem through "synchronicity"— say, when a book falls open to a certain page or we see a sign on a billboard that speaks directly to our situation. Occasionally, we will hear a strong voice inside ourselves, giving us an urgent message to do or avoid something.

In their book *Guardian Angels*, Hazel Whittaker and Cynthia Blanch

point out that this voice is completely different from the intrusive negative voices heard by people who are mentally ill. The strong angelic voice, they write, "is always good and loving, takes place only during an emergency or serious situation, and is very rare indeed."

It's not hard to tell whether you are really in contact with an angel or whether you are being guided by your own fears or human will. The key is to notice how you feel about the encounter. Most experts agree that when an angel communicates, there is always the most wonderful sense of peace and calm following the message, a feeling of being guided by someone you can completely trust. Even if the message you get contradicts your own desires, you will still carry away a peaceful certainty that "all will be well".

Making Yourself More Open to Angelic Communication

A good way to do this is to attune to the angels' energy field, which is like tuning your awareness in to the angelic frequency. Remember that angels are beings of pure light and spirit, vibrating at a higher frequency than the earthbound mind. "Angels fly because they take themselves lightly," as G. K. Chesterton wrote. We can tune in to their frequency by lightening our own mental load—by releasing such negative emotions as anger, fear, guilt and resentment, and replacing them with the more angelic qualities of love, forgiveness and acceptance. To hear the "still, small voice", we need to start by being still ourselves. That's why most angel meditations begin with calming the thought and releasing negative emotions.

A second prerequisite to seeking angelic assistance is to directly ask the angels to enter our consciousness for our highest good. The angels are always with us, watching over us all the time. It is up to us to acknowledge their presence and welcome them into our lives.

For unless it's a life-threatening emergency, angels will rarely intervene in a human life without being asked. But remember that asking is very different from invoking or compelling spiritual beings to do our bidding. This is emphatically not recommended. The latter involves ritual magic or sorcery, which seeks to "create an imbalance in nature by throwing the outcome in the doer's favour," according to Taylor. By contrast, she says, the purpose of angel rituals should be to open your heart to the universe and let go of any need to control.

Here are some specific ideas for inviting angels into everyday life.

Rituals and Ceremonies. Creating a sacred space, lighting candles and

Traditional Roman Catholic Angel Prayer

Angel of God, My Guardian dear,
To whom God's love entrusts me here;
Ever this day (or night) be at my side,
To light and guard,
To rule and guide.
Guardian Angel from heaven so bright,
Watching beside me to lead me aright,
Fold thy wings round me, and guard me with love,
Softly sing songs to me of heaven above.
Amen.

Angel Communication

I have seen a thousand times that angels are human forms, or men, for I have conversed with them as man to man, sometimes with one alone, sometimes with many in company.

—Italo Calvino, *If on a Winter's Night a Traveler*

saying a prayer or invocation are time-honoured ways of focusing your mind and inviting angelic help. The Roman Catholic Church has a wealth of prayers that call on guardian angels and different archangels to ask their intercession and protection.

Author Migene González-Wippler, who culls from many traditions as well as from her own mystical experiences, describes several elaborate rituals for invoking angels in her book *Return of the Angels*. Most involve detailed preparation and purification. For example, in a ritual to contact your personal guardian angel, she suggests that you do not consume solid foods or alcohol for twenty-four hours and that you bathe, dress in white and wear no shoes.

Other writers suggest more casual and spontaneous rituals. But all emphasize maintaining an attitude of gratitude. William Bloom, Ph.D., notes in *Working with Angels, Fairies, and Nature Spirits*, "While you are in the gentle and open state of contemplation and attunement, communicate an invitation to the spirit. In whatever way works for you, silently or spoken, call in the spirit. Then—and this is very important—thank the spirit for being present with you as if it were already there."

Affirmations. These are positive statements that acknowledge truths about our lives, claiming the presence of good here and now and countering a negative mental state. Whenever you have the opportunity, sit quietly and state an affirmation. Affirmations should be simple and easy to memorize, such as, "I know that my angel is taking care of me and guiding me in all that I do" or "I know that my angel is supporting me with strength and love."

Meditation and Visualization. Meditation is a quiet and relaxed state

Angel Communication

Meditation: "I Am One with the Light of God"

Angel communicator Jane M. Howard, in Commune with the Angels, *provides a longer angelic meditation:*

To begin, sit comfortably in a chair with your arms and legs uncrossed and your spine as straight as possible. Breathe in deeply. As you exhale, completely relax. Envelop yourself in a powerful field of white light. This field of light will prevent anything that is not of the light from interfering with your sacred activity of meditation.

Visualize an ornate golden throne. An angelic being beckons you to sit upon it. Keep breathing. With every breath, you breathe in the powerful white light. As your body fills with this light, visualize yourself transformed into a being of light. Your lungs, your arms, your feet, your body are all filled with the light. You are suddenly weightless. The light expands within your being. As you let your breath out slowly, see the light going forth from you and filling the space around you. The light expands around you. As you gently inhale and exhale the light, decree the following:

"I am awakening to the truth that God is shining in me always. I am one with all life and with all the angelic presence. God shines in me through intelligence and wisdom. I open my mind to God's radiant light, and all my thoughts of doubt, darkness and negativity dissolve. My thoughts are transformed into creativity, imagination and positive thinking . . .

"I, too, am a shining one because I am one with the light of God."

Gently return your awareness to your room. Experience the buoyancy and lightness you are feeling—the oneness you share with all life and with the angelic presence everywhere. Always thank the angels for their help.

that enables you to cleanse your mind of wandering thoughts and focus on a stillness inside or a spiritual image. Meditations can be simple or complex. Some include visualization, in which you take a guided journey to a place of peace and spiritual understanding. This level of consciousness makes you a clearer channel for angelic communication. Psychologist Doreen Virtue,

It came upon a midnight clear,

That glorious song of old,

From Angels bending near the earth

To touch their harps of gold:

"Peace on the earth; good will to man

From Heaven's all gracious King."

The world in solemn stillness lay

To hear the angels sing.

—Edmund Hamilton Sears

Ph.D., advises, "Visualizing angels is a powerful way to call them to your side. See the angels flying around you or your loved ones."

Keep an Angel Journal. According to many experts, communing with angels can be done by keeping a journal. Keeping a record of your own experiences, dreams and insights about angels will enable you to become more conscious of them and more grateful for all the good in your life. Journaling may also allow angels to speak directly to you or through you as you write, as if you were an "executive secretary", taking dictation.

You may start journaling by creating or buying a beautiful book with blank pages and a special pen. Calm and centre yourself. Offer prayers of protection and invocation. Greet your angel and feel its presence.

Let a question form in your mind and heart, and then write it down. In the stillness, open to the words that come to you from your angel. Without thinking about them, write them down. Continue writing your questions and the answers that come through an inner voice—without editing or judgment. Don't be surprised if the angel's answers employ a different handwriting or vocabulary from your own.

When you sign off, don't forget to thank your angel.

A few other thoughts: Dr. Virtue refers to the process of taking dictation from your angel as "automatic writing". She advises asking the archangel Michael to oversee this Q & A process so that only angels, rather than earthbound spirits, reply.

Prayer to St. Michael, the Archangel

Holy Michael, the Archangel, defend us in battle. Be our safeguard against the wickedness and snares of the devil. May God rebuke him, we humbly pray; and do you, O Prince of the heavenly host, by the power of God cast into hell Satan and all the evil spirits who wander through the world seeking the ruin of souls.

Amen.

In our computer-driven world, it's not uncommon for people to type out their angels' messages on a keyboard. If you used this method, be sure to clear your desk before starting—angels don't like mess and clutter. Saying a prayer, lighting a candle and bringing in fresh flowers can help create a sacred space.

Write Letters to Angels. Writing a letter to your angel is another way to focus and connect with your spiritual friend. Use special stationery. Start with a prayer and a relaxation exercise to centre yourself. Don't be afraid to write from your heart, pouring out your worries, anxieties or deepest wishes. You can also ask for help for someone else. Always thank your angel in advance for assisting. Then tuck your letter in a special place—a beautifully decorated box or even a bird feeder refitted as an angel "mailbox". Then let go of your problem. You may not get instant gratification, but an answer will come. Just be open to signs and symbols that the angels are with you.

Painting, Drawing, Singing, Dancing, Drumming, Gardening. Creative activities like these, when preceded by prayer and intentionally asking angels for their help, can be excellent ways to connect with celestial spirits and enter into a sacred relationship with them.

Frequently Asked Angel Questions

How Not to Seek Angelic Attention

With Brad and Sherry Steiger

I have read that it is possible to attract angels by lighting scented candles, using perfumed oils in the bath water or spraying a fragrant flowery essence around the room. Is this true?

You're asking whether angels can be lured to you by means of pleasant aromas. The lighted candles, perfumed oils and the flowery essence you mention may allow you to enter a relaxed or meditative state of mind that will

Angel Communication

encourage your receptivity to angelic inspiration, but angels cannot be lured or enticed or summoned to anyone's presence.

Angels are not physical beings. Aromas, sweet and flowery or rank and foul, have no effect on them.

In various apocryphal texts, when angels who had been living, dining and travelling with humans in order to accomplish a particular earthly mission finally reveal themselves to their astonished and bewildered hosts, they explain that they only appeared to be eating, drinking and sleeping.

As ethereal beings, they don't need to avail themselves of these earthly, physical human requirements. They gave the impression of dining so that their disguise as friends or kinsmen would seem more real and thus allow them to move undetected among the people whom they had come to help.

We caution against selfishly

Angel Stories
DREAM ENCOUNTERS

Once when I was very young, around 8–10 years old, I had a bad dream. It had something to do with the Devil. The next night, the same thing. The third night as the dream began again, a voice as clear as anything spoke to me, comforted me. I felt the presence of my Guardian Angel. My Angel told me not to be afraid. "God Loves You. God is Love, Love is All. He won't let anything happen to you because he loves you and he knows that you love him." I always will remember that happening. I felt it and heard it and I still feel it . . . The bad part of the dream never came back!

employing any methods that you believe will encourage the manifestation of angelic beings in your presence. Such eagerness or desperation on a human's part to entice a heavenly entity to appear may attract lower astral entities or fallen angels masquerading as an angelic guide in order to mislead the naïve and unwary.

We believe prayer, proper meditation, contemplation of the sacred and an earnest desire to lead a good life are still the best methods of establishing contact with the true heavenly beings.

Brad Steiger is the author of 140 books, both fiction and nonfiction, with more than 17 million copies in print. Sherry Hansen Steiger is the cocreator of the Celebrate Life program, the founder of the Butterfly Center of Holistic Education and a founding member of the Holistic Healing Board in Washington, D.C. She is the author or coauthor of more than 20 books, including Seasons of the Soul, The Power of Prayer to Heal and Transform Your Life *and* Angels around the World.

How to Hear Your Angels' Messages
Four Channels for Tuning In to Angels

By Doreen Virtue, Ph.D.

"We aren't that difficult to hear, if you will listen for us with an open heart. Most of the time, we are closer to you than you can imagine. A whisper, a thought, is the only signal we need from you to get a conversation started. We have enormous respect for what you're going through here on planet Earth at this time. We never seek to interfere with your lives, only to bring you blessings of insights and new ways of looking at yourselves."
—*Messages from Your Angels oracle cards*

Not everyone "hears" angelic voices as an audible sound. Many people receive divine messages through nonverbal means such as visions, feelings or a knowingness.

I heard an Angel singing,
When the day was springing,
"Mercy, Pity, Peace
Is the world's release."

—William Blake

Clairaudience: Hearing the voice of an angel is called "clairaudience", which means "clear hearing". An angel's voice may sound human, or it may sound different. The voice can emanate from within your body, within your mind or sound as if it's outside your head. When an angel warned me that my car was about to be stolen, his voice sounded as if he were talking through a paper towel tube, just outside my right ear.

You know that guidance comes from angels when it is loving, focused, consistent and not hurtful to anyone.

Clairvoyance: Your angels may speak to you in pictures or images. We call this "clairvoyance", or "clear seeing". Angelic messages may come to you as snapshots, visible to your eyes or simply floating or flashing in your mind. Or, you may see miniature scenes, as if from a movie. The images may be black and white or full colour.

Visual messages from angels are sometimes symbolic, such as seeing a stop sign indicating you should take a rest, slow down or stop what you are doing.

Clairsentience: A third way we receive angelic guidance is through our emotions and physical sensations. We call this "clairsentience", or "clear feeling". Clairsentients get divine guidance through bodily sensations or through strong or subtle emotions.

Each of our five senses has a corresponding spiritual sense. Clairsentients receive angelic guidance through an etheric sense of smell, taste and touch. For example, you may know that your beloved deceased grandmother is near when you smell her perfume or favourite flower fragrance. An angel may shower your room with the aroma of orange blossoms to tell you of an impending wedding.

Angel Stories

I was 11 years old in 1964 and our family went to the county fair for the first time. There was this fellow, average height, crew-cut hair, brown corduroys, blue windbreaker and the largest, deepest, most expressive brown eyes I have ever seen. He was working the crowd for dollar donations for the deaf and had approached my Dad who gave him the dollar.

Saw this same guy year after year for 25 years. I grew up and had a family of my own, and I still saw him once a year with my own kids in tow, like clockwork. He never changed; I, however, did. There came a time in my life when I grew to be too busy with life and was consumed by the world. It was marked by my attitude towards this deaf man.

I, as my dad had before me, had given him a dollar without question year after year. One year when he approached, I said no and waved him off. When my young son asked why I reacted so, I told him that with all the advances in medical science, there was no reason for this guy to be a bum—hard of heart, you better believe it.

This went on for five years until at the age of 38 I had a spiritual reawakening. Everything changed. That year I did not see the deaf man at the fair. That Christmas I was doing some late night shopping in a nearby city. It was cold, late and I wasn't happy about being in this city because there had been a lot of crime. The parking lot was full, yet no people were around. As I made my way towards the entrance, a figure slid out from between two cars as I passed. I quickened my pace but a hand reached out and grabbed my shoulder, amost scaring me to death. As I turned ready to confront what I thought was an attacker, a familiar face appeared. It was the deaf man.

An angel may be the guy on the corner, or the women short a dollar ahead of you in line. We never know when an angel may cross our path; we can only hope we treat them with the same love God treats us.

When anyone prays, the angels that minister to God and watch over mankind gather round about him and join with him in prayer.

—Origen

Clairsentients also receive a lot of guidance through their intuition, gut feelings and hunches. Much of our intuition comes from the stomach region, and the stomach flutters, relaxes and tightens according to the angelic guidance. Instinctively, the clairsentient interprets the meaning of these gut feelings, and a wise clairsentient follows these internal directives without much hesitation.

Clairsentients receive angelic messages through their heart and love-emotions as well. If a thought of doing something swells your chest with warm feelings of joy, this is a directive from God and the angels.

Claircognizance: We call the fourth means of angelic communication "claircognizance", or "clear knowing". Men are frequently claircognizant and may not even realize they naturally receive detailed and accurate information from the angels.

A claircognizant knows without knowing how he knows. Consequently, he may doubt the validity of his knowingness. This is a mistake because when divine wisdom enters our minds, it is a gift we can use to improve our lives and to serve the world.

We all have access to all four channels of communication. Usually, we have one primary means of receiving angelic guidance and one secondary or lesser channel of communication. With practice, you can become adept at receiving messages in all four ways. When first attempting to communicate with angels, however, most people focus on their most natural means of communication.

Doreen Virtue, Ph.D., is a metaphysician and psychologist who works with the angelic realm in her spiritual healing practice. She is the author of many books, including Healing with the Angels: How the Angels Can Assist You in Every Area of Your Life *(Hay House, Carlsbad, CA), from which this article is excerpted.*